5,000 YEARS OF
ROYALTY

KINGS, QUEENS, PRINCES, EMPERORS & TSARS

5,000 YEARS OF
ROYALTY

KINGS, QUEENS, PRINCES, EMPERORS & TSARS

THOMAS J. CRAUGHWELL

Tess Press

For Teri Natalicchio and Bill Mezzomo—New Jersey royalty

5,000 Years of Royalty was created by Black Dog and Leventhal in conjunction with Endeavour London Limited. Originally published as *The Book of Royalty*.

PHOTO CREDITS

Art Resource: 5, 55, 71, 137, 169, 205, 233, 267. **Corbis:** 11, 183, 369, 401, 465. **Granger:** 6, 7, 8, 57, 63, 65, 69, 71, 75, 89, 93, 121, 125, 139, 153, 163, 197, 201, 203, 261, 263, 269, 279, 281, 297, 304, 305, 307, 309, 319, 323, 329, 381, 385, 397, 403, 407, 411, 413, 445, 453. **Shutterstock:** 5, 21, 27, 29, 41, 49, 61, 97, 105, 149, 155, 161, 193, 195, 215, 235, 251, 265, 373, 391.

Bridgeman Art Library: 187, 241/Bibliotheque Nationale, Paris; 223/Tretyakov Gallery, Moscow/DACS/RIA Novosti; 237/Louvre, Paris/Giraudon; 337/Private collection/The Stapleton Collection, London.

All other images courtesy of **Getty Images** including the following which have additional attributions—

Agence France Presse: 127, 135, 479, 495; **Bridgeman Art Library:** front jacket (L), 9(R), 295/Palazzo Barberini, Rome; front jacket (2L), title page, 311/Stirling Maxwell Collection, Pollok House, Glasgow, Scotland; front jacket (2R), title page, 341/Private collection/Peter Newark American Pictures; front jacket (R), title page, 7(R), 10(L), 117, 207, 387, 395/Chateau de Versailles, France; spine, 317/Private collection/Bonhams, London; jacket flap, 11(L), 435/Summer Palace, Beijing; 5(L), 15/National Museum, Aleppo, Syria; 5(3L), 37/Private collection; 6(2R), 119/San Vitale, Ravenna, Italy; 7(2L), 147/Private collection/The Stapleton Collection, London; 7(3L), 177/Victoria & Albert Museum, London; 8(2L), 211/Bibliotheque Nationale, Paris; 8(R), 283/Kunsthistorisches Museum, Vienna; 9(2L), 10(2L), 313, 367/Tretyakov Gallery, Moscow; 9(3L), 10(3L & 2R), 321, 383, 419/Guildhall Art Gallery, City of London; 9(2R), 357/Musee Antoine Lecuyer, Saint-Quentin, France; 19, 25, 287, 371/Louvre, Paris; 31/Musee des Beaux-Arts, Angers, France; 33/Santa Maria della Salute, Venice; 47, 85, 299/Hamburger Kunsthalle, Hamburg; 67/Private collection/Agnew's, London; 81/Musee Crozatier, Le Puy-en-Velay, France; 99/Galleria Sabauda, Turin; 103/Basilica di San Marco, Venice; 107/Walker Art Gallery, National Museums Liverpool; 113/Archivio di Stato, Bologna; 129/Temple of the Inscriptions, Palenque, Chiapas State, Mexico; 191/Palazzo Ducale, Venice; 199/Bayon Temple, Angkor, Cambodia; 209/Bibliotheque des Arts Decoratifs, Paris; 225/Alcazar Gardens, Cordoba, Spain; 229/British Library, London; 239/Private collection/The Maas Gallery, London; 243/Private collection/Agra Art, Warsaw, Poland; 249/British Museum, London; 253, 333/Private Collection/Philip Mould Ltd., London; 275, 327/Palacio del Senado, Madrid; 291/Musee Dobree, Nantes, France; 315/Private collection; 317/Private collection/Bonhams, London; 325/Private collection; 349/Musee des Beaux-Arts, Beziers, France; 355/Ham House, Surrey, UK; 375/Nationalmuseum, Stockholm Sweden; 377/City of Edinburgh Museums & Art Galleries, Scotland; 379/Museum of Art, Serpukhov, Russia; 399/Private collection/Look and Learn; 421/Min.Defense-Service Historique de l'Armee de Terre, France; 425/Museu Historico Nacional, Rio de Janeiro, Brazil; **George Eastman House:** 231, 427; **hemis.fr:** 181; **Imagno:** 8(3L), 219, 331, 335, 353, 433, 451; **David Hume Kennerly:** 11(3L), 475; **National Geographic:** 6(3L), 79, 361, 389, 485; **Popperfoto:** 11(R), 175, 405, 443, 455; **Peter Rogers:** 131; **Tim Graham:** 459, 487; **Time & Life Pictures:** back jacket (R), 17, 23, 53, 95, 109, 111, 123, 171, 185, 343, 351, 409, 491, 493; **WireImage:** 11(2R), 489, 499

This edition published by Tess Press, an imprint of
Black Dog & Leventhal Publishers, Inc.
151 West 19th Street
New York, NY 10011

Manufactured in China

Paperback ISBN: 978-1-60376-275-5
h g f e d c b

Hardcover ISBN: 978-1-60376-118-5
h g f e d c b

CONTENTS

2700 B.C.

Gilgamesh

1370 B.C.

Akhenaton

991 B.C.

Solomon

432 B.C.

Dionysius I

540 B.C.
Leonidas

73 B.C.
Herod the Great

259 B.C.
Qin Shi Huang

100 B.C.
Julius Caesar

483
Justinian I

688
Charles Martel

742
Charlemagne

849
Alfred the Great

1005
Macbeth

1137
Saladin

1157

Richard I, the Lionheart

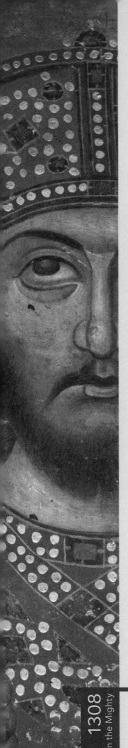

1308
Dusan the Mighty

1162
Genghis Khan

1214
Louis IX

1394
Henry the Navigator

1459
Maximilian I

1466
Montezuma

1530
Ivan the Terrible

1542
Mary I, Queen of Scots

1638
Louis XIV

1491
Henry VIII

1769
Napoleon

1672
Peter the Great

1738
George III

1819
Victoria

1822
Tawhiao

1841
Edward VII

1835

Cixi

1885

Faisal

1901

Hirohito

1926

Elizabeth II

INTRODUCTION

It would be difficult to find a society on the planet that did not, at one time or another, have a monarchy. For most of human history it was the established order that one royal family should stand at the pinnacle while everyone obeyed them, worked for them, and more often than not, fought and died for them. In exchange kings were expected to provide their people with security and prosperity.

The allure of monarchy was so strong that the ancient Israelites complained that they felt inferior to their neighbors because they did not have a king.

Even people who should have known better longed for a king. In the 19th century, when Greece finally won its independence from the Ottoman Turks and Italy was finally united into a single nation, the Greeks did not introduce the type of democracy the Athenians had enjoyed 2,300 years earlier, nor did the Italians try to revive the Roman Republic. Instead, both countries installed kings.

For anyone who loves a good story, the lives of kings and queens makes for fascinating reading. Conflict. Glory. Romance. Tragedy. Bloodshed. Monarchs have always understood that inheriting a throne is the easy part—how to hang on to the throne is what kept kings and queens up nights. All of them found that prisons and the executioner's block were useful, but monarchs also looked for more sophisticated ways to win their subjects' loyalty. In Egypt and Japan the royal family claimed that they were untouchable because they were descended from the gods. The Stuart kings of Great Britain advanced the principle of divine right, saying that God had made them kings and only God could remove them.

With all the stories of intrigues and wars and rebellions, it's easy to overlook the extraordinary contributions monarchs have made to civilization. They built the pyramids in Egypt and in Central America, the Colosseum in Rome, Versailles outside Paris and the Forbidden City in Beijing. They were the patrons of Haydn and Mozart, of da Vinci, of Chaucer and Shakespeare.

The stars of the entertainment industry are the new royals, but celebrities always take a backseat to real royalty: in the 1990s, anything Princess Diana did was newsworthy. And when she died, two billion people across the globe turned on their televisions to watch her funeral. Only a real princess could attract that kind of audience.

GILGAMESH

King of Uruk (c. 2700 B.C.)

If you travel to the site of ancient Uruk, you will see traces of a vast complex of battlements that once stretched for nine kilometers around the city—all the work of Gilgamesh, a king whose greatest ambition was to be remembered. And he was. The scribes who compiled the list of Mesopotamian kings certainly embellished his biography: it says that he was the son of a king and a goddess. According to the *Epic of Gilgamesh*—a legendary account of his life that is also celebrated as the world's first epic poem—the boy took after his mother's side of the family, being two-thirds a god and only one-third mortal man.

The theme of Gilgamesh's epic is the pursuit for lasting fame and the quest for the meaning of life and death. In the poem, the veil between heaven and earth is very thin, and gods and goddesses interact with humans on an intimate level. For example, on one occasion Gilgamesh is confronted by Ishtar—the goddess of sexual love and war—who desires him as her husband. But Gilgamesh, for reasons that are obscure, rebuffs the goddess. Enraged that a mortal should insult her, Ishtar sends a celestial bull to attack Gilgamesh, but the king, with the help of his closest friend Enkidu, kills the bull. Tragically, the struggle weakens Enkidu so severely that he falls ill and dies.

Deprived of his dearest friend, Gilgamesh almost goes mad with grief. He abandons his desire for fame and sets out to wander the world in search of the meaning of existence. During this quest he meets an old man who tells him the story of a great flood (which may have been the inspiration for the story of Noah and the flood found in Genesis). But the old man also teaches the king a vital lesson: each man's fate is fixed, and he who struggles against it saps all the joy from his life.

2700 B.C.

14

Relief depicting Gilgamesh between two bull-men supporting a winged sun disk

SARGON THE GREAT

King of Akkad (c. 2316–2261 B.C.)

The founder of the world's first empire, Sargon began his career very humbly: his father was a gardener, his mother a priestess, and while still a boy, Sargon found work as the cupbearer of King Ur-Zababa of Kish. Sargon's opportunity came when a local warlord conquered Kish. In the chaos that followed, Sargon, by now an ambitious young man, moved to a backwater town named Akkad. This became his power base; from there, assisted by adventurous men who knew how to profit from the collapse of a civilization, he carved out his own kingdom that stretched from the Persian Gulf to northern Syria.

Sargon's success came from his original approach to warfare. At the time, most armies marched onto the field weighted down with heavy arms and armor and arrayed in tight formation. Sargon's warriors wore light clothing and carried only a sword and a dagger. They could attack the clumsy battalions of the enemy in a kind of blitzkrieg charge, then break ranks to reform and attack again before their enemies had time to recover.

While his new method of attack was impressive, Sargon's major innovation was introducing archers to the battlefield. Hand-to-hand fighting was unpredictable and cost the lives of too many troops, but archers could bring down scores of the enemy without suffering many casualties themselves.

At his court, Sargon assembled representatives of the ruling elites from all the lands he conquered. They were treated as his advisors, but everyone understood they were also hostages—one uprising back in their homelands and these lords would be executed.

In the peace that followed Sargon's conquests, he expanded commerce, standardized weights and measures throughout his empire, and posted guards along the roads so travelers could move about in safety.

Although he was a man of the people, who came to the throne from the bottom of society, Sargon was no democrat. Once his power was secure, he ruled as an absolute monarch who shared power with no one.

Bronze profile of Sargon of Akkad

HAMMURABI

King of Babylon (c. 1795–1750 B.C.)

In 1901, archaeologists working amid the ruins of the ancient city of Susa in Persia uncovered an eight-foot-long black stone slab. At the top of the stele was a carving of a king standing before the Babylonian god Shamash; below the carving the stone was covered with inscriptions. This was the Code of Hammurabi, the world's first-known example of a king presenting his subjects with a complete body of laws. It had been set up in Babylon where every passerby could read it; it came to Susa long after Hammurabi's death, when his city was conquered and the conqueror carried off the massive slab as a trophy of war.

Hammurabi's code enshrined ideas about justice, motive, and proof that have been the hallmarks of virtually every legal code in the West ever since. For example, under Hammurabi's code it was not enough to suspect a person of theft, the missing goods had to be found in his house or on his person. Furthermore, a man who killed in self-defense or by accident was not guilty of murder and therefore not liable for the death penalty. Negligence, however, was another matter: a physician found guilty of malpractice was sentenced to have both of his hands cut off.

With 282 laws "on the books," as it were, the code covers virtually every facet of day-to-day life, from divorce and the custody of children to reparations for injuring a slave to penalties for a contractor's shoddy work.

Hammurabi had expanded Babylon from a city-state into an empire that covered all of Mesopotamia (all of present-day Iraq, as well as parts of Turkey, Syria, and Iran). Permitting each ethnic group in the empire to maintain their own ideas about law and order was a recipe for chaos; it was essential, then, for Hammurabi to create a legal system that would apply to everyone in his empire.

In recognition of his achievements as lawgiver, a portrait of Hammurabi is included among carvings of twenty-three other influential legal minds in the chamber of the House of Representatives in the United States Capitol. As for the black stele, it is on display in the Louvre Museum in Paris.

Hammurabi, king of Babylon, at prayer

HATSHEPSUT

Queen of Egypt (c. 1504–1458 B.C.)

Hatshepsut was not the first woman to rule Egypt in her own right. However, she was shrewd enough to realize that the royal court, the army, the temple priests, and perhaps the Egyptian people would have been more comfortable with a man on the throne. So she used the traditional title of the pharaohs, King of Upper and Lower Egypt, and from time to time she strapped on the little false beard that was part of the pharaoh's regalia. The priests of Amun threw their support behind her, even spreading the story that Hatshepsut was literally the daughter of the king of the gods.

During Hatshepsut's twenty-one-year reign, Egypt enjoyed long periods of peace. Early on she waged brief, successful wars in Nubia, Syria, and what is now Lebanon, but Hatshepsut was more interested in enriching her land through trade. She opened new trade routes to Asia, the Aegean Islands, and to Punt, a land in eastern Africa. And wealth poured in: gold, frankincense, myrrh, ivory, ebony, slaves, and exotic wild animals such as baboons. There was an enormous market for all of these luxury items, both in Egypt and in all the lands of the eastern Mediterranean. Thanks to Hatshepsut's economic policy, Egypt was fabulously wealthy for decades to come (witness the treasures of her descendant, King Tutankhamen).

Like all the pharaohs who came before her, Hatshepsut commissioned great monuments to record the glories of her reign. With her two favorite architects, Ineni and Senemut, she launched a massive building campaign grander than anything any previous pharaoh had attempted since the construction of the pyramids. Her masterpiece was her mortuary temple designed by Senemut at the entrance to the Valley of the Kings. It is a series of impressive terraces built into the face of a massive cliff. The crowning achievement is the Djeser-Djeseru, or "the Sublime of Sublimes," an elegant colonnade that is a masterpiece of symmetry the likes of which the world would not see again until the Parthenon.

For decades archaeologists sought the mummy of Hatshepsut without success. Then in 2007 Zahi Hawass, the renowned archaeologist and secretary general of Egypt's Supreme Council of Antiquities, announced that the mummy of Hatshepsut, forgotten and unidentified, had been found—in the Egyptian Museum in Cairo.

Amenhotep III

King of Egypt (c. 1416–1353 B.C.)

Only twelve years old when he became pharaoh, Amenhotep III inherited an Egypt that was at the height of its power. He ruled an empire that stretched from present-day Iraq to Sudan.

While he was a child, his mother, Queen Mutemwia, acted as regent, but when he reached adulthood, Amenhotep took a firm command of his power and introduced some interesting innovations. He was the first king to issue regular news bulletins; carved on large scarabs (stones shaped like beetles), the bulletins reported on the progress of his building projects, which new wives he had acquired, even what type of game he had bagged on his latest hunting expedition. Messengers carried these bulletins to foreign courts and to governors of important cities and provinces throughout the empire.

Of his three wives, Tiy was the woman Amenhotep loved and respected above all others. She was the daughter of a chariot driver, but Amenhotep was indifferent to her status—she was self-assured, intelligent, and lovely, and their marriage appears to have been a love match. He gave her the title Great Royal Wife, and Tiy became Amenhotep's political partner, handling requests and solving dilemmas for Egyptian government officials as well as neighboring kings and princes.

Egypt in the day of Amenhotep was immensely rich, thanks to the empire's gold mines in Nubia. Between the country's natural wealth and the tribute that poured in from all parts of the empire, the pharaoh's treasury had never been so full. In the classic pharaonic style, Amenhotep showed off his wealth by initiating a grandiose building program. He erected a magnificent palace in Thebes, then ordered work crews to dig an immense harbor and system of canals to link his palace with the Nile. He also built the largest funerary temple Egypt had ever seen; actually, he built two temples side by side—one dedicated to himself, the other to Tiy. Tragically, the site he chose was too close to the Nile; within two hundred years the temples were virtually destroyed by floods.

Amenhotep bears another distinction: approximately 250 of his portrait sculptures have survived, the largest number of any king of Egypt.

AKHENATEN AND NEFERTITI

King (c. 1378–1336 B.C.) and Queen (c. 1370–1330 B.C.) of Egypt

The son of Amenhotep III originally came to the throne with the name Amenhotep IV. Like his father, the new pharaoh had a beautiful, intelligent wife, Nefertiti, whom he treated as his co-ruler, so much so that he permitted artists to portray Nefertiti in the act of killing Egypt's enemies—a depiction previously restricted to the pharaoh alone.

The royal couple introduced dramatic changes to Egypt. First they called on artists to abandon the traditional method of portraying the royal family in a graceful but highly idealized manner; in future, Egyptian artists were to adopt a naturalistic style that represented the pharaoh and his queen as they truly appeared. In the pharaoh's case, the result would not be flattering: he had a long face, thin arms and legs, a protruding belly, and big, broad hips. As for Nefertiti, she was stunning. A magnificent painted bust of her was discovered by the German archaeologist Ludwig Borchardt in the ruins of Tell el-Amarna in 1912. The discovery proved that Nefertiti's name, which means "a beautiful woman has come," could not have been more accurate.

In or around the year 1348 B.C., Amenhotep IV made a surprising decision: he shut down all the temples in Egypt. Although he permitted his subjects to worship the many Egyptian gods privately, he urged them to join him in the worship of only one god, Aten, the sun god. To commemorate this tremendous change, the pharaoh changed his name to Akhenaten, which means "effective spirit of Aten." Never before in the ancient world had a country made the shift from the worship of many gods to the worship of only one god.

Then Akhenaten made another break with Egypt's past: he built a new capital city, Tell el-Amarna, two hundred miles north of the old capital, Thebes. When Tell el-Amarna was ready to be inhabited, the pharaoh ordered the entire population of Thebes—twenty thousand people—to pack up and move to the new city.

Upon Akhenaten's death, everything he had tried to do fell apart. His court deserted Tell el-Amarna, the priests revived the old cults and dismantled the temples of Aten, and artists returned to the idealized style of portraying the pharoah. As for Akhenaten, for centuries his name was purposely omitted from the list of Egypt's kings; the forgotten pharaoh was not rediscovered until the late nineteenth century.

Statuette of Amenhotep and Nerfertiti, from Tell el-Amarna, Amarna Period, New Kingdom, 1353–1337 B.C.

MUWATALLIS

King of the Hittites (c. 1320–1272 B.C.)

The Hittites ruled from what is now eastern Turkey to Lebanon. With the Hittites looking to expand farther south, and the Egyptians always eager to expand their empire farther north, this was a recipe for trouble that finally came to a boil when two aggressive kings occupied the thrones of these empires at the same time.

Muwatallis had begun his reign securing his hold over the unruly vassal kingdoms of the Hittite empire and hammering out a mutual defense treaty with the kingdom of Troy. The Trojan treaty was especially important since the Hittites occupied a narrow strip of the Aegean coast and did not want to lose it to a hostile neighbor. With Troy, the greatest power on the Asian side of the Aegean, as its ally, the Hittites felt their toehold on the Aegean was secure. Egypt, however, remained an unresolved problem.

Ramses II, arguably the greatest of the warrior pharaohs, wanted Syria; Muwatallis was determined not to let him have it. The showdown came at the Syrian walled city of Kadesh on the Orontes River. Ramses led an army of approximately forty-one thousand men on a thousand-mile march north. Muwatallis met him with an army of more than forty-seven thousand men. In addition to having a numerical advantage, Muwatallis had a secret weapon: his military engineers had invented a new, larger type of chariot that could hold three men instead of two. In the traditional war chariot, such as that used by Ramses, one man was the driver while the second man was the warrior. With two fighting men in each chariot, Muwatallis doubled his firepower on wheels.

The clash of these two ancient superpowers came on May 12, 1274 B.C.. Both kings suffered heavy losses, but neither had a decisive victory. Ultimately, Ramses gathered his men and marched back to Egypt, leaving Kadesh and Syria in the hands of the Hittites. Historians consider the Battle of Kadesh a draw, but from Muwatallis's perspective, the Egyptians had retreated and he was the victor.

Frieze of Ramses II, Mutwallis's nemesis, on his chariot at the Battle of Kadesh

Ramses II the Great

King of Egypt (c. 1303–1213 B.C.)

Toward the end of his life, Ramses II boasted that he had fathered eighty sons and sixty daughters by his eight wives and many concubines. It's possible: the king lived to be over ninety years old, an astonishing achievement at a time when most adults considered themselves lucky to reach their fortieth birthday.

There is a popular misconception, abetted by Cecil B. DeMille's 1956 epic film *The Ten Commandments*, that Ramses was the pharaoh who refused to let Egypt's Hebrew slaves go and so was punished by God with the Ten Plagues. But the facts of Ramses's reign do not mesh with the story of the plagues, found in *Exodus*.

During his long life, Ramses did more than simply father an army of offspring; his building projects are among the most ambitious in Egypt, in many cases making the tombs and temples built by his predecessors look puny. He erected the two temples of Abu Simbel and the mammoth Colossus of Ramses II (the statue is incomplete, but the surviving fragment is almost thirty-three feet long). As for his funerary temple, the Ramesseum, it took an army of artists and workmen twenty years to complete this spectacular structure.

In an age when kings were expected to be fierce and victorious warriors, Ramses broke with tradition by forging the world's first peace treaty. After many years of on-again, off-again warfare with the Hittites (which culminated in the bloody stalemate at the Battle of Kadesh), Ramses made a treaty in which he and the Hittite king promised not only to put an end to hostilities but also to come to each other's assistance against an aggressor. The text of the treaty survives, complete with Ramses's promise regarding the king of the Hittites: "He is a brother to me and he is at peace with me; and I am a brother to him and I am forever at peace with him."

Although grave robbers looted Ramses's tomb, his well-preserved mummy has survived. He was a man with a pronounced hooked nose, a strong jawline, red hair, and he stood five feet, seven inches tall, which was a bit below average in ancient Egypt.

1303 B.C.

Priam

King of Troy (died c. 1250 B.C.)

One of the most colorful characters of nineteenth-century archaeology was Heinrich Schliemann, a German entrepreneur, *Iliad* enthusiast, and amateur archaeologist who was determined to prove through excavations that Homer's account of the Trojan War was literally true. He did find the remains of Troy, but Schliemann's assertion that the cache of gold ornaments he found amid the ruins was King Priam's treasure was wishful thinking.

Then, in the 1980s, something unexpected occurred: archaeologists found three thirteenth-century B.C. Hittite letters and a treaty that referred to individuals and places that sounded strangely familiar. The earliest documents discuss the trouble caused around the city of Wilusa by a local warlord or guerrilla leader named Piyama-Radu; later documents mention the king of Wilusa, Alaksandu, who has made a treaty with the Hittites in which Alaksandu invokes the god Apaliunas.

Scholars have suggested that Piyama-Radu could have been the inspiration for Priam; Alaksandu for Priam's son Alexander (better known by his nickname, Paris); Wilusa for Ilios, the Greek name for Troy; and Apaliunas for Apollo, the god who favored the Trojans in their ten-year war against the Greeks. In other words, these Hittite documents suggest that there is a historical basis for at least two of the main characters of the *Iliad*.

The Priam of Greek mythology was a heroic figure who created a great kingdom for himself in what is now western Turkey. He is said to have fathered fifty sons, including Hector, the greatest of the Trojan warriors, and Alexander, or Paris, whose passion for Helen, the wife of the Greek king Menelaus, sparked the Trojan War.

When the war broke out, Priam was too old to fight; instead he suffered the tragedy of seeing his splendid sons cut down on the battlefield, one by one. The death of Hector at the hands of Achilles was Priam's greatest grief. The old king's appeal to Achilles to let him take the body of his son home for a proper burial is one of the most affecting passages in the *Iliad*.

According to Homer, when the Greeks captured Troy, Priam fled to an altar for sanctuary, but Achilles's son, Neoptolemus, violated the law of sanctuary by dragging the old man away from the altar and slitting his throat.

The Death of Priam by Pierre Narcisse Guérin

SAUL

King of Israel (c. 1067–1007 B.C.)

Between approximately 1400 B.C. and 1050 B.C., the Israelites were ruled by judges who settled disputes and enforced the Law of Moses. When the Israelites complained that they wanted a king like all the surrounding nations, their prophets, judges and priests reminded them that God was their king. But that was not enough for a nation the Old Testament describes as "a stiff-necked people."

Finally the prophet Samuel, with the approval of the Lord, gave the Israelites a king. The man selected to rule the Chosen People literally stood head and shoulders above all other contenders: "From his shoulders upward he was taller than any of the people" (I Samuel 9:2). The man's name was Saul.

Saul's greatest challenge was defending his little kingdom against such aggressive neighbors as the Philistines, the Ammonites, and the Amalekites, but he did not have complete autonomy—he was obliged to follow the directions that God sent him through Samuel. Driven by pride, Saul began to act independently, even flagrantly disobeying a direct command from the Lord to wipe out the Amalekites, their king, and even their livestock. Instead, Saul spared the life of the king and rounded up all the best-quality sheep and cattle. That was the beginning of the end of Saul's reign. "Because you have rejected the word of the Lord," Samuel told him, "he has also rejected you from becoming king" (I Samuel 15:23).

Saul fell into a depression. In an effort to soothe the king's troubled spirit, members of his family invited a shepherd boy named David to come play the harp and sing for Saul. Usually the music did calm the king, but on one occasion, in a violent fit, he hurled a spear at David, narrowly missing him.

Following the death of Samuel in the year 1011 B.C., Saul felt more lost than ever. On the eve of a major battle, Saul violated a cardinal principle of the Hebrews; he had a witch conjure up the spirit of Samuel. The prophet appeared, and was angry that Saul has disturbed his rest and committed such a great sin. Then Samuel predicted that Saul would be defeated and slain with all of his sons. Samuel's last prophecy proved true: at Gilboa, the Philistines routed the Israelites and killed all of the king's sons. Saul, badly wounded and afraid the Philistines might take him prisoner, fell on his own sword and died.

Painting of Saul from the church of Santa Maria della Salute, Venice, Italy

DAVID

King of Israel (c. 1037–970 B.C.)

David was a boy shepherd, the youngest of eight brothers, when the prophet Samuel anointed him king to succeed Saul. But everyone involved in the anointing kept it secret so as not to stir up the vengeance of Saul.

The most famous story about the boy David is his battle with Goliath, a Philistine giant who stood about ten feet tall and was armed with massive weaponry. Every day Goliath challenged the Israelites to send out a champion for man-to-man combat, but no one in Israel would take on the giant, so David said he would go. Taking only his slingshot and five round stones, he walked out onto the battlefield. With a running start, he placed a stone in his sling and hurled it at Goliath. It embedded itself in the giant's forehead and he fell facedown on the ground, dead. But just to be on the safe side, David cut off Goliath's head.

Years later when he was king, David spied a beautiful woman named Bathsheba as she was bathing. Bathsheba was married, but David had a solution for that: he had her husband, Uriah, assigned to the front ranks in the next battle. When the man was killed, as the king expected he would be, David married Bathsheba.

As was customary at the time, David had many wives and many children. Although he was a beloved king, he was an inconsistent father who could never bring himself to discipline his children. Consequently his sons grew up spoiled and arrogant but also insecure, since David had never announced which of the princes would succeed him. In fact, he had decided that his heir would be Solomon, the son he fathered with Bathsheba, but he never disclosed this decision to the rest of his family. Two of David's sons, Absalom and Adonijah, led rebellions against David, and both nearly succeeded in toppling their father from his throne. It was David's loyal military commanders who saved him from the rebels.

An ancient legend claims that David composed the 150 psalms of the Bible. It is possible, even likely, that he composed some of them, including one that must have been written by someone who spent years guarding flocks of sheep: Psalm 23 reads, "The Lord is my shepherd, I shall not want."

King David in his old age

David.

SOLOMON

King of Israel (c. 991–831 B.C.)

The crowning achievement of Solomon's reign was the construction of the Holy Temple in Jerusalem. For centuries, since the days of the Exodus, Israel's most sacred object, the Ark of the Covenant (which enshrined the original tablets bearing the Ten Commandments, along with other relics) had been housed in a pavilion. Essentially, the house of the Lord was a tent—a very opulent tent, but still a tent. David had wanted to build a temple, but God had forbidden it, saying, "You may not build a house for my name, for you are a man of war and have shed blood" (I Chronicles 28:3). Instead, David accumulated gold, silver, bronze, silk, cedar wood, and other precious objects for the day the Lord would permit a king of Israel to build him a proper temple. That king was Solomon, and the temple he constructed was the most magnificent structure the people of Israel had ever seen.

When he was still a novice king, Solomon asked God to give him wisdom. God answered the king's prayer and also gave him vast wealth, power, and an empire that extended from what is now southern Iraq to the Red Sea. The highest tribute to Solomon's glory was the state visit of the Queen of Sheba, whose empire embraced modern-day Ethiopia, Somalia, Eritrea, and Yemen. There is an ancient legend that Solomon and Sheba had an affair, and on her return home she gave birth to a son, Menilek I, whom Ethiopians regard as the founder of a royal line that endured until the death of Emperor Haile Selassie in 1975.

In his old age, Solomon's wisdom left him. He married hundreds of foreign princesses, all of them pagans. To keep his attractive young wives happy, he erected altars and shrines to their gods, and even prayed at them himself. As if this were not enough to antagonize his people, Solomon kept up a lavish building program that obliged him to increase taxes and even to force free Israelite men to work at the construction sites. The tensions begun during the final years of Solomon's reign would lead to the breakup of the kingdom of Israel.

Illustration of Solomon from a 19th century edition of the Bible

AHAB AND JEZEBEL

King (c. 897–850 B.C.) and Queen (died c. 845 B.C.) of Judah

One of the most notorious royal couples of the ancient world, Ahab and Jezebel shocked their subjects as few monarchs have before or since.

Ahab was the great-great-great-great-great grandson of Solomon. Jezebel was a Phoenician princess. In the ninth century B.C., the Phoenicians were the merchant princes of the Mediterranean world. By his marriage to Jezebel, Ahab's kingdom suddenly had access to the markets of the world. Judah became immensely rich, and Ahab's share was staggering; he was so wealthy he built himself a palace covered with thin sheets of ivory.

Jezebel brought more than wealth to Judah, she also brought her gods: Baal, the god of rain, thunder, crops, and fertility; and Astarte, the goddess of fertility and sexuality. It was customary in other countries for consorts of the king to continue to worship the gods they had revered back home, but in Israel such a thing was forbidden by law. Finding this law uncongenial, Ahab and Jezebel chose to ignore it.

Ahab erected shrines to Baal and Astarte wherever Jezebel liked, including sites the Israelites considered sacred to the Lord God. Soon Jezebel was acting independently of her husband—persuading leading Israelites to worship at her temples, declaring publicly that she was the sworn enemy of the God of Israel, murdering Hebrew prophets by the dozens, even having a poor farmer named Naboth stoned to death on false charges of blasphemy so Ahab could acquire the man's vineyard. And against all these outrages, Ahab did not lift a finger. The Bible tells us, "Ahab did more to provoke the Lord, the God of Israel, to anger than all the kings of Israel who were before him" (I Kings 16:33).

Ahab had been king about nineteen years when he went to war against the Assyrians. He died in a battle fought along the Jordan River. As for Jezebel, she lived on for a few more years, raising her children to be vicious little heathens and continuing to outrage her Hebrew subjects. Finally Jehu, a member of the royal family who had had enough of the queen's depravity, persuaded Jezebel's eunuchs to kill her. The slaves threw her out a palace window. No one bothered to take the queen's broken body away for burial—it was left on the pavement for stray dogs to eat.

Ahab upset that Naboth would not sell him his vineyard

ASHURBANIPAL

King of Assyria (c. 695–627 B.C.)

Ashurbanipal was one of those rare kings who was both a warrior and a scholar. His warlike qualities came to him naturally—the Assyrians were the most ferocious fighters of the ancient Middle East, notorious for committing the most shocking atrocities against their enemies. In 667 B.C., the year after he became king, Ashurbanipal displayed his military gifts in a war against Egypt that resulted in the Assyrians seizing control of the Nile Delta. Three years later Ashurbanipal invaded Egypt again, this time capturing and sacking the cities of Memphis and Thebes. In fact, much of the king's reign was taken up with wars. One moment he especially savored came in 639 B.C. when he hitched the kings of four nations to his chariot and forced them to pull it in a victory parade.

But Ashurbanipal was also a book lover. He built the greatest library in the Middle East, filled with twenty thousand to thirty thousand books (actually they were clay tablets). Among these works were some of the earliest scientific texts written by Assyrian scholars who were trying, through direct observation, to understand the natural world and the movement of the stars and planets. Ashurbanipal's library also contained many religious works, as well as works of literature, including the *Epic of Gilgamesh*.

The library had a section that today we would call "closed stacks," to which general readers were not admitted. This chamber held tablets relating to affairs of state and reports from the king's spies.

Ashurbanipal ruled from Nineveh, a spectacular capital near modern-day Mosul in Iraq. The city stood on the eastern bank of the Tigris River and was enclosed within seven miles of defensive battlements. Broad boulevards led to lovely gardens and parks, thriving marketplaces, and glorious palaces and temples. One of these palaces, known as the North Palace, was built by Ashurbanipal; its walls were covered with sublime carvings of the king hunting lions and gazelles, destroying his enemies, worshipping the gods, and celebrating at banquets. Today most of these masterworks of art are on display at the British Museum in London.

Statue of Ashurbanipal clutching a lion

NEBUCHADNEZZAR II

King of Babylon (c. 630–562 B.C.)

Babylon lay in what is now Iraq, fifty-five miles south of present-day Baghdad. In the seventh century B.C., Babylon was a rising power, and its king Nebuchadnezzar wanted to expand his kingdom into Syria, Judah, and, if fortune smiled on him, Egypt.

In 605 he led a successful expedition against Egypt, but the little kingdom of Judah proved to be more problematic than expected. Judah fell quickly before the Babylonians, and the king Jehoiakim swore to be Nebuchadnezzar's vassal. But soon Jehoiakim was scheming with the Egyptians. Nebuchadnezzar invaded Judah a second time, executed Jehoiakim and left his body in the sun to rot. He then rounded up more than three thousand Jewish hostages and marched them to Babylon. He gave the throne of Judah to Jeconiah, Jehoiakim's son, but Jeconiah proved to be a schemer, too.

Barely three months passed before Nebuchadnezzar was forced to invaded Judah again. This time he rounded up the entire royal family and ten thousand of the most distinguished men, women, and children of Judah and led them all to exile in Babylon.

Once again Nebuchadnezzar appointed a puppet king to rule Judah—Jeconiah's uncle, Zedekiah. For nine years Zedekiah did as he was commanded by his Babylonian overlords, but conniving must have been a family trait because, in the end, he tried to make a deal with the Egyptians to break the Babylonians' hold over Judah.

Now Nebuchadnezzar was merciless. He stormed the walls of Jerusalem, looted all the sacred vessels from the Temple of Solomon, then destroyed the holy place along with the rest of city. He captured Zedekiah and ordered him to watch as Babylonian troops slaughtered all of Zedekiah's sons. Finally, Nebuchadnezzar had Zedekiah blinded, loaded down with chains, and dragged to Babylon, where he was left in a prison cell to die.

Aside from his troubles with Judah, Nebuchadnezzar has another claim to fame: as a gift for his queen, Amytis, who missed the gardens of her homeland, he built one of the Seven Wonders of the World, the Hanging Gardens of Babylon. Planted on a series of elaborate terraces, the garden got its name from the lush vines and vegetation that spilled, or hung, over the balustrades and terrace walls.

According to the biblical Book of Daniel, Nebuchadnezzar threw three of his Israelite captives into a furnace

CYRUS THE GREAT

King of Persia (c. 600–530 B.C.)

Cyrus the Great was the first man to conquer an immense swathe of his world. Within twenty years he forged an empire that stretched from India to the borders of Greece.

Unlike many empire builders, Cyrus was a popular king, even among the people he conquered. He won over the Babylonians by attributing his victories to the chief god of the Babylonian pantheon, Marduk. In other words, he identified himself with his Babylonian subjects.

In Babylon, at this time, were the Jews who had been dragged there by Nebuchadnezzar. In 538 B.C., Cyrus released the Jews and gave them permission to return to their homeland, rebuild Jerusalem, and reconstruct their temple. According to the biblical book of Ezra, Cyrus issued a proclamation stating, "The Lord, the God of heaven, has given me all the kingdoms of the earth, and he has charged me to build him a house at Jerusalem" (Ezra 1:2). Consequently, both Jewish and Christian historians came to regard Cyrus as a messianic figure.

Cyrus's empire marked the end of the kingdoms of Mesopotamia. For at least five hundred years they had been major power players in the Middle East; now they were vassal states of Persia. They would never regain their former political influence.

At the time Cyrus began his conquest, there were a string of Greek colonies clinging to the Aegean coast of present-day Turkey. All of these colonies fell to Cyrus, of course. This marked the first clash between Greeks and Persians, a state of affairs which would dominate Greek foreign policy for the next two hundred years until Alexander the Great turned the tables on the Persians by invading and conquering their empire.

What became of Cyrus is a mystery. The Greek historians Herodotus and Ctesias say that he died in battle, while another Greek historian, Xenophon, says the great king died peacefully in his bed. Even his legacy is open to dispute. It is popular these days to cite Cyrus as an early champion of human rights and religious tolerance. More likely he was a shrewd practitioner of public relations, a man who understood that it was easier to rule people if you treated them with sympathy and generosity.

Croesus (c. 546 B.C.), last king of Lydia, faces Cyrus the Great, emperor of Persia, after defeat and capture at his hands.

CROESUS

King of Lydia (c. 595–547 B.C.)

Croesus is the king who inspired the saying "rich as Croesus." It is said that, thanks to his gold and silver mines, as well as trade routes that brought wealth into his kingdom by the boatload, Croesus outstripped all other monarchs of his day for luxurious living. Plutarch describes him as "decked out with everything in the way of precious stones, dyed raiment, and wrought gold that men deem remarkable, or extravagant, or enviable, in order that he might present a most august and gorgeous spectacle."

Croesus is one of those figures whose story is caught somewhere between history and mythology. For example, it is said that Croesus invented coins. While it is true that coins were first used in the kingdom of Lydia, they were put into circulation not by Croesus but by his ancestor King Gyges around the year 650 B.C..

There is another story, which tells how the great Athenian philosopher Solon visited Croesus at his court. Croesus took great pleasure in showing his distinguished guest all the treasures of his palace; then he asked Solon if he did not believe that he, Croesus, must be the happiest man alive. Solon replied, "Count no man happy until he is dead."

When Cyrus the Great of Persia planned to attack Lydia, Croesus formed an alliance with the Spartans, the Egyptians, and the Babylonians. Even here a bit of mythology enters the narrative. Before preparing for war against Cyrus, Croesus is said to have consulted the oracles of Delphi and Thebes; they both told him that if he led an army against the Persians, he would destroy a great empire. Believing that the prophecy meant that he would defeat Cyrus, Croesus went forward with his battle plans.

The armies met on the Halys River in modern-day Turkey, but the battle was inconclusive. Croesus fell back to the city of Sardis, and Cyrus followed. The Persians stormed the city and captured Croesus, whom Cyrus sentenced to be burned alive. As the flames rose around him, the king must have remembered what the Athenian philosopher had said about happy men; the last word Croesus spoke was "Solon!"

Croesus among his treasures, 1624

LEONIDAS

King of Sparta (c. 540–480 B.C.)

One of the greatest Greek heroes, Leonidas's story has reached a wider audience than ever before thanks to the success of the film *300*, based on Frank Miller and Lynn Varley's graphic novel of the same name.

In 480 B.C. Xerxes I, king of Persia, led an immense army to conquer Greece. The ancient Greek historian Herodotus later claimed that Xerxes had more than 2 million men; modern estimates set the strength of the Persian troops at approximately two hundred thousand. Xerxes entered Greece from the north, following the country's eastern coastline. In a meeting of representatives of all the Greek city-states, the allies agreed to a two-part strategy: to halt, or least impede, the Persian invasion by holding the narrow mountain pass of Thermopylae while a navy of Greek ships would attempt to destroy or turn back the Persian armada. Leonidas of Sparta volunteered to defend Thermopylae.

But a problem of timing arose: it was the time of the Carneia, a sacred festival in honor of Apollo, when Spartan law forbade the army to participate in a military campaign. Leonidas could lead only his personal bodyguard of three hundred men and a small force of Spartan troops to Thermopylae. Other Greek city-states sent reinforcements numbering between three thousand and six thousand men.

For two days Leonidas commanded a brilliantly simple defensive strategy. Standing shoulder to shoulder, the Greeks blocked the narrow pass, inflicting serious casualties on Xerxes's men.

At the end of the second day, however, the Persians, led by a Greek traitor, took up position at the Greeks' rear. Rather than have thousands of men slaughtered, Leonidas dismissed his allies; as for the Spartans, they were forbidden by law to retreat from any battlefield. They would remain. Seven hundred Thespians and four hundred Thebans volunteered to remain and fight with the Spartans.

Surrounded and outnumbered, the Greeks put up a desperate fight until the Persians fired repeated volleys of arrows that killed every Greek.

Today at Thermopylae, a monument commemorates Leonidas and his valiant Greek troops. Engraved on the monument is the epitaph "Go tell the Spartans, stranger passing by, that here, obedient to their laws, we lie."

Statue of Leonidas in Sparta, which features his response to Xerxes demand to lay down their weapons: "Come and take them"

Xerxes I

King of Persia (c. 519–465 B.C.)

Every hero needs a villain, and for Leonidas of Sparta that role was filled by Xerxes I, a Persian king who has gone down in history as despotic, vengeful, and cruel.

When Xerxes succeeded to the throne of Persia in 486 B.C., he had one thought on his mind: to punish the Greeks for the defeat his father, Darius I, had suffered four years earlier. At the Battle of Marathon, a Greek force, outnumbered perhaps nine to one, slaughtered more than six thousand Persians while taking barely two hundred casualties.

In 480 B.C., after assembling an army of two hundred thousand men from every corner of his empire, Xerxes marched on Greece. Leonidas, his three hundred Spartans, and their allies delayed the Persians for three days at Thermopylae. In the end, Xerxes massacred the Greek defenders of the pass.

As he advanced into Greece, he turned his troops loose on the inhabitants. They burned towns and cities to the ground, killed the men, gang-raped the women, and kept any survivors as slaves. When the Persians reached Athens, they found the lower city deserted—the entire population had fled—but a Greek garrison defended the Acropolis along with a few dozen civilians who had chosen to remain. The Persians stormed the upper city, killed everyone on the Acropolis, then set fire to the Temple of Athena.

The final battle of the war was fought not on land but at sea. The navy of the Greek alliance had larger, heavier ships than Xerxes, and imitating the strategy of King Leonidas, they picked a constricted area for their sea battle. The Persians, finding it difficult to maneuver in the little Bay of Salamis, became easy targets for the Greeks, who rammed their ships and set them on fire. With half his navy sunk, Xerxes turned over the command of the invasion to his general Mardonius and returned to Persia.

The Greek historian Herodotus says that Xerxes spent the last fifteen years of his life immersed in "the intrigues of the harem" until at last his own bodyguard killed him.

King Xerxes of Persia loses his fleet to the Greeks at the Battle of Salamis, in the Gulf of Aegina near Athens, September 480 B.C.

ARTEMISIA I

Queen of Caria and Ionia (Died c. 480 B.C.)

One of the ancient world's craftiest warrior queens, Artemisia became queen of Caria and Ionia (in what is now Turkey) after the death of her husband. It is not known when she was born, or what occurred in her early life, or even her husband's name. Most of the facts concerning Artemisia come from the Greek historian Herodotus. He wrote that she ruled her kingdom from the city of Halicarnassus and allied herself with the Persians against the Greeks, contributing five war ships—which she commanded herself—to Xerxes's navy.

On the eve of the Battle of Salamis, Xerxes held a war council with his admirals, all of whom urged him to attack the Greek ships. Artemisia disagreed. Pointing out that he had conquered a great part of Greece and destroyed Athens and that the rest of the country was likely to fall to him soon, the queen begged him, "Spare your ships and do not fight at sea, for the Greeks are infinitely superior to us in naval matters." In spite of Artemisia's advice, Xerxes followed the counsel of his admirals.

The next day, like a loyal ally, Artemisia brought her five warships to the battle, but when she found herself surrounded by Athenian ships, she adopted a daring method of escape. She rammed and sank a Persian ship. Xerxes, watching from a distance, assumed that Artemisia had successfully destroyed a Greek ship. The Greeks, seeing her turn on a Persian vessel, assumed she was allied with them. With neither the Persians nor the Greeks making any attempt to stop her, Artemisia made her getaway.

From her shrewd game of playing both sides at Salamis, a legend grew that Queen Artemisia went on to become a pirate who flew the Persian flag when she was hunting Greek ships and flew the Greek flag if any Greek ships pursued her.

What became of Artemisia is another mystery; we do not know how or when she died, but we do know that she was succeeded by her grandson.

480 B.C.

Greeks defeating Persians at the Battle of Salamis

Dionysius I

Tyrant of Syracuse (c. 432–367 B.C.)

In ancient Greece, the title tyrant meant an absolute ruler who had seized power illegally. "Tyrant" did not become associated with cruelty and despotism until the fifth century B.C., and certainly Dionysius I helped give the word its new meaning.

He began life as an ordinary bureaucrat, but in 409 B.C., when his city-state, Syracuse, went to war with the Carthaginians over control of the island of Sicily, Dionysius enlisted. He discovered that he had unexpected talents as a warrior and as a public speaker. After Syracuse suffered a nasty defeat at the hands of the Carthaginians, Dionysius rose in the city assembly to urge the election of a new staff of generals—and he offered himself as one of the candidates. The motion passed, Dionysius was elected, and within a year he had seized absolute power. As supreme commander, with the entire Syracuse military behind him, he could do as he pleased.

Because he regarded the Greek colonies in southern Italy as a threat, he destroyed the cities of Croton and Thurii, stormed the city of Rhegium (now Reggio di Calabria), and sold all the surviving citizens into slavery.

The dream of his life was to drive the Carthaginians from Sicily and become lord of the entire island. In spite of repeated attempts, he never managed to conquer more than two-thirds of the island.

Dionysius regarded himself as a sophisticated man. He invited historians, poets, and philosophers—including Plato—to his court and sometimes recited his poetry for them. But Dionysius's literary gifts were uneven. When his poems were read at the Olympic Games, the crowd hissed, although toward the end of his life he won a prize for his play, *The Ransom of Hector*. There is a story, perhaps apocryphal, that Dionysius overheard the poet Philoxenus criticizing his poetry; he had the man arrested and sentenced him to forced labor in the quarries. A few days later he had Philoxenus brought back to the palace for another poetry reading. When Dionysius had finished, he asked the poet what he thought of his work. Philoxenus replied, "Take me back to the quarries."

54

PHILIP II AND OLYMPIAS

King (c. 382–336 B.C.) and Queen (c. 376–316 B.C.) of Macedonia

At age fourteen, Philip of Macedon was given to the Greeks as a hostage to ensure that his father and elder brother would not attack Greece. Although Greece was a world power at this time, the Greeks regarded Macedonia as an up-and-coming threat. For three years Philip lived in Greece, and during that time he observed how the Greek military operated—and how it could be beaten.

When the Greeks sent Philip home, he immediately set to work retraining and reorganizing the Macedonian army. One of his innovations was arming his troops with sixteen-foot spears. These very long spears, combined with complicated maneuvers and formations on the battlefield, made it almost impossible for enemy troops to get anywhere near the Macedonians.

The kingdom Philip inherited at age twenty-one was on the verge of disaster, with enemies on all sides, but within a year he stabilized the political situation. He made peace with the king of Thrace (present-day Bulgaria) by presenting him with lavish gifts. He won the friendship of Athens by ceding to it a city on the Macedonian coast. And he met a rival claimant to the throne on the battlefield, where he defeated him.

Two years later Philip traveled to the island of Samothrace to be inducted into the mysterious cult of Dionysius, the god of wine and ecstasy. There he met Olympias, a fifteen-year-old initiate. They married, and in 356 B.C., Olympias gave birth to a son they named Alexander—the future Alexander the Great.

The royal couple's marriage was stormy, not least because Philip married seven or eight times, forcing Olympias to give up her position as the principal wife. Although hopeless as a couple, they were devoted parents who saw great promise in Alexander.

In 337 B.C. Philip took another wife, but this marriage was different—this time he divorced Olympias and even repudiated Alexander as his legitimate heir. A year later a Macedonian noble named Pausanias stabbed Philip to death. There is a long-standing suspicion that Olympias hired the assassin.

PTOLEMY I SOTER

King of Egypt (367–282 B.C.)

When Philip of Macedonia hired Aristotle to tutor his son Alexander, he permitted a handful of fortunate young boys also to join the class; one of these boys was Ptolemy. Alexander and Ptolemy remained close friends all their lives; when Alexander became king and began his conquests, Ptolemy was one of his Companions, his inner circle of comrades and trusted advisors.

Alexander's empire did not survive him: after his death, his friends and generals divided up his empire, and Ptolemy got Egypt. As a Greek, he had no idea how to be a pharaoh, but he was determined to learn. He brought in a team of Egyptians to teach him the ancient customs of the kings of Egypt.

One of Ptolemy's first acts was to kidnap the body of Alexander. A general named Perdiccas was escorting it home to Macedonia when Ptolemy's men waylaid it in Damascus. They carried it back to Alexandria, the city Alexander had founded on the Mediterranean near the western edge of the Nile Delta. It may sound macabre, but Ptolemy believed that he and his successors would gain prestige if they were the guardians of the remains of Alexander the Great.

Ptolemy received his nickname Soter (Greek for "savior") in 304 B.C. when he came to the rescue of the people of Rhodes, who were besieged by an enemy of Ptolemy's, Demetrius, the ambitious son of one of Alexander's generals. Over the next decade, Ptolemy added southern Syria and Palestine to his Egyptian empire and extended his political influence into what is now Turkey.

Although warfare absorbed most of his energy, Ptolemy was also interested in bringing Greek culture and civilization to Egypt. He founded the great Library of Alexandria and established the Museum, an academy for artists, scientists, and philosophers. He also wrote a biography of Alexander the Great, but sadly, no copy of it has survived.

Ptolemy's descendants ruled Egypt for nearly three hundred years, his dynasty of Greek pharaohs coming to end when Cleopatra killed herself.

Ptolemy I Soter, one of Alexander the Great's greatest generals and King of Egypt

J. Chapman   sculp.

ALEXANDER THE GREAT

King of Macedonia (356–323 B.C.)

Alexander was a restless young man whose desire for glory led him to attempt to conquer the entire known world —in a space of only thirteen years. And he almost succeeded. He swept through the Balkans and Thrace. All of present-day Turkey, Syria, and the nations of the Middle East fell to him. Egypt did not even put up a fight. The Persian Empire, long considered the mightiest in the world, collapsed, and its king, Darius, was murdered by his own men. Alexander marched through the mountains of Afghanistan (although it is debatable how much of the country he actually controlled) and into India, where finally, he was forced to stop—his army refused to go any farther.

As an empire builder, Alexander was remarkably innovative. His dominion embraced countless ethnic groups who spoke a babel of languages. How was such an empire to be ruled? Alexander's solution was first to give preference to no nation or tribe and to treat all of his subjects as equal citizens of his empire. Second, he introduced Greek civilization to people the Greeks derided as barbarians. In this way, he hoped to diminish resentments while setting up a culture with which all of his people could identify.

Alexander's pride often got in the way of his ideals. He liked to think of himself as an ordinary Macedonian trooper, yet he liked to wear the gorgeous robes of a Persian king—dress his Macedonian soldiers considered outrageously foppish. He also enjoyed seeing his Persian subjects prostrate themselves before him, an act the Macedonians regarded as sacrilegious since one only prostrated oneself before a god. When Alexander demanded that Macedonians and Greeks prostrate themselves if he was in the company of his Persian in-laws (he had married a Persian princess), he nearly had a mutiny on his hands.

Although he had acquiesced to his troops' demands to withdraw from India, Alexander still dreamed of other worlds to conquer. In 323 B.C. he was in Babylon, planning a new campaign, when he became ill and died. He was only thirty-three years old. Because he had named no heir, Alexander's empire died with him.

HAMILCAR BARCA

Dictator of Carthage (c. 275–228 B.C.)

Hamilcar Barca's family was one of the most distinguished in Carthage—they traced their ancestry back to the semi-legendary Carthaginian queen Dido. She had fallen hopelessly in love with Aeneas. When he abandoned her to continue his quest to found the city that would become Rome, she killed herself, cursing Aeneas and his Roman descendants as she died.

The story is almost certainly mythical, but the intense hatred Carthaginians and Romans felt for one another was real. For centuries the Carthaginians had dominated the western Mediterranean militarily, culturally, and commercially. In the third century B.C., the Romans completed their conquest of the entire Italian peninsula and were ready to start flexing their muscles in the Mediterranean. The first clash between Carthaginians and Romans occurred on Sicily. It was the largest island in the Mediterranean, situated at the center of all the trade routes, and famous for its abundant harvests of everything from grapes to grain to lemons.

At the beginning of this war with Rome—known as the First Punic War—Carthage was already fighting the Libyans; consequently, the Carthaginians could not send a great mass of troops to Sicily. Working with what he had at hand, Hamilcar transformed a small fighting force of Carthaginians and mercenary troops into a cohesive unit. Over a period of six years it harassed the Romans in Sicily and sapped their resources of men, arms, and supplies. Although Hamilcar went from victory to victory on land, the Carthaginian navy was defeated by a newly constructed Roman navy. After this defeat, Hamilcar and his men returned to Carthage, where by popular acclaim the general was made absolute ruler, or dictator.

During the eight years of his administration, Hamilcar raised a new army to protect Carthaginian territory from the next assault from Rome (which he knew would come) and invaded the Iberian Peninsula—a move intended to expand Carthage's empire and flank the Romans. He died in what is now Spain, drowning in the Jucar River during the siege of an Iberian town.

QIN SHI HUANG

Emperor of China (c. 259–210 B.C.)

It is the rare ruler who does not create some grand work of art or architecture as a monument to himself, but the work Qin Shi Huang left for posterity is one of the most remarkable in the world. He ordered the finest artists and craftsmen in China to create for him a life-size terracotta army—eight thousand soldiers, archers, cavalrymen with their horses, and chariots complete with charioteers. Each statue was hand painted, each face individualized, which has led some scholars to believe that living persons served as models. Upon the emperor's death, these extraordinary figures were lined up in battle formation, then buried with him in his immense tomb.

Qin Shi Huang was a man of great vision, great ambition, and tremendous ego. He began his reign by subduing rival clans and regions and uniting them into a single state; this was the beginning of the nation we know as China. He divided his realm in to thirty-six prefectures, or provinces, administered by men loyal to him alone. He built a system of roads to enable the swift passage of commerce as well as information throughout the empire. He standardized Chinese script and introduced uniform coinage. These were all necessary and praiseworthy innovations, but Qin Shi Huang went well beyond them.

To protect China's northern borders, he sent tens, perhaps hundreds, of thousands of slaves and convicts to erect a massive fortification. This was the beginning of the Great Wall, an epic building project that would take a century to complete and cost approximately one million lives.

To control the beliefs and culture of his empire, the emperor ordered all books written before his reign to be burned. To suppress rebellion, he executed anyone who criticized him or any of his actions, and for good measure, the emperor executed the critic's family, too. Confucian scholars were especially resistant to the emperor's suppression of philosophy: he arrested 460 such scholars and, as a lesson to all other Chinese philosophers, had these men buried alive.

Toward the end of his reign, Qin Shi Huang took up a new obsession—an elixir would that would make him immortal. The potion his doctors prescribed contained a tiny amount of mercury that slowly poisoned the emperor.

Hannibal

Ruler of Carthage (c. 247– c. 183 B.C.)

Hannibal's entire life was shaped by a single desire: to destroy the power of Rome and make Carthage supreme in the Mediterranean. It's said that when he was only nine years old, his father, Hamilcar Barca, insisted that he place his hand on the altar of the gods of Carthage and swear a sacred oath of undying hatred for Rome.

At age twenty-six, Hannibal was named commander of the armies of Carthage. War had just broken out with Rome, and he was about to display the daring and insight of a much more mature man. Hannibal took his army to Iberia, then drove across Gaul (present-day France), and through the Alps. In October 218 B.C., the people of northern Italy saw thirty-eight thousand Carthaginian infantry, eight thousand cavalry, and a horde of war elephants marching through their countryside.

For the next two years Hannibal defeated, sometimes even annihilated, every army Rome sent against him. Finally, in the summer of 216 B.C., the Roman senate sent eighty thousand men to fight against the Carthaginians. The two armies met near Cannae on the east coast of Italy. Hannibal arrayed his men in the shape of a convex crescent. As the Romans attacked, the Carthaginians slowly gave way until their formation changed to a concave crescent. Then the Carthaginian cavalry attacked from the rear, completely encircling the Romans and destroying them.

Meanwhile, Rome dug in for a fight. Hannibal failed to seize vital Roman ports, which made it almost impossible for Carthage to send him reinforcements. As one Roman army drove him into southern Italy, another Roman army, led by Publius Cornelius Scipio (later Scipio Africanus), conquered Iberia and attacked Carthage. Hannibal rushed home only to be defeated by Scipio at the Battle of Zama.

Rome imposed humiliating treaty terms on Carthage, yet the Carthaginians did not blame their commander—they elected Hannibal *suffete*, or ruler. In the face of this setback, Hannibal continued to look for an opportunity to collect an army and finally crush his great enemy. Hannibal's scheming attracted the attention of the Romans and he was forced to flee, first to Syria, then to Bithynia on the Black Sea. As the Romans closed in on him, Hannibal made his final escape by taking poison.

Hannibal swearing eternal enmity to Rome

Judas Maccabeus

Ruler of Judea (c. 205–160 B.C.)

The Jewish festival Hanukkah celebrates the high point of Judas Maccabeus's life. He had driven the Syrians and Greeks out of Jerusalem, tossed the idols of their gods out of the Temple, and was preparing to have Jewish priests rededicate it for the worship of God. However, he learned that during the Syrian-Greek desecration, virtually all of the Temple's sacred oil had been destroyed. Only one small jar remained, enough to burn in the Temple's menorah for a single day, but the purification ritual called for the menorah to burn continuously for eight days. Nonetheless, the priests poured the oil into the menorah and lit it. Miraculously, the menorah burned for the required eight days.

Much of Judas's life was as miraculous, or at least had an astonishing quality. In 175 B.C., when King Antiochus IV Epiphanes outlawed the practice of the Jewish religion and tried to compel all the people of Judea to worship the gods of Syria and Greece, Judas, the son of a Jewish priest, was living quietly in an obscure village. As anti-Jewish persecution intensified, Judas, his father, and his four brothers led a guerrilla movement that harassed Antiochus's forces.

As more Jewish men joined Judas, his raids became battles. Inspired by Judas, whose strength and fearlessness in combat won him the nickname Maccabeus—the Hammer—the Jews won a string of victories.

After eleven years of fighting, in 164 B.C., Judas and his army drove the Syrians and Greeks from Jerusalem. But the war was not over. The last four years of Judas's life were spent fighting new Syrian invasions and trying to restore traditional Jewish religious life. His efforts were opposed by two high priests, Menelaus and Alcimus, who wanted to graft Greek religious practices onto Judaism. Menelaus became such a menace that Judas had him executed.

In 160 B.C. the Syrians sent an army of twenty thousand men to retake Judea. Judas's army fled, except for a small number of loyal fighting men. These, Judas led into battle, where they were all slaughtered.

Judas's sacrifice became an inspiration, a turning point that united the Jews and gave them the confidence to drive out the Syrians at last. Judas was succeeded by his brothers, who founded the Hasmonean dynasty that ruled the Kingdom of Israel for 103 years.

Judas Maccabeus pursuing Timotheus

SOPHONISBA

Queen of Numidia (died c. 203 B.C.)

One of the saddest stories of the ancient world is the life of Sophonisba, a Carthaginian noblewoman who should have enjoyed a happy, privileged life as the Queen of Eastern Numidia (present-day Algeria as well as a portion of Tunisia).

The trouble began in 206 B.C., when her betrothed, Massinissa, King of the eastern Numidians, had second thoughts about allying himself with a Carthaginian family. The Romans were becoming the dominant power in the Mediterranean, Massinissa thought it might be best to find a wife who brought with her a lot less political baggage. But before he could break off the engagement, the king of the western Numidians, Syphax, invaded and seized Massinissa's kingdom.

Meanwhile poor Sophonisba was still at home, unmarried. Her father, however, was a pragmatic man and approached Syphax to see if he might be interested in marrying his daughter. Syphax most certainly was interested in a marriage to Sophonisba and an alliance with Carthage.

For a time after Sophonisba's wedding, the Numidian-Carthaginian alliance was a success. When the Romans invaded North Africa and tried to capture the city of Utica, Syphax and his Carthaginian allies drove them back. Sadly, their success was short-lived. The Romans returned with additional troops supplied by Massinissa. As the Romans rolled across North Africa, Syphax and Sophonisba fled east to the Numidian city of Cirta, where Massinissa pursued and captured them.

The Romans sent Syphax to Italy as a prisoner of war. Sophonisba should have gone, too—the Romans liked to parade conquered royalty through the streets—but Massinissa had a change of heart again. He hoped the Romans would install him as king of all Numidia, and he imagined he would appear more legitimate to his subjects if their queen was his wife.

The Roman commander, Scipio Africanus, did not approve of the marriage. Sophonisba had spoken too strongly against Rome—clearly she was a queen who could not be trusted. It is not known whether Scipio demanded that Sophonisba kill herself or if Massinissa suggested it to spare her the indignity of being made a spectacle in Rome. Whoever was responsible, Sophonisba drank a cup of poison and died.

Sophonisba receives poison from her husband, Massinissa

Wu

Emperor of China (157–87 B.C.)

The Han people of China had a quasi-religious fascination with horses, and this was no less true of Wu, the sixth emperor of China's Han dynasty. He learned that the king of Fergana, in what is now Uzbekistan, had a sublime breed of horses that were strong, fast, had great stamina, and stood sixteen hands high (over five feet). He sent an emissary with a fortune in gold to purchase some of these "Celestial Horses," as Wu called them. But the king refused to sell and emphasized his unwillingness to do business with Wu by murdering the emissary. So Wu went to war, ultimately destroying Fergana's capital, and returning home with a herd of thousands of Celestial Horses.

The horse story illustrates Wu's determination to cultivate the best of everything in China. During his fifty-four-year reign, he established trade routes known as the famous Silk Road that carried Chinese luxury items to the markets of Asia Minor, Arabia, North Africa, and Europe, while welcoming into China goods from her far-flung trade partners. The Chinese scholar Confucius (551–479 B.C.) had formulated a system in which every action, whether within a family or in the political sphere, was guided by the desire to do what is virtuous, and Wu declared this would be the official philosophy of his realm. To attract the best minds to government service, he established an empire-wide examination system, and whoever tested well received an offer of a government job.

Although China was a vast realm, Wu insisted that all power must be centralized. All coins would be minted and distributed by the imperial government. The manufacture and distribution of such necessities as salt and iron were nationalized.

As a military leader, Wu defeated the Xiongnu, a central Asian tribe that might have been the Huns, and pushed his empire's borders north to modern-day Kyrgyzstan and east to Vietnam.

Tragically, the final years of his reign were marred by a paranoid persecution of people Wu believed were witches. Hundreds, perhaps thousands, of individuals, including members of the royal family, were charged with witchcraft and executed, along with their families. For this reason, some historians regard Wu as a despot on par with Qin Shi Huang.

TIGRANES II THE GREAT

King of Armenia (c. 135–56 B.C.)

In 95 B.C. the king of Armenia died, and his son, Tigranes, who had been a hostage of the Persians for a decade, was permitted to return home to rule Armenia as one of Persia's satellite kings. But before letting the hostage go, the Persian king demanded control of the Seventy Valleys, a region of strategic passes and valleys in the mountains of southern Armenia that ran along Persia's border. With no other option, Tigranes surrendered the territory.

Meanwhile, Rome had become the dominant player in the Mediterranean and was showing interest in adding Asia Minor to its sphere of influence. Rather than challenge the Romans, Tigranes declared his neutrality and even evacuated his garrison from Cappadocia when Roman general Sulla advanced on the region. Tigranes had no interest in a war with Rome; he wanted to defeat the Persians, reclaim lost Armenian territory, and transform his vassal country into an empire so mighty that no king in the region would try to tangle with him. He began by avenging the humiliation he and his father had suffered at the hands of the Persians by recapturing the Seventy Valleys. Next he attacked the Medes, seizing what is now northern Iran. In the years that followed he enjoyed a string of military successes until the Armenian Empire stretched from the Caspian Sea to Gaza, from the Caucasus mountains to Cappadocia.

But Rome was a problem that would not go away. In 73 B.C., when the Romans defeated the king of Pontus, Mithridates VI, the king took refuge at Tigranes's court. The Romans demanded that Tigranes surrender Mithridates; Tigranes considered such a request dishonorable, and refused.

The war between Rome and Armenia that followed was brutal. The Romans looted the Armenian capital; Tigranes led the Romans deep into his territory where cold, hunger, and exhaustion took their toll on the invaders. In response, the Romans sent in a new commander, Pompey, who cut off Tigranes from his allies. Isolated and short on troops, Tigranes had no choice but to surrender.

Pompey treated Tigranes honorably, permitting him to keep his throne (in exchange for 360,000 pounds of silver). Tigranes, who had overthrown the Persians, spent the last eleven years of his life as a vassal of Rome.

MITHRIDATES VI THE GREAT

King of Pontus (132–63 B.C.)

Mithridates VI was the houseguest who brought down an empire. He was king of Pontus, a land along the southern shore of the Black Sea. It was a region where for five hundred years, Greek colonists had had a strong presence, and so Mithridates identified strongly with Greek culture. In fact, he regarded himself as a new Alexander the Great who would bring the Greeks and the people of Pontus to a new level of glory and international prominence.

One of the first territories Mithridates seized was Cappadocia, a land directly on Rome's route of eastward expansion across what is now Turkey. The Romans did not like this act of interference, so the senate sent Mithridates a message warning him that it would be wise if he withdrew his troops. Mithridates did as the senate suggested—he was not ready for a war with Rome.

But there was still tension in the region: a Roman consul named Aquillius foolishly offered to assist one of Rome's allies in Asia Minor if he invaded Pontus. Mithridates annihilated the invaders and their Roman allies, then, in retaliation for the unprovoked attack, rounded up eighty thousand Roman residents in the region and massacred them. It was the beginning of an on-again, off-again war that would consume the rest of Mithridates's life.

The end came in 73 B.C. when the Romans destroyed Pontus's fleet, defeated the king at Cabira, and sent him fleeing to the king of Armenia, Tigranes, for safety. Since Tigranes's wife was Mithridates's daughter, he felt obliged to shelter his father-in-law. Nonetheless, it put the Armenian king in a terrible position: if he did not surrender Mithridates to the Romans, Tigranes could expect a Roman invasion of his empire. Tigranes did the honorable thing, shielded Mithridates, and went to war with the Romans. The result was the loss of his empire and his independence. The Romans permitted Tigranes to stay on as king, but as king firmly under Rome's thumb.

As for Mithridates, he drank poison, but the poison did not take effect; desperate to escape the vengeance of the Romans, he had one of his soldiers run him through with a sword.

132 B.C.

76

King Mithridates asked one of his soldiers to kill him

Julius Caesar

Dictator of Rome (100–44 B.C.)

Romans hated kings. In 510 B.C. they had driven the last one from the city and instituted a republic. Yet more than four hundred years later, Julius Caesar toyed with the idea of assuming kinglike powers.

He came from an ancient patrician family, and like all Roman aristocrats, he became involved in politics and the military. In 58 B.C., when the senate sent him with four legions to govern Rome's provinces in Gaul (modern-day France), he saw an opportunity to expand the empire, enhance his reputation by becoming a war hero, and vastly enrich himself through plunder and the sale of captive Gauls. While Caesar conquered Gaul, his ally Gnaeus Pompey looked after Caesar's political interests in Rome.

Caesar's power base was the army and the common people of Rome. He won their love by showering them with gifts of money and loot from his campaigns. As Caesar's popularity increased, Pompey looked for his own power base and found it among the aristocrats who despised Caesar as a demagogue. The senate ordered Caesar to resign his command; instead, he broke with an ancient tradition and marched his legions on Rome. Pompey, charged by the senate with the defense of Italy, found that most of his troops were loyal to Caesar. Rather than risk defeat, Pompey and most of the senate with their troops fled to Greece. For the next three years, Caesar pursued the armies of Pompey and the senate around the Mediterranean, scoring one victory after another. By 46 B.C. Pompey was dead, as were Caesar's other enemies, and Caesar celebrated with a magnificent triumphal procession, during which he showered more money on the people and his veterans.

Named dictator for life, Caesar began to adopt some regal habits, including permitting his statues to be crowned with laurel wreaths. Meanwhile a large number of senators were plotting to assassinate Caesar.

On March 15, 44 B.C., senators lured Caesar into the portico of a theater to read a petition. As he read, they attacked. As many as sixty senators stabbed the defenseless man, including Brutus, a direct descendant of the Roman aristocrat who drove King Tarquin from Rome. As Brutus, a trusted friend, plunged his dagger into Caesar, the dying man said, "You too, Brutus?" A moment later, Julius Caesar was dead.

Vercingetorix

King of the Averni (c. 82–46 B.C.)

In 52 B.C. the Carnutes, a Gallic tribe that occupied the territory between the Seine and the Loire rivers in what is now central France, rebelled against Roman rule in Gaul. A thirty-year-old chieftain, Vercingetorix, urged his people, the Averni, to join the uprising. While a few warriors joined him, the majority of the Averni—including members of Vercingetorix's own family—considered the revolt too risky and drove the chieftain and his followers out of their city, Gergovia (near modern-day Clermont-Ferrand).

Undeterred, Vercingetorix visited one Gallic tribe after another, forming alliances and collecting an army of 120,000 men. Such success brought the Averni around, and they gave Vercingetorix the title of king.

Vercingetorix's strategy was to keep ahead of Julius Caesar's legions, burning towns and crops so the Romans could not live off the land, and avoiding major battles whenever possible. Caesar responded by destroying the city of Avaricum (modern-day Bourges), massacring tens of thousands of inhabitants, then marching on Vercingetorix's birthplace and capital, Gergovia. Outside the city, Vercengetorix met the Romans. The fight that ensued was especially hard, and each side lost several hundred men. Although the Gauls won the battle, Vercengetorix needed reinforcements before he could face Caesar again. He pulled back to his stronghold, Alesia, but the Romans pursued him. Vercingetorix had intended Alesia to be a place where he and his men could rest and regroup, but now it was a trap: the Romans built nine miles of siege works around Alesia, and there was no escape from the fortress. In desperation, Vercingetorix led out his men, hoping to break through the Roman lines, but their attempt failed and they retreated back to Alesia.

What happened next is uncertain. One account says the Gallic chiefs, to save their lives and the lives of their people, handed over Vercingetorix to Caesar. Another version tells how Vercingetorix came to Caesar's camp and threw down his weapons at the Roman's feet. Whatever the details, the Gallic king became Caesar's prisoner.

For five years, Vercingetorix was kept in a windowless underground cell. In 46 B.C. he was exhibited before the entire city of Rome during Caesar's triumphal procession. While the Romans were still celebrating, Vercingetorix was taken back to his prison and strangled to death.

Vercingetorix throws down his arms at the feet of Julius Caesar

HEROD THE GREAT

King of Judea (73–4 B.C.)

It was Octavian (the future Augustus Caesar) and Mark Antony who persuaded the Roman senate to make Herod king of Judea. Although Herod was technically Jewish, he gave thanks for his crown in the temple of the Roman god Jupiter. Once back in Judea, he ingratiated himself with his Jewish subjects by marrying Mariamne, a member of the popular Hasmonean family whose illustrious ancestors included Judas Maccabeus. In time Herod came to regard the Hasmoneans as too popular. He had his wife's grandfather, her mother, and her seventeen-year-old brother murdered, and then he arranged Mariamne's death, too.

As a tribute to Augustus, Herod built a splendid new city, Caesarea, on the Mediterranean and filled it with theaters and arenas as well as temples to the Roman gods. Once again to keep his Jewish subjects quiet, he built a magnificent new temple in Jerusalem so lavish it was said to rival the original built by Solomon.

Meanwhile, Herod's murderous streak surfaced again: he killed three of his sons because he suspected they planned to assassinate him. He also attempted to kill the infant Jesus, described to him by the magi as the newborn king of the Jews, by sending a troop of soldiers to Bethlehem with orders to slay every male baby aged two years and under. The account of the murder of these innocent children is found only in Saint Matthew's gospel, and although there is no corroborating evidence from other sources, this much is certain: it sounds like something Herod would do.

Toward the end of his life, Herod suffered from a painful skin disease. Hoping for a cure, he traveled to hot springs near the Dead Sea, but the waters did him no good. As he lay dying, unloved by his family, despised by his subjects, he had his troops fan out across Judea, arrest all the most prominent Jewish men in the country, and shut them up inside the hippodrome at Jericho. Upon the king's death, the soldiers were to massacre all the prisoners. In Herod's warped mind, it was one way to ensure that at his death there would be mourning throughout Judea. The king died, but the soldiers did not obey his final order.

Herod the Great orders his troops to massacre the baby boys of Bethlehem

ICI FAIT HERODE OCIRRE LES INNOCÉNS.

2

IST LI SIRE
A LOUENT SEW
NUR SÉ VE VERS
LES OOLES DESTRES
Desque reo pose
le cuens enemif:
amel clete̊z piez.

4

Cleopatra VII Philopator

Queen of Egypt (69–30 B.C.)

Portraits of the Queen of the Nile from her own day tell us that she was not a classic beauty: she had mannish features and a large hooked nose. But the portraits do not capture Cleopatra's seductive qualities, her ability to enchant men.

When Cleopatra was seventeen or eighteen, she married her twelve-year-old brother, Ptolemy XIII (such incestuous marriages were common among the pharaohs, and when the Macedonian Ptolemies took the throne of Egypt, they kept up the custom). Cleopatra tried to dominate her little brother/husband, but Ptolemy had a wily advisor who helped the boy depose Cleopatra and drive her into exile. Cleopatra and Ptolemy were on the verge of war. When Julius Caesar arrived in Egypt, he announced that he would mediate between Ptolemy and Cleopatra. Egypt was one of Rome's most important sources of grain, and if this family feud disrupted the Egyptian grain shipments, Rome would starve. To win the great man over to her side, Cleopatra entered his residence in Alexandria concealed inside a carpet. When a slave unrolled the rug, out sprang the queen. That night Caesar and Cleopatra became lovers.

Soon thereafter Cleopatra gave birth to a son, Caesarion. Caesar brought Cleopatra to Rome, showered her with honors, and acknowledged Caesarion as his son. But the idyll ended when Caesar was assassinated.

As Rome sank into civil war, Cleopatra studied the two chief rivals: Octavian, Caesar's adopted son, and Mark Antony, Caesar's closest friend. Of the two, Cleopatra believed she could most easily enchant Antony, a vulgar, pleasure-loving man. And she did: Antony and Cleopatra became a romantic couple and political partners ambitious to seize Rome's provinces in the east.

Such imprudence gave Octavian an excuse to declare war. The decisive battle was fought at sea, near Actium, off the coast of Greece. When it appeared to Cleopatra that Antony's ships were being overwhelmed by Octavian's, she set sail and fled. Antony left the scene of battle, too, in pursuit of Cleopatra. But Octavian followed the lovers, and as he closed in, Antony stabbed himself in the stomach while Cleopatra killed herself by holding a venomous snake to her breast. With the death of Cleopatra, the line of the pharaohs of Egypt came to an end.

The Death of Cleopatra

AUGUSTUS CAESAR

Emperor of Rome (63 B.C.—A.D. 14)

At his death, Julius Caesar had no living legitimate child, but in his will he declared that he had adopted his great-nephew Octavian as his son, and named him his heir. Twenty-one-year-old Octavian proved to be a remarkably shrewd young man. In the turmoil that followed Caesar's murder, he first sided with the senate to create the impression that he would restore the republic, then allied himself with Mark Antony to hunt down and kill Caesar's assassins, and finally waged war against Antony, whom he recognized as his chief rival.

All the while, Octavian conducted a public relations campaign to persuade the people of Rome that he had their best interests at heart. In reality, Octavian planned to become king. Once the assassins were dead, Antony and Cleopatra were dead, and Egypt had become a Roman province, Octavian declared that the Roman republic was restored—although he possessed all the real power in Rome. He changed his name to Augustus, which means "divinely ordained." He also used the title imperator, which originally meant commander but came to be understood as emperor.

He kept the army loyal by giving each soldier gold and land, and he kept the Roman people happy by giving them free food and lavish public entertainments. Yet for all his power, Augustus faced a serious dilemma: who would be his heir? He had only one child, a daughter, Julia. His grandsons died when they were young men. In the end, Augustus's only possible successor was his stepson Tiberius, the child of his wife, Livia. There are stories that Livia was a murderous schemer who poisoned or otherwise arranged the deaths of virtually every relative in Augustus's family so her son Tiberius would become emperor. This is mere gossip. The historical record offers no evidence that Livia was an imperial serial killer.

After reigning for forty-five years, Augustus died peacefully in his bed. Within a month, the senate declared Augustus a god—a first in Roman history.

Caesar Augustus, in the garb of a Roman Commander

THUSNELDA

Princess of the Cherusci (c. 10 B.C.—A.D. 17)

The Germanic tribes were divided between those who refused to give up their independence and those who believed the Romans were unstoppable and it was wise to come to some mutually agreeable arrangement. Thusnelda's father, Prince Segestes, had convinced his people, the Cherusci, to bow to the inevitable and accept the Romans as their overlords. Thusnelda made her position clear by eloping with Arminius, a Cherusci nobleman who rejected Segestes's accommodationist policy.

In A.D. 9 it appeared that Thusnelda had made the right choice. That year, Arminius planned a daring blow against the Romans. He lured the general Quinctilius Varus and his three legions deep into the Teutoburg Forest, where Arminius sprang his trap. Unable to maneuver in the dense woods, the Roman infantry and cavalry were slaughtered by thousands of Germanic tribesmen. Rather than be taken alive, Varus killed himself, which was a prudent decision considering what the Germans did to their prisoners after the battle. The Germans stretched out captured Roman officers on stone altars and sacrificed them to their gods, and stuffed the Roman soldiers inside wicker cages and burned them alive.

Once Augustus Caesar got over the shock of the disaster, he sent fresh troops under Tiberius (Augustus's stepson) and Germanicus (Tiberius's nephew) to put down the German revolt. Segestes fought with the Romans, and in A.D. 15, when Germanicus overran a German camp and captured Thusnelda, it is likely that her father was a witness. Germanicus treated Thusnelda (who was pregnant) with respect, permitting her to live with her father. As for Arminius, he was still at large and he used the capture of his wife to raise more support among the German tribes. Meanwhile, Thusnelda gave birth to a son, whom she named Thumelicus.

In A.D. 17, Germanicus returned to Rome for a triumphal procession through the city. Prominent among the captives paraded through the streets were Thusnelda and her little boy. Her father, Segestes, was among the spectators. Shortly after Germanicus's triumph, Thusnelda and her son were exiled to Ravenna in northern Italy. It appears that Thusnelda died within weeks or months of their arrival. As for Thumelicus, he was sent to train at Ravenna's gladiatorial school. He died fighting in the arena when he was about sixteen years old.

Roman general Germanicus Caesar captures Thusnelda, wife of Arminius, following his victory over German forces near the Weser River

CARTIMANDUA

Queen of the Brigantes (died c. 69)

The Brigantes were the largest tribe in Britain, inhabiting all of the present-day northern counties of Yorkshire, Lancashire, and Cumbria. Cartimandua, the Brigantes' queen, made peace with the Romans and became one of the empire's client rulers.

In 43, the British king Caratacus led a rebellion against Rome, but Cartimandua remained neutral. Several years later, the Romans defeated Caratacus, who fled to Cartimandua's court. Considering her status as a vassal of Rome, this was a risky decision. When the Romans demanded that Cartimandua surrender Caratacus to them, she felt that she had no other option but to do so. As the Roman historian Tacitus put it, "There is seldom safety for the unfortunate, and Caractacus . . . was put in chains and delivered up to the conquerors."

The Roman emperor Claudius richly rewarded Cartimandua for handing over his greatest enemy in Britain, but Cartimandua's husband, Venutius, was outraged by her betrayal of a fellow British king. Cartimandua responded by divorcing her husband and marrying Vellocatus, Venutius's armor bearer.

This was too much for Venutius. He gathered an army of anti-Roman Brigantes as well as warriors from other British tribes and made war on Cartimandua. Gallus, the governor of Britain, rushed a Roman legion northward to defend Rome's loyal ally, and Venutius and his army were scattered.

Cartimandua was still queen in A.D. 69, the tumultuous Year of the Four Emperors in Rome, when four emperors ruled in quick succession. Taking advantage of the upheavals, Venutius raised another army and attacked his ex-wife. The Roman governor sent some troops, but not enough this time. Since they could not defeat the British rebels, the Romans evacuated Cartimandua to a place of safety in Roman-controlled Britain. We don't know what became of her after that; her name simply disappears from the histories of the period.

Berenice

Queen of Judea (28– c. 82)

Berenice was the great-granddaughter of the murderous Herod the Great. Her aunt Salome had danced before the ruler of Galilee in exchange for the beheading of John the Baptist. And her father, Herod Agrippa I, believed he was a god.

Berenice married her uncle Herod of Chalcis and had two sons with him. Even the Romans regarded such a marriage as incestuous, but Berenice suffered no pangs of guilt. A few years later, when Herod of Chalcis died, she formed an even closer liaison with her brother, Herod Agrippa II. If the brother and sister lived in Jerusalem, their affair would have set off riots in the streets, so they settled in Caesarea, the Roman city their great-grandfather had built on the Mediterranean. With its theaters, gladiator games, horse races, and baths, the sibling lovers had found a congenial home.

Yet even in Caesarea, Berenice and her brother were the butt of vulgar jokes. To refurbish her reputation she married again, this time to Polemon II, king of Cilicia, a kingdom on the southern coast of present-day Turkey. It was not a happy match; after two or three years the couple parted and Berenice returned to her brother. She had scarcely settled in when a new Roman governor named Florus began antagonizing the people of Judea: desecrating synagogues, stealing from the Holy Temple, and crucifying the most distinguished men of Jerusalem on trumped-up charges. The Jews rose up in rebellion.

When the Romans invaded to put down the rebellion, Berenice seduced the commander, twenty-seven-year-old Titus. He was intoxicated by this notorious queen, and she found herself profoundly attracted to the handsome, sophisticated young general. Their love affair blossomed as Titus's army destroyed Jerusalem, looted the Holy Temple, and carried off ninety-seven thousand Jews to the slave markets of Rome. When Titus returned home with his booty and his captives, Berenice went with him. In Rome, Titus's father had become emperor, and Berenice expected a marriage proposal that would make her the next empress of Rome. But although they lived together, Titus never did marry Berenice, and they split up before he became emperor.

Titus died in A.D. 81, and Herod Agrippa II died around the year 92, but no one knows what became of Berenice.

BERENICE.

E. Picart sculp.

NERO

Emperor of Rome (37–68)

Most films portray Nero as mad; this is a mistake. Nero was cruel, intolerably vain, and monstrously self-deluded, but he was not insane.

He was only sixteen when he became emperor, yet in spite of his youth and inexperience, he began his reign well—thanks to the sound advice he received from his tutor Seneca; the captain of the Praetorian Guard, Burrus; and his mother, Agrippina. But once Nero reached his twenty-first birthday, he began to assert himself. He divorced his wife, Octavia, to marry Poppea, a woman who was ambitious, ruthless, and sexually adventurous. He had his mother murdered. And when Burrus retired, Nero made a man named Tigellinus commander of the Praetorians. Tigellinus then strengthened his influence over the emperor by revealing to him an endless string of plots and conspiracies—most of which were nonexistent.

Disaster struck in A.D. 64 when a fire broke out in Rome and destroyed most of the city. Legend says that Nero played the lyre and sang while Rome burned, but it is not true—he was not even in the city at the time of the conflagration. Although he fed and sheltered the homeless, Nero also took advantage of the disaster, seizing a large area that had once been filled with private homes so he could build a new palace. The resentment this caused among the people led to the accusation that Nero had set the fire. To deflect the blame, he announced that an obscure religious sect, the Christians, had burned down the city. In this first persecution of the Christian church, he sentence countless men, women, and children to horrific deaths, including being smeared with pitch and set ablaze to illuminate his garden. Among the martyrs were the apostles Saint Peter and Saint Paul.

In 66, Nero traveled to Greece to compete in a series of artistic and athletic competitions. Although he was at best a mediocre musician and no athlete at all, he won first prize in every event. While he was in Greece, Rome's governors in Gaul, North Africa, and Spain rebelled against Nero. The senate denounced him as an enemy of the people, and the Praetorian Guard deserted him. Alone and frightened, he took refuge in the villa of a freedman named Phaon, where he killed himself. He had been the last surviving member of the family of Augustus Caesar.

Nero at the burning of Rome

BOUDICA

Queen of the Iceni (died 60 or 61)

Boudica was probably not this queen's actual name, but there is a good chance it comes closer to it than the traditional form, Boadicea. The Roman historians are the source of the inaccuracy—they couldn't quite get used to the sound of British speech and filtered it through their own language, Latin.

Boudica was queen of the Iceni, a British tribe who, after the Romans began their conquest of Britain in A.D. 43, allied themselves with the invaders. This must have been a relief for the Romans because the British, as members of the Celtic race, were tough fighters who lived for war. British warriors prized physical strength and physical courage, and to display both to their enemies, they came into battle naked. In addition to courage, the British took pride in their independence: as long as the Romans treated the Iceni as free people, they could count on the tribe's loyalty.

When Boudica's husband, King Prasutagus, died, the Roman who administered the finances of the province sent in armed men to confiscate the late king's entire estate. In addition, the Romans looted the homes and estates of the Iceni nobility. As for the royal family, the Romans flogged Boudica and raped her two daughters. It was this combination of treachery and brutality that sparked an Iceni revolt.

The Roman historian Dio Cassius tells us that Boudica was tall, had a mass of red hair that fell to her waist, and spoke in a loud, harsh voice. In an assembly of the British tribes, she declared what the Romans had done to her, to her daughters, and to her people, and she called for revenge. Tens of thousands of British warriors flocked to her side, and in her chariot she led an attack on the Roman towns of London, Colchester, and Saint Albans, sacking the cities, setting them ablaze, and massacring the inhabitants.

But the Romans regrouped, and at an unknown location along the Roman road known today as Watling Street, they defeated Boudica's army of angry but disorganized Britons. Roman historians claimed that eighty thousand Britons fell in the battle, although that is undoubtedly an exaggeration. According to tradition, Boudica escaped and killed herself by taking poison. No one knows what became of her daughters.

Boudica with her two daughters

MARCUS AURELIUS

Emperor of Rome (121–180)

Marcus Aurelius was Rome's only philosopher-emperor, but because he inherited an empire that was being pressed on all sides by enemies, he was obliged to spend most of his time on battlefields rather than in libraries.

Marcus embraced Stoicism, a philosophy formulated in Greece in the third century B.C.. The Stoics believed in strict self-control, especially of such violent emotions as anger and envy. They strove to be virtuous and to accept without complaint whatever life, or fate, brought them. The Stoics believed that if one possessed peace of mind, personal suffering would be diminished, possibly even eliminated altogether. This became Marcus's religion.

During military campaigns in what is now Serbia and Hungary, Marcus used his spare time to jot down his personal interpretation of Stoic philosophy. This collection of the emperor's aphorisms is known as the *Meditations*; it is a handbook for self-improvement, one of the world's earliest self-help books.

"The best way of avenging yourself is not to become like the wrongdoer."

"A cucumber is bitter. Throw it away. There are briers in the road. Turn aside from them."

"Never regard something as doing you good if it makes you betray a trust or lose your sense of shame or makes you show hatred, suspicion, ill-will or hypocrisy."

Although Marcus's advice is not especially original, the fact that he wrote a book that people have read and admired for more than eighteen hundred years makes him stand out from all the other Roman emperors.

Naturally, Marcus's desire to do good extended to his empire, especially the weakest members of Roman society. He appointed honest officials who ensured that food was distributed fairly to the poor and that orphaned children were cared for.

On March 17, 180, while in Vindobona (present-day Vienna), Marcus died suddenly. Tragically, this virtuous man produced a monstrous son. Commodus was a cruel man who murdered anyone who irritated him. He imagined he was Hercules reborn, and liked to dress like the ancient hero and kill animals in the arena; it is said that during one of his Herculean performances, Commodus killed one hundred lions in a single day.

The Triumph of Marcus Aurelius

ZENOBIA

Queen of Palmyra (220– after 274)

Like Boudica, Zenobia became queen after the death of her husband, but unlike her British counterpart, she did not lead an uprising against Rome; she established a rival empire. She was a remarkable woman of Arab descent (perhaps even Jewish, or mixed Arab-Jewish background), who was as intelligent as she was daring and beautiful. Her closest advisor was Longinus, a philosopher thought to be the greatest intellect of his time.

At the time of the king's death, the treasury was empty, barbarians from the east were raiding along Palmyra's borders, and the people were chafing under Roman rule. So Zenobia resolved to establish a Palmyran empire that would be strong enough to resist Roman interference. She expelled the Roman governor and conquered Antioch, then Egypt. She collected the old Roman coins, melted them down, and issued new coins bearing her own image.

It was not in the character of a Roman Caesar to let a valuable province such as Palmyra break away from the empire. When Emperor Aurelian led an army against Palmyra, Zenobia mounted an energetic defense as she waited for help to come from the king of Persia. She was confident that she could outlast the Romans because, although Palymra stood amid a desert, the city was well watered with springs and full of gardens that grew abundant fruit and vegetables. As for the Romans, their foraging expeditions brought in little food or water.

To feed his men, Aurelian bribed the desert tribes to stop raiding his supply trains. Next he defeated the Persian reinforcements before they reached Palmyra. Fearing that her situation had become hopeless, Zenobia mounted a camel and fled into the desert, but after a sixty-mile chase, a detachment of Aurelian's cavalry caught up with her and took her prisoner.

Aurelian took Zenobia and her son to Rome, where he dressed them in their finest clothes, draped them with jewels, then locked golden chains around their necks and led them through the streets of Rome as trophies.

After the humiliation of walking in Aurelian's triumphal procession, Zenobia moved into a country villa where she spent the rest of life, living so obscurely that no one knows when she died.

DIOCLETIAN

Emperor of Rome (244–311)

By the end of the third century, the Roman Empire was so vast and so beset by problems that it had become too big a job for one man. Diocletian, who had exceptional problem-solving skills, remedied the situation by choosing three men to rule with him. As his coemperor he selected Maximian, his closest friend and an experienced military commander. Diocletian and Maximian would each use the title Augustus. They would each have an assistant, known by the title Caesar. Diocletian was emperor of the eastern half of the empire while Maximian was emperor of the western half. Diocletian's assistant was Galerius, a herdsman-turned-soldier who rose through the ranks. Maximian's assistant was Constantius I Chlorus, also a herdsman who had used the army to rise above his lowly birth. Together these rulers were known as the tetrarchs, from the Greek term for "four leaders."

In February 303, Diocletian issued an edict calling for the first-ever empire-wide persecution of the Christians. They were ordered to surrender all copies of the scriptures and liturgical books to be burned; their churches were to be destroyed; and Christians who would not sacrifice to the Roman gods would be executed. Some historians believe the persecution was the work of Galerius, who was devoted to the gods and traditions of Rome. It is possible, but he would not have been a lone voice calling for an attack upon the Christians, as almost all of Diocletian's advisors were ardently anti-Christian. No one knows how many men, women, and children throughout the empire died in the persecution. The generally accepted estimate is twenty thousand.

Although his tetrarchy made it easier to govern, Diocletian appears to have overlooked the practical problems involved in sharing imperial power. In 305, he and Maximian retired, and their Caesars moved up to the rank of Augustus. The next question was how to arrange the succession. It had been a simple matter when there was only one emperor, but now that four men were involved, it was infinitely more complicated. While he was at a conference attempting to sort out the issue, Diocletian died.

The Four Tetrarchs, from the Basilica of San Marco in Venice, Italy

Constantine I the Great

Emperor of Rome (272–337)

Constantine made a complete break with Rome's past, spiritually and physically. Barely a decade after Christians suffered a savage persecution, he not only made their religion legal throughout the empire, he favored it above the traditional Roman cults. Just as dramatic was his establishment of a new capital on the Bosphorus in present-day Turkey. He named his city Constantinople, but it was also known as New Rome. As for old Rome, it would no longer be the center of the world.

When Constantine was twenty years old, his father, Constantius I Chlorus, was selected by Maximian Augustus to serve as his Caesar, or assistant, in the new tetrarchy system Emperor Diocletian was creating. The position came with perks: Constantius would marry Maximian's stepdaughter and Constantine would complete his military training fighting Rome's enemies in Egypt. Constantius accepted Maximian's offer and immediately divorced Helena, his wife of twenty-two years.

In 305, while Constantine was in northern England with his father, fighting the Picts, Constantius I Chlorus died. The legions proclaimed Constantine emperor, but it would be seven more years before he had eliminated his rivals and could feel secure in his title. It was before the final, decisive battle at the Milvian Bridge outside Rome that Constantine is said to have had his vision of a shining cross that led to his conversion to Christianity.

Constantine was generous to his fellow Christians. He built churches in Jerusalem, Antioch, Rome, and Constantinople. He gave the pope a Roman palace. He called a council of bishops to rule on the unorthodox teachings of an Egyptian priest named Arius. But Constantine put off baptism until he was on his deathbed—he wasn't quite ready to fully commit himself to the Christian faith.

Like so many emperors, Constantine feared plots to overthrow him. When his wife, Fausta, whispered that his eldest son Crispus (her stepson) was scheming to seize the crown, Constantine had his son executed. Soon thereafter, however, he learned that he had been duped, that Fausta had made up the story to get Crispus out of the way so one her sons by Constantine would inherit the empire. Constantine avenged his son's death by having Fausta suffocated.

Julian the Apostate

Emperor of Rome (331–363)

Constantine was Rome's first Christian emperor, and Julian was the last pagan emperor. He received his title Apostate because as a young man he rejected the Christian faith in which he had been raised and returned to the worship of the gods of Rome.

Julian had a quiet childhood spent almost entirely in the company of his tutor, who immersed the boy in Greek philosophy. But as a member of the imperial family (Constantine was his uncle), Julian was expected to take an active role in government. At age twenty-four, he was sent to Gaul, where two Germanic tribes, the Alamanni and the Franks, had been raiding Roman outposts and attacking Roman cities. He defeated the tribes in battle, then negotiated a truce with their chieftains. For a scholarly young man with no military experience, this was a genuine accomplishment, and Julian remained proud of it for the rest of his life.

In 360, Emperor Constantius II died and Julian succeeded him. One of his very first acts as emperor was to revive traditional Roman religion. He did not openly persecute Christians, but he did everything he could to push them to the margins of Roman society. Christians were barred from attempting to make converts, and they were forbidden to teach classical literature, rhetoric, or grammar. Julian cut off the subsidies the government made to church charities and revoked the Christian clergy's tax-exempt status.

Recognizing that Christian charitable institutions brought about many conversions, Julian established rival pagan charities. He hoped these institutions would revitalize the cult of the gods and persuade the people of the empire that they could turn to their emperor for help and security rather than to the Christians. To Julian's annoyance, in spite of all his measures, the church still enjoyed a steady stream of converts.

Meanwhile trouble broke in Persia. Given his success in Gaul, Julian expected he could put down this uprising easily enough, but the Persians proved to be a much more formidable enemy than the Alamanni and the Franks. Although the Romans won major battles and captured Persian cities, they were harassed constantly by guerrilla raids. In June 363, Persian guerrillas struck the part of the Roman column where Julian was riding. In the skirmish, a Persian stabbed the emperor in the belly with a spear. Julian died surrounded by his officers. Supposedly his final words were addressed to Jesus Christ: "Galilean, you have conquered." But this is almost certainly apocryphal.

ALARIC I
King of the Visigoths (370—410)

Beginning in the fourth century, the Romans developed an ingenious way to neutralize the barbarian nations that raided their provinces: they hired them as mercenaries. Soon, thousands of Goth warriors and their families had settled within the borders of the Roman Empire. Some became officers in the Roman legions. Many converted to Christianity. But for many Romans, the Goths would always be outsiders.

At age twenty-four, Alaric led an army of Goth troops in defense of Emperor Theodosius I against a would-be usurper. At the Battle of Frigidus River, Alaric and his men charged the enemy's position repeatedly. These heroic assaults took the lives of ten thousand Goths—half of Alaric's force. Yet after the battle, when Theodosius handed out gifts to his troops and promotions to the officers, the Goths received almost nothing, and Alaric was not even acknowledged. Stung by the insult, Alaric turned his back on the Romans.

In the first years of the fifth century, Alaric planned a move that would stun the world—he would capture the city of Rome. In 410, the Goths laid siege to the city. As food ran low and disease spread, the Romans grew desperate. They sent two senators to negotiate a truce. Alaric received the ambassadors and presented them with his demands: he wanted all barbarian slaves in Rome liberated, five thousand pounds of gold, thirty thousand pounds of silver, plus many other luxury items.

The Romans paid the ransom, and Alaric led his army away from the city. En route he sent a message to the emperor demanding that he be named commander of all of Rome's legions in the western provinces. The emperor replied that such high rank could never be given to a barbarian. With that, Alaric turned his army around and besieged Rome once again.

On the night of August 24, 410, someone inside the city—the identity of the traitor has never been discovered—opened the Salarian Gate and the Goths poured through. For three days the Goths ransacked Rome, rounding up captives to be sold as slaves, torturing rich men and women to force them to reveal where they had concealed their valuables. Once the city was virtually stripped bare, the Goths marched out. Alaric had achieved the unthinkable: for the first time in seven hundred years, Rome had fallen to an enemy army.

Alaric the Goth entering a Greek city

GAISERIC

King of the Vandals (c. 389–477)

The Vandal nation Gaiseric knew as a child and a teenager was a starving band huddled along the Rhine. But on New Year's Eve 406, when Gaiseric was about seventeen years old, a brutal cold snap struck Germany and the Rhine froze. If the Vandals stayed where they were, they faced famine and attacks by the Huns, but across the river lay the rich cities and fat farms of Roman Gaul. En masse, the Vandals gathered their belongings and walked across the ice to make a new life for themselves.

Over the next sixteen years, the Vandals fought and looted their way across Gaul and Spain, becoming ever stronger and more confident. When Gaiseric became king in 422, the Vandals were settled in southern Spain near the port town of Cartagena. One of the things the Vandals had learned during their travels was how to build and sail ships. In 428, when the Roman governor of North Africa hired the Vandals to assist him in a quarrel with the emperor, Gaiseric put his people to work building a fleet, then sailed eighty thousand Vandal men, women, and children to what is now Morocco. By the time Gaiseric and his people arrived at Carthage, the governor had changed his mind, but the Vandals were not about to go back to Spain. North Africa was a paradise of lush farms and magnificent Roman cities. Gaiseric decided to conquer it, and within five years he was the master of the central portion of North Africa, including the province's greatest city, Carthage.

Gaiseric turned his fleet into a navy that challenged the emperor. In 455, he invaded Italy and marched virtually unopposed to Rome, where he was met by Pope Saint Leo I the Great. Leo pleaded with Gaiseric to leave the city in peace, but the Vandal king refused—he could not pass up such a prize. However, since Gaiseric was a Christian, he made some concessions: the people would not be tortured or slaughtered, and the city would not be burned. He would only take the valuables.

During their two-week occupation, the Vandals stripped everything of value from every house, temple, church, and government building. They also took prisoner patricians who would bring a tidy ransom.

Gaseric was about eighty-seven when he died. He had transformed his people into a world power, the greatest naval threat in the Mediterranean, and the wealthiest of all the barbarian nations.

Vandals attacking Rome

THEODOSIUS II
Emperor of Byzantium (401–450)

As the baby of the Byzantine imperial family, Theodosius was raised by his three older sisters, particularly the eldest, Pulcheria. They were a pious little group—each of the sisters had taken a vow of perpetual virginity and they lived in the palace like nuns in a cloister. Theodosius, although devout, had more boisterous interests. He loved hunting, riding horses, and swordplay, and it is thought that he introduced to Byzantium the Persian game of *tsukan*, what we call polo.

Once he was old enough to rule on his own, Theodosius developed a foreign policy designed to address the three major headaches of his time: keeping peace with Persia, protecting the empire's borders from the Huns, and trying to restore order to western Europe where the barbarians were already chipping away at the provinces of Gaul, Spain, Britain, and even Italy. There was also trouble in his own house; his sister Pulcheria grew bitter and jealous after Theodosius married a beautiful Greek woman named Eudocia. The rivalry became so nasty that after years of jockeying for position, Eudocia finally gave up and moved out of the palace. It was an empty gesture because by that time Theodosius was in his late thirties and no longer sought advice from his wife or his sister.

Theodosius attempted to be a great military commander like the emperors of old, but both the Huns and the Vandals inflicted humiliating defeats upon his legions. The Vandals seized North Africa, including the great city of Carthage, attacked Sicily, and looted Rome, and Theodosius hadn't the military strength to defend these territories. Meanwhile, to placate the Huns, Theodosius paid Attila an annual tribute of twenty-one hundred pounds of gold.

Theodosius was pivotal in shaping the Byzantine Empire. Ultimately, he was forced to face reality and write off the provinces in western Europe as unrecoverable from the barbarian nations. He shifted his focus to the eastern provinces. Unfettered by the perceived need to cling to the provinces that had been conquered centuries earlier by Julius Caesar, the Byzantines were free to develop their flourishing civilization. Ironically, Theodosius's decision to give up started Byzantium on the road to a golden age.

Theodosius (right), with Pope Paul II, founds the University of Bologna

Attila

King of the Huns (406–453)

In the fifth century, the idea of a king was new to the Huns—they had always lived and fought in small independent bands. But as they swept west from their home on the steppes of Central Asia, they found it useful to fight under a supreme commander. The first king of the Huns was Rugila; he was succeeded by his nephew, Attila.

The Huns were unique among the barbarian nations that dismantled the Roman Empire. The Goths, the Vandals, the Franks, the Lombards, the Saxons—all settled in the territories they conquered. The Huns kept on the move, looting, killing, and destroying everything in their path. They acquired carts piled high with plunder, but they never felt the desire to stop, build a town, and farm the land.

Attila did not look regal: he was short, broad in the chest and shoulders, with a large head, small dark eyes, and a flat nose. And his clothes were no different from those of any other Hun, except his were cleaner.

Attila's appetite for war was insatiable. The utter destruction of the Roman Empire appears to have been Attila's goal, although what he planned to do afterward no one knows.

He was rolling across France when an army of Romans with Goth mercenaries resolved to stop him and drive him back. The two armies met at Châlons-sur-Marne: the Huns occupied the plains, their favorite ground for fighting on horseback; the Romans and Goths dug in on the hills where the Huns' horses could not get up the slopes. The fighting was brutal, often hand to hand, as the Huns dismounted to scramble up the hills to reach their enemies. At sundown neither the Romans nor the Huns were certain who, if anyone, had won. But the next morning, instead of attacking, Attila ordered a retreat to the Huns' base camp on the Danube.

About two years later Attila took a new wife. During the wedding night Attila suffered a massive nosebleed and choked to death on his own blood. The Huns diverted the Tisza River, buried their king in the riverbed, then let the river return to its course, covering and concealing Attila's grave forever.

Death of Attila the Hun

CLOVIS

King of the Franks (c. 466–511)

For centuries, the Franks were closely allied with the Romans. Many Franks served proudly in the legions and some rose to high office, including one who became commander of the imperial guard. In the fifth century, as the Roman Empire crumbled, the Franks took over Gaul. Unlike other barbarians, they did not destroy Roman culture in the province; they embraced it, so much so that they gave up their Germanic language and adopted Latin.

At age twenty-one Clovis, King of the Franks, conquered the last remnant of Roman territory in Gaul. With that victory he became king of what is now France, Belgium, and Rhineland, Germany. In 493, he married an eighteen-year-old Burgundian princess, Clotilde. Clovis worshipped the old Germanic gods; Clotilde was a devout Catholic. In 495 when she gave birth to a son, she persuaded Clovis to have the child baptized. Soon after the ceremony, the infant fell ill. While Clotilde prayed that her boy's life would be spared, Clovis blamed himself for not dedicating his son to the gods. But when the baby recovered, Clovis was impressed: he respected power, and clearly this Christ Clotilde worshipped had power.

A year later, during a desperate battle in Tolbiac against the Alamanni, Clovis watched as the enemy charged and his own army began to fall back. The men were on the verge of fleeing the battlefield when Clovis thought of Clotilde's God. "I have called upon my gods," he prayed, "but they are far from helping me. If you will grant me victory over my foes . . . then I will believe in you and will be baptized in your name." As he made his vow, the Franks rallied, launched a counteroffensive, and scattered the Alamanni. True to his word, on Christmas Day 496, Clovis, along with almost all of his officers, was baptized in the cathedral of Rheims.

The conversion of Clovis to the Catholic faith was not just one more link between the Franks and Rome; it also laid the foundation for closer ties between the Franks and the Gallo-Roman inhabitants of Gaul. The two nations now shared the same cultural and religious perspective, which led to intermarriage, which in turn led to the formation of a new people known ultimately as the French.

Clovis at the Battle of Tolbiac

Justinian I and Theodora

Emperor (483–565) and Empress (c. 500–548) of the Byzantine Empire

It was the dream of Justinian's life to restore the Roman Empire, and he nearly succeeded. He took back from various barbarian nations Italy, North Africa, and southern Spain, and he built a navy so powerful that the Mediterranean became a Byzantine lake. But Justinian's revived empire did not last—within two years of his death, the barbarians reasserted themselves, and the Byzantines abandoned almost all of the provinces of western Europe.

Justinian also believed that society was happiest when the church and the state worked in harmony. "There are two great gifts which God, in his love for man, has granted from on high," he wrote, "the priesthood and the imperial dignity." To this end he tried to arbitrate between the church and Christian sects that held unorthodox opinions: he banned the worship of the old gods and even closed down Plato's Academy in Athens because he viewed it as a bastion of paganism. His most lasting physical monument was a church, Hagia Sophia, Holy Wisdom, an architectural marvel that is still on the must-see list of every visitor to Istanbul.

Justinian's most influential act was creating a new legal code that updated and moderated many of the old Roman laws. For example, he made it easier for masters to liberate their slaves, he gave women and children more rights and legal protections, and he reduced the number of crimes that called for the death penalty.

His empress, his beloved wife, and his best advisor was Theodora, a former actress and, so it was said, ex-prostitute. She was also a tougher character than Justinian. During the notorious Nika riot when a mob overran Constantinople and appeared on the verge of overthrowing the emperor, Justinian dithered about whether he should stay or flee. Theodora said he could go if he liked, but she would remain. Then she added that an emperor's purple robe made a good burial shroud. Theodora's courage revived Justinian's and he sent loyal troops into the hippodrome, the headquarters of the insurrection, with orders to massacre the crowd.

Justinian I from a mosaic in the Church of San Vitale in Italy

RECCARED I

King of Visigothic Spain (c. 565–601)

By the sixth century, Spain was isolated from the rest of western Europe. Two hundred years earlier the Goths had converted to the Arian form of Christianity; meanwhile, the other nations of Europe—Italy, Germany, France, England, Ireland—converted to Catholicism. The Arian Visigothic kings found that their European neighbors were reluctant to ally themselves with this outpost of unorthodox opinions.

Reccared was a teenager when his older brother, Hermenegild, converted to Catholicism, an act that outraged their father the king and sparked a civil war in Spain. When the king offered peace terms, Hermenegild, all too trusting, accepted and was immediately seized and imprisoned in Seville. There, his father had the prince murdered.

A year later, 586, the old king died and Reccared succeeded him. In 587, the new king announced that he had become Catholic. The reason for his conversion is unknown—perhaps conviction, perhaps as a tribute to his murdered brother, perhaps political expediency, perhaps a combination of all these motives. By this time, Catholics outnumbered Arians in the general population, but Arians still dominated the aristocracy. Most of the nobles and even Arian bishops followed Reccared's example, but there were pockets of fierce resistance in the Pyrenees and around Merida. Reccared even had to deal with a conspiracy that originated with his own stepmother. Eventually, on the battlefield and by banishing the most outspoken dissidents, Reccared overcame the Arians.

Interestingly, although Recarred encouraged all his subjects to become Catholic, he did not extend that policy to Spain's large Jewish community. The Arian Visigothic kings had been tolerant of the Jews, and Reccared did not alter that policy.

After the religious question had been settled, the history books of the period tell us almost nothing else about Reccared. The last document is a friendly letter written to him by Pope Saint Gregory I the Great to accompany a gift of relics: a piece of the True Cross, some bits of the chains that had bound Saint Peter in prison, and some hairs from the head of Saint John the Baptist.

The first baptisms among the Goths in Spain following the conversion of King Reccared from Arianism to Catholicism

TAISHI SHOTOKU

Prince Regent of Japan (574–622)

At a time when leading Japanese were looking for a way to unify their country and enhance the prestige of the emperor, Prince Taishi Shotoku offered a religion and a philosophical system that would change the character of Japanese culture forever. From the Koreans he borrowed Buddhism, and from the Chinese the ethical system of Confucius. Buddhism gave the Japanese a common faith, and Confucianism, with its ideal that emperors ruled with "the mandate of heaven," exalted the role of the emperor, making him a figure around whom all of Japanese society could coalesce. It would also be good for Shotoku's family—he was the second son of Emperor Yomei.

Inspired by the teachings of Confucius, Shotoku wrote the Seventeen Article Constitution, which set ethical standards for Japan's ruling class, the most important article (and the most innovative for Japan at the time) being the appointment of government officials based on their skills, character, and merits rather than their status in society.

He also encouraged the spread of Buddhism in Japan; in fact, he is revered as the father of Japanese Buddhism, a man of great holiness and intellect who wrote commentaries on the important Lotus Sutra, Vimalakirti Sutra, and Sutra of Queen Srimala. It is believed that the prince built the Shitenno-ji Temple in Osaka—the first Buddhist temple in Japan. There is evidence that Shotoku also built the Horyu-ji Temple in Ikaruga—in 1939 archaeologists found the remains of his palace at one end of the temple complex.

This reverence has obscured the historical figure. While the Japanese tell many legends about Shotoku, very few facts about his life have survived. He came to be worshipped as a bodhisattva, a being who out of compassion for humankind forgoes entering nirvana in order to assist those still on earth.

Taizong

Emperor of China (599–649)

Taizong had a saying, "The waters can both float and capsize a boat." By the waters he meant the peasantry of China, and by the boat he meant the emperor. As a boy he had seen such a thing happen. Sick of endless wars, excessive taxes, and the extravagance of the emperor and his court, the peasants of China rose up in a violent rebellion. Taizong's father was one of the emperor's military commanders at the time, and he saw the uprising as an opportunity to depose the emperor and seize the throne for himself, but he feared he did not have enough troops for a successful coup. Taizong, who was only sixteen at the time, suggested that his father hire as mercenaries the fiercest warriors in the region—the Huns. It was sound advice. In 618, thanks to the victories of his Chinese-and-Hun army, Taizong's father was in position to proclaim himself China's first emperor of the Tang dynasty.

Taizong was a perceptive young man, but he was not the eldest son. His older brother, fearing that the clever Taizong would find a way to displace him, conspired to murder Taizong. But Taizong struck first, assassinating his elder brother and thus clearing the way for his own accession to the throne in 626.

Having seen how angry peasants can destabilize a government, Taizong enacted a series of new laws to win the support of the ordinary people of China. He reduced their taxes, streamlined the bureaucracy, eliminated extravagant government expenditures, and abolished the harsh penal code of his predecessors. He also sponsored new irrigation programs that opened up more land to farmers and encouraged talented young men to take the civil service examination: in Taizong's government, rank did not matter, only ability.

The emperor also encouraged new cultural and commercial ties with the Middle East and Europe. Scholars and artists were as welcome to his court as merchants, and the country prospered as the West demanded such luxury goods as silk, tea, porcelain, and paper.

After a reign of twenty-three years, Taizong died and was mourned by his people as an emperor who brought peace, unity, and prosperity to China.

ALI IBN ABI TALIB

Caliph of Islam (600–661)

Ali was the prophet Muhammad's cousin and son-in-law, and the father of his grandsons Hasan and Hussein. Muhammad made their bond even closer by adopting Ali as his son.

While still a boy, Ali accepted Muhammad's revelation, becoming the first male convert to Islam. As an adult he became one of the prophet's most trusted advisors, a member of his inner circle known as the Companions. It might have been expected that Muhammad would have named his adopted son as his heir, but at his death (according to the Sunni version of events), Muhammad named no successor. Abu Bakr, a member of the prophet's tribe and a Companion, was elected caliph, or political leader of the Muslim faithful. The Shia, however, believe that Muhammad did name Ali as his successor, and it was the other Companions who flouted the will of the prophet. Apparently there was tension at the time of the election, which Ali tried to suppress by keeping out of the spotlight and concentrating on religious rather than political matters.

Ultimately Ali was elected caliph, but he was reluctant to accept—perhaps because Muhammad's widow, Aishah, opposed him. When at last he did accept the caliphate, he was immersed in trouble. Two of the Companions, Talhah and az-Zubayr, who had long been among his supporters, deserted him when he failed to make them governors of Basra and Kufa. Muawiyah, one of Islam's foremost military commanders, also opposed Ali, believing he himself should be caliph.

Ali's power base was Iraq, Arabia, Egypt, and Hejaz, but by 660 he found the number of his supporters shrinking. Muawiyah raided Iraq and Arabia, and Egypt and Hejaz went over to the commander. Incredibly, the rule of Ali, the son of Muhammad, had almost no support among Muslims.

In 661, Ali was praying in the mosque of Kufa when an extremist slashed him with a poisoned sword.

Ali's grave became a place of pilgrimage. Shia Muslims especially revere him as a man to whom Muhammad passed the divine light of revelation, and whose murder is one of the great tragedies of their history.

An Iraqi Shiite woman kisses the picture of Ali

PACAL II THE GREAT

King of Palenque (603–686)

When Pacal was twelve years old he became king of the Mayan kingdom of Palenque. There is a carving that commemorates the moment. It shows Pacal receiving the crown from his mother, who had ruled as queen in her own right—a rare thing among the Maya.

Mayan civilization extended from what is now Mexico into Guatemala. For many years the city of Tikal (in Guatemala) had been preeminent, but during Pacal's sixty-eight-year reign he initiated a lavish building program of palaces and temples in Palenque that put Tikal in the shadow. Nonetheless, Pacal kept up good relations with the kings of Tikal as well as the Mayan kingdom of Yaxchilan, aiding them in war and conquering at least six neighboring kingdoms.

One of the monuments Pacal erected in Palenque was the Temple of the Inscriptions, named for incised tablets that recount episodes from Mayan history.

For decades archaeologists had assumed that the temple was Pacal's funerary monument, but they could find no clue of where the tomb might be. Then, in 1948, archaeologist Alberto Ruz Lhuillier noticed something that had escaped his colleagues—a stone slab with stone plugs along the edges. When the plugs were removed they revealed holes drilled through the slab. Lhuillier raised the slab and spent four years clearing out the rubble he found beneath it. The rubble covered a flight of stairs that led down to a chamber. Inside was an undisturbed tomb, covered with an intricately carved lid depicting Pacal descending into the Mayan underworld. When the lid was raised, Lhuillier and his team found the skeleton of a man, his face covered with a jade mask. There is ongoing debate whether the skeleton is Pacal, since some anthropologists believe the remains are of a man in his forties or fifties, and Pacal died at age eighty.

The tomb and its adornments were undoubtedly made for Pacal, so it is very likely that the body is also his.

Tomb slab of King Pacal II

SONGTSÄN GAMPO

King of Tibet (c. 605–649)

Songtsän Gampo is one of those extraordinary individuals who changed the character of his country forever. He was born into a Tibetan royal family at a place called Gyama, northeast of present-day Lhasa. When Songtsän was thirteen years old, his father was poisoned and the boy became king. History tells us that child rulers are rarely successful—either they become the puppet of their elders, or they are killed off to make room for some ambitious adult. Songtsän, however, proved to be a remarkable king.

Tibet had no written language, so Songtsän sent one of his ministers to India to work with scholars on devising a Tibetan script. China possessed wonderful technology, so he invited Chinese artisans who were skilled at making silk, wine, paper, and ink to come to his country and teach these skills to his people.

In Tibetan history, Songtsän is listed as the first of three dharma kings, the rulers who established Buddhism in Tibet. (Dharma is the term for the teachings of Buddha.) The king founded the Jokhang Temple, the most sacred in Tibet; his wives, Bhrituti and Wencheng, donated Buddhist statues and other holy images to adorn the temple.

Several times Songtsän went to war against China, conquering some of its territory and creating the first Tibetan Empire, yet he greatly admired Chinese culture. He encouraged Tibetan nobles to send their sons to study in China, and gave up the traditional Tibetan national dress of felt and furs to dress as the Chinese emperor did, in robes of silk and brocade.

In the 1960s, during Mao Tse-tung's cultural revolution, thousands of Tibetan Buddhist sacred images were destroyed or carted off to China, including the famous Belsa Buddha said to have been a gift to Songtsän by one of his wives. In 1983, the Chinese adopted a new policy of restoring to Tibet some of its surviving sacred artifacts. The upper portion of the Belsa statue was found in a factory in Beijing, and the lower portion in a pile of rubbish in Lhasa. The two halves were rejoined and the Belsa Buddha was restored to the Jokhang Temple.

A Tibetan shrine built in honor of Songtsän Gampo

CHARLES MARTEL

Prince of the Franks (688–741)

Charles Martel has been hailed as the savior of Europe, and that is not hyperbole. In 732, on a battlefield between the cities of Poitiers and Tour, Charles stopped an army of Muslim invaders and drove them back across the Pyrenees into Spain. The armies of Islam, which had swept across the Middle East and North Africa and conquered Spain and Portugal, were considered unstoppable. Many in western Europe believed their civilization was doomed, that they would be overrun, too. During the battle, and then in follow-up campaigns in the next few years, Charles stopped every Muslim attempt to advance north out of the Iberian Peninsula. For his success on the battlefield he acquired the nickname "Martel," from the Latin word *martellus*, meaning hammer.

Charles was the illegitimate son of Pepin II, the mayor of the palace. The title sounds odd today, but in Charles's time the mayor was usually the de facto king of the Franks. As a bastard son, Charles should not have inherited his father's office, but his legitimate half brothers were all dead and their sons were all children, so Charles seized the office. There was opposition, of course, from his brothers' relatives, but Charles's mother was well connected, and her relatives and friends supported Charles's claim. By 719, Charles was mayor of the palace and there were no more challenges to his authority.

Then Charles took a new, more regal title—Prince of the Franks. A born warrior, he subdued the Frisians, the Saxons, and the Alamanni. He understood that the German tribes would be less aggressive if they were part of the greater European Christian culture. For that reason he provided support and assistance to Saint Boniface, an English missionary bishop who worked to convert the Germans.

Although illegitimate, Charles founded one of the great dynasties of early medieval Europe—the Carolingians (the Latin form of Charles is *Carolus*). The greatest of his descendants was his grandson, born the year after Charles died: he was also named Charles, but is better known as Charlemagne.

Charles Martel at the Battle of Tours in 732

AL-MANSUR
Caliph of Baghdad (712–775)

It was Al-Mansur's brother, Al-Saffah, who ousted the ruling Umayyad family and began the Abbasid dynasty of caliphs. Al-Saffah had been a brutal ruler who hunted down and killed every Umayyad he could find, and then desecrated their bodies. Such brutality sent the Umayyad and their supporters running for shelter to the farthest corners of the Islamic world.

Al-Saffah died in 754 and Al-Mansur came to power; in many ways he was as nervous about his keeping position as his older brother had been. Al-Saffah had sent out assassins to exterminate his rivals, but Al-Mansur killed his allies, the people who had brought the Abbasid to power. His rationale was simple—he would tolerate no one who believed that he was in their debt. To emphasize that he had power over life and death, an executioner always stood in his presence, ready to dispatch anyone who broke his laws or in some way displeased him.

His second goal, closely related to the first, was to make the power of the caliph absolute. He already had the support of the army, but his chief advisor, Ibn al-Muqaffa, urged him to win the loyalty of the landowning class by granting them concessions and making the ulama, the Islamic religious scholars, an official group attached to the caliph's court. Al-Mansur adopted all of these suggestions, but he was still insecure, so he instituted a network of spies to watch for any conspiracies such as the one his own family had hatched to drive the Umayyad from power.

But Al-Mansur was not simply a paranoid monster. He founded the city of Baghdad on the Tigris River, at a place that was a crossroads for international trade. The Tigris and Euphrates rivers gave merchants access to the Persian Gulf and the Mediterranean Sea, while the city itself became a destination for caravans from Arabia, Yemen, Egypt, and beyond. Under Al-Mansur, Baghdad became a beautiful city where science, scholarship and the arts, as well commerce, all flourished—in spite of the constant presence of Al-Mansur's executioner.

Bronze head depicting Caliph Abu Jaafar Al-Mansur, the Abbasid Caliph and founder of Baghdad

WIDUKIND

Duke of the Saxons (c. 730–808)

In summer 776, Charlemagne celebrated an event he considered equal to a victory on the battlefield: thousands of Saxons had assembled outside a log church at Paderborn to be baptized. For the king, this marked the decisive moment when a barbarian nation entered the civilized world, when they would no longer be enemies but part of his empire.

The joy of that day did not last, however. Widukind, Duke of the Saxons, refused to make peace with Charlemagne and urged his people to reclaim their independence. One of the first places the Saxons struck was Paderborn, where they slaughtered the priests who had baptized them six years earlier.

Widukind would not become a vassal of Charlemagne. He would not give up his culture to accept the Greco-Roman and Christian civilization Charlemagne was determined to impose upon his empire. The war that broke out between the Saxons and the Franks was especially bloody. "Over all Saxonland," one chronicler wrote, "Charles the king stretched out his powerful arm." At Verden, he reportedly ordered the execution of forty-five hundred Saxons who had returned to pagan worship. The precise number killed is in dispute, but the incident set off three years of warfare between Charlemagne and Widukind.

Widukind retreated deep into the northern forests, drawing Charlemagne and his army far from their own territory and their supply bases. He confused them by leaking contradictory intelligence reports—he was in Denmark, or in the Teutoburg Forest, or he had gone east to the wild unknown lands along the Baltic. Charlemagne believed Widukind had gone toward the Baltic, so he marched his army into a region where no Roman legion had ever gone, but the tribes who lived there declared they knew nothing of Widukind. At the end of summer, Charlemagne and his army turned back.

For three years, Widukind harassed Charlemagne's forces, burned Christian Saxon towns, killed missionary monks, but ultimately Charlemagne's superior numbers were able to outlast the duke and his Saxons. In 785, Widukind made peace and agreed to be baptized, with Charlemagne acting as his godfather.

It is said that Widukind's conversion was sincere, that he became an exemplary Christian and never waged war again. He even came to be venerated as a saint—in Germany he is known as Blessed Widukind.

The tomb of Widukind in Enger, Germany

ABD AL-RAHMAN I

Emir of Cordoba (731–788)

Abd al-Rahman was born in Damascus, where his family, the Umayyad, had ruled for nearly a century. In 750, however, they were driven from power by their rivals the Abbasid, and al-Rahman was obliged to flee for his life. He sought refuge first in Palestine, then in Egypt, and finally among his mother's people, the Nafza Berber tribe in Morocco. He tried to assume leadership of the tribe, but the Berbers rejected his authority. He traveled then to Spain, where many Muslim adventurers hoped to become wealthy and powerful.

The Muslims in Spain were a mass of tribal and ethnic rivalries. There was squabbling between the Berbers and the Arabs, and between the Yemeni and the Syrians. Al-Rahman saw in this mess an opportunity: there were men still loyal to the Umayyad, and he organized them into an army. In 756, he defeated Yusuf al-Fihri, the governor of al-Andalus (the Arabic name for Muslim-occupied Spain), and declared himself emir of the territory. Then al-Rahman sent a message to the Abbasid caliph in Damascus that, while he recognized his title, he would not swear allegiance to him.

Al-Rahman could not resolve every petty war and rivalry in Muslim Spain, so he made an agreement with local Muslim warlords: as long as they recognized him as emir and sent him a portion of their taxes, he wouldn't interfere with their administration of their own territory. His arrangement restored some semblance of order in al-Andalus. Meanwhile, as the Umayyad and their supporters elsewhere in the world learned of al-Rahman's success, they came to Spain to join him, thereby boosting his power and influence.

In one regard al-Rahman made no headway: with the Muslims divided, he never had the military strength to defeat the Spanish Christian forces or even recover the cities and towns that had once been Muslim occupied but had fallen to the Spanish.

Al-Rahman's greatest and most memorable achievement was the construction of the Great Mosque of Córdoba, an architectural wonder of the world, famous for its graceful red-and-white arches supported by a thousand columns of jasper, onyx, marble, and granite. The building still stands, although the Spanish converted it into a cathedral.

Statue of Abd Al-Rahman in Spain

CHARLEMAGNE

Holy Roman Emperor (742–814)

Charlemagne's dream was to unite the warring tribes and nations of western Europe into a cohesive empire, the first in the west since the fall of Rome. By and large, he succeeded—at his death Charlemagne ruled a realm that extended from the Vistula to the Atlantic, from the Baltic Sea to the Pyrenees. In recognition of his achievement, and in appreciation for his loyal service in defense of the interests of the Catholic Church, on Christmas Day 800, Pope Leo III crowned Charlemagne emperor of the Romans. Later the title became Holy Roman Emperor.

Charlemagne was an impressive figure, standing six feet three inches tall. He was powerfully built, although toward the end of his life he developed a potbelly. His hair was such a light shade of blonde that it appeared white.

Because he never learned to read, Charlemagne had great respect for education. He invited the best teachers and scholars to settle at his court; among those who accepted were Alcuin from England, Theodulf from Spain, and Paul the Deacon and Paulinus II of Aquileia from Italy. Charlemagne opened a school at his court and founded new schools in monasteries throughout his realm. He also established scriptoria where monks copied the Greek and Roman classics. He was so lavish in his support of writers, artists, and architects that he set off a cultural golden age that has come to be known as the Carolingian Renaissance.

Charlemagne enjoyed stunning military successes: the Saxons and the Bavarians submitted to his authority; he drove back the Slavs and the Avars (a pagan tribe in present-day Hungary); he occupied Corsica, Sardinia, and the Balearic Islands, all of which had suffered frequent attacks from Muslim pirates; and he tried to extend his power into Spain. It was during a skirmish at the Roncevaux Pass in the Pyrenees that a member of his household, Roland, was killed; the event inspired one of the great poems of the Middle Ages, "The Song of Roland."

After a forty-six-year reign Charlemagne died peacefully in his palace at Aachen. During the Middle Ages it was said that he was buried seated on a throne, wearing a crown and holding a scepter. The story is impossible to prove because in 1165 Emperor Frederick I opened the tomb and laid Charlemagne in a gold and silver casket.

The coronation of Charlemagne as king of Lombardy at Pavia in 774

Harun al-Rashid

Caliph of Baghdad (763–809)

Harun al-Rashid is the caliph of The Thousand and One Nights. He ruled at a time of great prosperity, when the cultural life of Baghdad had reached unprecedented heights.

Al-Mansur had ensured that the caliphs would be absolute monarchs; by al-Rashid's day the caliphs were above the tawdry concerns of running a kingdom. A vast bureaucracy governed, reporting to various department heads or to the vizier who supervised the bureaucracy in the caliph's name. The caliph sat above it all in splendid isolation as the court of last appeal, but also as the primary patron of the arts. And it was in the last function that al-Rashid excelled.

He founded an academy where linguists translated the works of the ancient Greeks into Arabic. He established libraries and schools—including medical schools. He opened hospitals, an asylum for the mentally ill, and shelters for the poor. He was a patron of poets and musicians. It was said that the caliph's generosity was based on his personal experiences: every night he went out into the streets in disguise to see firsthand how his subjects lived and what they needed.

Al-Rashid was also a great diplomat who established friendly relations with the emperor in China and Charlemagne in Europe. The Frankish king sent the caliph Spanish horses and hunting dogs; the caliph sent Charlemagne silks, an ivory chess set, and an elephant named Abul-Abbas. But he was also a shrewd negotiator. Realizing he was the greatest threat to the Byzantine Empire, al-Rashid came to an amicable arrangement with the empress, Irene: in exchange for an annual tribute of seventy thousand pieces of gold, he would leave Constantinople in peace. Irene accepted al-Rashid's terms.

In 807, al-Rashid's army invaded and occupied the island of Cyprus. Two years later he made a state visit to the island. While he was praying in a mosque an assassin attacked him, inflicting terrible head wounds. Harun al-Rashid died the next day.

EDMUND

King of East Anglia (c. 841–869)

In 865, thousands of Vikings landed in England. The terrified English called them "the Great Heathen Army," and they swept across the country, as unstoppable as a war god.

Directly in the Vikings' path lay the kingdom of East Anglia, ruled by a peace-loving, religious twenty-four-year-old king named Edmund. If he marched his army out against the Vikings, his troops would be slaughtered and his people defenseless, so Edmund tried to buy the goodwill of the invaders. He offered their leaders, Ivar the Boneless and Ivar's brothers Halfdan and Ubbe, a "gift" of hundreds of horses. Ivar accepted Edmund's offering, and marched through the kingdom, leaving it relatively unscathed.

The Vikings continued north. They swarmed into the kingdom of Northumbria, stormed its capital city, York, and captured and executed the Northumbrian king Aella. For the next three years, King Edmund and his people heard reports of Viking victories and atrocities. Then, in 869, they learned that the Vikings were returning to East Anglia. Ivar sent Edmund a message: if he wanted peace, he must renounce Christianity and worship the Norse gods. This was less a religious matter for Ivar than a way to force a king to act like a coward. Edmund rejected the offer, gathered his army, and met the Vikings in battle, probably at the village of Hoxne (the exact location is a matter of dispute among historians). The Vikings routed the East Anglians and captured Edmund.

Once again, Ivar offered Edmund peace if he renounced Christianity, and once again Edmund refused. The Vikings beat the king with cudgels, tied him to a tree and whipped him with leather straps, then invited their archers to use Edmund as target practice. The earliest account of Edmund's death says that "he was all covered with their missiles as with the bristles of a hedgehog," but he was still breathing, so the Vikings cut him down and hacked off his head.

Once the Vikings had moved on, Edmund's people recovered the mutilated body. Almost immediately Edmund came to be venerated as a saint. Around his tomb, a monastery and a town grew up, Bury Saint Edmunds, which endured until 1539 when Henry VIII destroyed both the shrine and the abbey.

St. Edmund, standing on the far left, holding an arrow, the symbol of his martyrdom

Alfred the Great

King of England (c. 849–899)

No one expected Alfred to become king—he had three older brothers. But one by one they died, the last one, Aethelred, of wounds he received fighting Danish Vikings. Overnight Alfred, twenty-two years old, was King of Wessex, which covered the southern counties of England. At this time the country was divided into four kingdoms and had no central authority; by the time Alfred became king, the Vikings had picked off the kingdoms of Northumbria, Mercia, and East Anglia—only Alfred's Wessex held out against the invaders.

That Wessex survived was essential—it was the last outpost of western civilization in England. The Vikings had reduced other English towns, farms, monasteries, and convents to smoldering ruins. Whole sections of the island were depopulated, with the surviving inhabitants hiding in the marshes of England or in the mountains of Wales. Of all the depredations of the Vikings, their attacks on the monasteries were most grievous. In addition to being religious communities, the abbeys were centers of English culture with schools and libraries as well as studios for artists and musicians. Alfred understood that by destroying the monasteries, the Vikings were threatening the future of English civilization.

To get himself some breathing space so he could formulate a strategy, Alfred bought off the Vikings; in exchange for a large sum of gold, they agreed to leave Wessex in peace for five years. But the Vikings broke their word, raiding the kingdom repeatedly. Then, in the middle of night on January 6, 878, the Vikings attacked the royal palace at Chippenham. Alfred and his family, with a few armed men, barely escaped to Athelney in the Somerset marshes. But in May the king emerged from the marsh, raised an army, and surprised the Vikings at Edington, inflicting such a serious defeat that they agreed to a treaty that divided the realm into two kingdoms—England ruled by Alfred and the Danelaw ruled by the Vikings.

For the rest of his reign, Alfred worked hard to revitalize cultural life in England, even translating Latin texts into English himself. He has been hailed as the savior of England—the king who united the country under one monarch, the warrior who restored English civilization.

OLGA

Princess of Kiev (c. 879–969)

When her husband, Igor, was murdered by the Drevlians, a neighboring tribe, Olga took it hard. When Mal, the Drevlian chief, sent a delegation to Kiev to explain that he had killed Igor because he was "like a wolf, crafty and ravening," and suggested that Olga should put aside her mourning and marry Mal, Olga saw a way to avenge herself and her dead husband. Assuming a pleasant expression, she suggested the ambassadors return the next day for her answer; when they did, Olga had her people throw the Drevlian embassy into a deep pit and bury them alive.

Next Olga sent a message to Mal—she was on her way, but before the marriage ceremony she wanted to hold the customary funeral feast for Igor, with Mal and several hundred of his most distinguished retainers as Olga's guests. At the banquet Olga ensured that the Drevlians' cups were always filled; the more they drank, the less the Drevlians noticed that neither Olga nor any of her people were drinking. Once the Drevlians were dead drunk, Olga gave the signal and her men slaughtered every Drevlian in the banqueting hall.

Still, Olga's rage had not run its course. She returned to Kiev, summoned her army, and marched on the Drevlian capital. The Kievan troops stormed the walls, set fire to the city, killed most of the inhabitants, and then rounded up the survivors and sold them into slavery. Now, finally, Olga's desire for vengeance was satisfied.

About a decade later Olga traveled to Constantinople to discuss an alliance with the emperor. This was her first encounter with a great city and with Christianity, and she was dazzled by what she saw. The magnificence of the place, the beauty of the churches, and the sublime spectacle of the liturgy filled her with awe. After lengthy conversations with bishops and monks, Olga decided to convert and bring the Christian message to her people.

Sadly, when she returned home and began to speak of her new faith, scarcely anyone would listen to her. That such a cruel, bloody-minded woman would suddenly encourage people to turn the other cheek struck most Kievans as ludicrous. Even Olga's family refused to listen to her. She died at age ninety, greatly disappointed that she had been such an unsuccessful missionary.

GUTHRUM

King of the Danelaw (died 890)

In 851, the Vikings altered their strategy from raiding England to conquering it outright. That year, 350 dragon ships anchored at the mouth of Thames. When winter set in, the Vikings did not return home but settled on the island of Thanet. Fresh waves of invaders kept coming until, in 866, an immense Viking force the English called "the Great Heathen Army" landed and began to pick off the four kingdoms of England, one by one.

One of the Viking chieftains was Guthrum, a Dane, who concentrated his attacks on Wessex, where an inexperienced young English prince named Alfred had just become king. In 872, Alfred had tried to buy off the Vikings, and although Guthrum accepted the king's gold, he had no intention of keeping the truce. He raided Wessex in 874, and in 876 mounted a major attack that captured a place called Wareham and its nearby fortress (the exact location of Wareham is unknown). More raids followed in 877, but Guthrum's most daring attack came in the small hours of the morning in January 878 when he led his army against Alfred's royal residence at Chippenham. The Vikings captured the manor, but the king and his family and a few retainers escaped.

By May, Alfred had regrouped, raised an army, and marched on Guthrum and his Vikings at Edington. Guthrum and his men took refuge inside Alfred's own manor house, Chippenham. After a two-week siege, the food ran out and Guthrum was obliged to ask Alfred for terms. Drawing a diagonal line from the Mersey River in the west to the town of Maldon in the east, the king and the chieftain worked out an arrangement that divided England in two. Alfred's realm covered Wessex and half of central England, and included the cities of Winchester (his capital) and Canterbury (the spiritual heart of England). Guthrum ruled over northern and eastern England, a region that became known as the Danelaw. Alfred demanded that Guthrum disband his army and accept baptism. To all these terms Guthrum agreed.

In 885, Guthrum attacked Alfred one last time, and for the last time Alfred defeated him. During the last four years of his life Guthrum gave Alfred no more trouble. He died in Hadleigh, where, according to a local tradition, the Viking king lies buried somewhere in St. Mary's Church.

English troops attack Guthrum's fleet of dragon ships

ERIK BLOODAX

King of York (c. 895–954)

Erik received his nickname after he murdered several of his brothers so he could be the sole surviving heir to the throne of Norway. A Latin account of his life gives him the nickname *Fratris interfector*, Brother-killer. In 933 he became king, but he held on to his title for only two years; the people of Norway grew fed up with Erik's brutal rule and threw their support behind his half brother, Haakon the Good, who drove him into exile.

Erik went to England, settling in Jorvik—modern-day York—which was a prominent Viking settlement in the northern part of the country. Exactly how he became king is murky; it is likely that he won the support for his title from the English king Aethelstan by promising to defend the northern part of the country against raids from the Scots and the Irish. In fact, Erik turned the tables by leading raids against Scotland and Ireland. But in time he was driven from power in York, too, this time by Aethelstan's half brother King Eadred. Over the next four years Erik built alliances with Viking rulers in the Hebrides and the Orkneys until he was ready to take back York; in 952, he succeeded.

York was a rich prize. The Vikings, with their wide-ranging commercial ties, had made York arguably the greatest center of international trade in the British Isles. Craftsmen and artisans manufactured amber jewelry, fine knives, locks and keys, and beautifully dyed textiles, as well as humbler items such as wooden cups and bowls—all of these goods they sold in markets across Europe. Among the luxuries that flowed into York were German wines and Byzantine silks. Little wonder that Erik wanted the city as his own.

In 954, Erik was traveling through the Pennine mountains. At a lonely place called Stainmore he was ambushed by a Viking rival named Maccus. A Norse skald, or poet, wrote a song describing Erik's entry into Valhalla, where the god Odin welcomed him because "many lands . . . with his sword he had reddened."

After Erik, there were no more Viking kings of York; the city became English again, which has led some historians to suspect that King Eadred was involved in Erik's murder.

A Viking ship displayed in Oseberg, Norway, such as Erik would have used.

WENCESLAS

Duke of Bohemia (c. 907–929)

"Good King Wenceslas" of the Christmas carol was a real king, although the episode recounted in the lyrics is based on legend rather than an actual event in Wenceslas's life.

Wenceslas grew up at a time when Bohemia was torn by two factions: one led by Wenceslas's mother, Dragomir, who wanted the country to remain pagan and Slavic, and the other led by Wenceslas's grandmother, Ludmila, who wanted to see Bohemia as part of the European Christian civilization that was expanding into eastern Europe.

Ludmila made herself responsible for her grandson's education, and ensured he was as fluent in Latin—Christian Europe's international language—as he was in his native language. When Wenceslas's father died, Dragomir seized power and arranged for Ludmila to be strangled. Enraged by the murder of the good old woman, Bohemian nobles who favored ties with Europe, backed by a large percentage of the common people, proclaimed sixteen-year-old Wenceslas duke of Bohemia.

The young duke banished his mother, gave his grandmother a lavish funeral, adopted a policy that was pro-Western and pro-Christian, and placed his country under the protection of the powerful king of Germany, Henry I the Fowler.

The faction Dragomir had led was taken up by Wenceslas's brother, Boleslaus, who concealed what he was really plotting by pretending to become a Christian. In 935, Boleslaus sent his brother an invitation to an occasion he knew Wenceslas would not be able to resist—the dedication of a new church. At the banquet that followed, men loyal to Wenceslas warned him that his life was in danger, but the duke brushed them off. The next morning, as Wenceslas was walking to the church, he met his brother. Boleslaus struck him, Wenceslas hit back. As the brothers struggled, two of Boleslaus's henchmen emerged from their hiding place and attacked Wenceslas, killing him.

In the wake of the murder, the Bohemians rejected Boleslaus and his party; Christianity became more firmly rooted in the country than ever and the people rallied around pro-European nobles. As for Duke Wenceslas, they laid his mutilated body in a shrine in Saint Vitus' Cathedral in Prague and venerated him as the patron saint of Bohemia.

Stained glass depiction of Wenceslaus, on the left

OTTO I THE GREAT

Holy Roman Emperor (912–973)

A forceful man, Otto single-handedly revived the Holy Roman Empire and made Germany the most important political power in Europe. Otto's father, Henry I, had been widely admired, even beloved, but he had not strengthened the monarchy. Consequently, during the first years of his reign, Otto had to contend with ambitious nobles who tried to restrict his royal power, and plots led by two of his brothers, Thankmar and Henry, to kill him and seize his throne. Otto hamstrung the nobility by replacing the dukes, the most powerful rank of the German aristocracy, with members of his own family. As for his brothers, they schemed against Otto for eleven years, until Thankmar died and Henry begged Otto to forgive him.

The eastern borders of Germany were under almost constant attack from Slavic tribesmen from what is now Poland and the Czech Republic, and Magyar tribesmen from present-day Hungary. Otto, a skillful military commander, invaded the Slavic and Magyar lands closest to his border. There he established a string of strongly garrisoned forts to control the tribes, and he established missions to convert and pacify the Slavs and Magyars. In 955, after a stunning victory over the Slavs, Bohemia and a large portion of Poland became part of Otto's German empire.

Like Charlemagne, Otto saw himself as a protector of the church, so when Pope John XII found himself assailed by enemies, Otto rushed an army into Italy and scattered the pope's adversaries. As a reward for his service, Pope John crowned Otto Holy Roman Emperor, just as his predecessor had crowned Charlemagne.

Otto's military successes and his clever method of disempowering the nobles made Germany stronger and more secure than it had been in decades. It was also much wealthier, thanks to the discovery of silver mines at Goslar in Lower Saxony. Otto became the premier monarch of Europe, the man other kings turned to as mediator. When he died in 973, Otto was mourned throughout Germany and across the continent.

BRIAN BORU

Emperor of the Irish (941–1014)

Brian Boru was born the youngest son of an Irish minor royal family. Brian's dream was to expel the Vikings from Ireland and unite all the petty Irish kingdoms under a single ruler—himself. After the deaths of his older brothers, he began pursuing his ambition in earnest.

He adopted the Viking way of making war: he built a fleet of ships and sent them up the rivers of Ireland to make lightning attacks on cities and castles, while his infantry attacked on land. One by one the Irish kingdoms fell to him, only Ulster in northern Ireland and the Viking kingdom of Dublin held out. The Uí Néill clan who ruled Ulster never submitted to Brian, but Sitric Silkbeard, king of Dublin, seeing that Brian was too strong to resist, surrendered and became Brian's vassal.

In 1005, Brian traveled to Armagh to the tomb of Saint Patrick, where he gave thanks for his victories. In the guest book he signed his name and wrote after it the title *"imperator Scottorum,"* emperor of the Irish. It was not hyperbole—Brian was the greatest king and most powerful ruler the Irish had ever known. But he had enemies.

Maelmorda, the former king of Leinster whom Brian had deposed, schemed with Sitric to bring a huge Viking army into Ireland to destroy Brian and restore the island's many kingdoms. Word of the plot reached Brian, now an old man of eighty-eight. He called out his army, and on April 23, 1014, the Irish and the Vikings met on the field of Clontarf outside Dublin. Brian, too old to fight, had his tent erected on high ground where he could watch the battle. It was a bloody, desperate fight, but toward the end of the afternoon the Vikings threw down their weapons and ran for their ships. One of the escaping Vikings, a warrior named Brodir, got lost and found himself outside Brian's tent. He recognized the king, raised his battle axe, and rushed at the old man, splitting his skull in two.

The Battle of Clontarf broke the Vikings' hold on Ireland, but Brian's united empire of the Irish did not survive him. However, it was not invaded again for another 150 years.

The assasination of Brian Boru

Vladimir I

Prince of Kiev (c. 956–1015)

In temperament, Vladimir resembled his grandmother Olga's pre-Christian character. As an illegitimate son he had no right to become prince of Kiev, but Vladimir was not the kind of man to let a technicality get in his way. He murdered his half brother and seized the title.

Vladimir was the type of pagan prince who gave his Christian neighbors nightmares: he erected an immense temple full of idols of pagan gods and consecrated it with human sacrifice (the victims he selected were a father and son, both members of Kiev's tiny community of Christians). He kept seven wives and about three hundred concubines—among them his half brother's widow.

As a warlord Vladimir had no peer, a quality that attracted the attention of the Byzantine emperor, Basil, who was having trouble with rebellious subjects and Bulgar raiders. When Emperor Basil asked for his help, Vladimir assembled an army of six thousand Kievan warriors, who scattered both the rebels and the Bulgars. As his reward Vladimir demanded that Anna, the emperor's sister, become his eighth wife. Basil countered that such a marriage could not take place so long as Vladimir was a pagan polygamist. If Basil was bluffing, Vladimir called his bluff: he agreed to be baptized and promised to dismiss his wives and his harem. Once Vladimir fulfilled his side of the bargain, Anna had no choice but to submit and marry the prince of Kiev.

It was the general consensus in Kiev and Constantinople that Vladimir was going through the motions of conversion, that back in his own country he would revert to his old ways. So it came as a shock to Vladimir's retinue and his new wife when he invited a small crowd of bishops and monks to accompany him to Kiev. There he ordered his temple destroyed and began building churches. He issued a decree that the poor and helpless would be fed free of charge at the prince's residence every day, while wagons full of food would visit the homes of invalids.

Then Vladimir did something truly unexpected: he abolished the death penalty. Impressed by their prince's dramatic change of heart, the people converted by the thousands. Half a century after her death, Olga's dream of a Christian Kiev became a reality.

Vladimir raises his right hand to make the sign of the cross as priests minister to his people

OLAF TRYGGVASON

King of Norway (c. 960–1000)

Olaf Tryggvason was a Viking chieftain who became king almost by accident. Yet once he had power, he did all he could to increase the authority of the king in Norway, even extending it to the Norse settlements on far-off Iceland.

Like all Viking warlords, Olaf made his fortune and his reputation raiding the British Isles. In 995, he was back in Norway just in time for an insurgency against the ruler of the country, Earl Haakon. The earl had outraged the farmers by his habit of carrying off and raping any of their wives and daughters who caught his eye. When Haakon demanded that a well-to-do farmer surrender his wife to him, the proud man refused, then called upon his neighbors for help. Haakon ran off, with the irate farmers in pursuit. During the flight, one of Haakon's own slaves turned on him and killed him.

Meanwhile, Olaf had a chance meeting with Haakon's three sons. Harsh words were exchanged, and in the skirmish that followed, Olaf killed one of the young men, while the other two escaped. Relieved to be free of Haakon and unwilling to submit to either of his surviving sons, the people of Norway proclaimed Olaf Tryggvason their king.

Olaf had converted to Christianity, and like other Viking rulers, he demanded that his subjects accept the new religion, too. He was met with strenuous opposition, including from the farmers who had been his most loyal supporters since the death of Haakon. When they rose against him, he killed their leader, Jarn-Skeggi, then tried to mollify the farmers by marrying Jarn-Skeggi's daughter Guthrun; it was futile gesture—Guthrun tried to kill Olaf on their wedding night.

Despite his struggles, Olaf succeeded in establishing Christianity in the coastal areas of Norway and in Iceland and Greenland, although his methods were harsh—men who refused to convert might be executed, maimed, or at the very least banished.

In 1000, the kings of Denmark and Sweden along with one of Earl Haakon's surviving sons decided to take advantage of Olaf's precarious position and invade Norway. Olaf met them in a sea battle at a place called Svolder in the western Baltic Sea. He had only eleven ships against an enemy fleet of seventy. One by one his ships were captured until only his flagship remained. Rather than be killed by his enemies, Olaf leaped into the sea and was presumed dead, although reports of sightings of the vanished king persisted for years.

A Norse raid led by King Olaf Tryggvason of Norway

Boleslaw I the Brave

King of Poland (967–1025)

The German, or Holy Roman, Empire reached to Poland's borders, and Boleslaw's father, Mieszko, always worried that the Germans would try to swallow up his country. Consequently, when Mieszko decided to become a Christian, he traveled to Rome to be baptized, because he feared that if he permitted himself to be baptized by a German bishop, the German emperor would interpret it as an act of submission.

When Boleslaw came to the throne, he adopted a policy of appearing to appease the Germans as long as it did not involve compromising the independence of Poland. The Poland Boleslaw inherited was a little place, almost entirely limited to the Warta River valley, but Boleslaw expanded his territory. He acquired Silesia in southern Poland, Eastern Pomerania on the German border around the present-day city of Gdansk, the city of Cracow and all the surrounding territory, as well as Moravia and a portion of Slovakia. Previously, Poland's chief ruler had been called duke, but Boleslaw was strong enough to call himself king—the first king of Poland.

Because his army was considered one of the finest in eastern Europe, his relatives and in-laws asked Boleslaw to send Polish troops to help in their wars. Poles tried to prop up the rule of Boleslaw's son-in-law Sviatopolk I of Kiev, and fought with Boleslaw's nephew, Canute the Great, during his conquest of England.

One of the innovations Boleslaw introduced to Poland was towns and marketplaces. He invited craftsmen to settle with their families around the castles that were scattered across the land. The garrisons offered protection, the craftsmen produced the necessities the lord, his family, and the soldiers required, and on market days farmers brought produce to sell to the town dwellers and the residents of the castle.

Boleslaw made Poland an influential player in European politics, expanded its borders almost to those of present-day Poland, and gave fresh impetus to the national economy.

STEPHEN I
King of Hungary (c. 970–1038)

Stephen is regarded as the founder of the Kingdom of Hungary. He took a land of many tribes and by force of will forged them into a united people.

Stephen abolished the old tribal territorial designations and divided Hungary into several provinces that he called "lands," over which he appointed governors and magistrates. He also curtailed the independence of the nobility, compelling them to swear fealty to him. Like other rulers in eastern Europe at this time, Stephen believed that fostering Christianity in his realm was a way to bring Hungary into the mainstream of European culture and politics. To achieve this he suppressed pagan customs, outlawed blasphemy against the Christian God, and required that every ten towns within his kingdom pool their resources to build a parish church and support a parish priest.

In appreciation for Stephen's efforts, Pope Sylvester II recognized Stephen's title, King of Hungary, and sent him a crown. Saint Stephen's crown, one of Hungary's most prized possessions, is not the diadem Pope Sylvester sent, but it may include jewels or enamels from the original.

Stephen had a strong sense of justice, which led him to make himself accessible to any of his subjects who had a complaint. Humble farmers and tradesmen especially flocked to him because Stephen could be relied upon to give a sympathetic hearing to their complaints.

While Stephen was convinced that the changes he was implementing were for the good of his kingdom and its people, he was aware that some nobles and common people resented his program. The king found a strong ally in his son, Emeric, who offered his father such sound advice that Emeric became, in essence, his father's co-ruler. With Emeric as his successor, Stephen felt confident that the renewal of Hungary would continue. Therefore it was the tragedy of Stephen's life when, while out hunting, Emeric was attacked by a wild boar and fatally wounded.

At Stephen's death the nobles and tribal chiefs who had opposed the king's policy selected one of their own to be king, and he did what Stephen and Emeric had always dreaded—rolled back the reforms.

Statue of St. Stephen on the Fishermen's Bastion, Budapest, Hungary

HENRY II AND CUNEGUND

Holy Roman Emperor (973–1024) and Empress (c. 975–1040)

Emperor Otto III died without an heir, a situation that sparked a brief civil war in Germany among rival contenders. Ultimately, through battle and negotiation, the various parties agreed to accept Otto's cousin Henry as king. He was crowned in 1002, yet tensions among various nobles and ethnic groups in the kingdom plagued Henry throughout his reign.

Unable to consolidate the nobility, Henry cultivated another great power in the country—the Catholic Church. He was pious by nature, so much so that it was rumored that he and his queen, Cunegund, did not have children because they had both taken a vow to live together as chastely as brother and sister. Be that as it may, Henry won the support of the church by naming excellent men to the country's most important bishoprics and abbeys, and lavishing upon the church gifts of land and art. Together the royal couple founded the Bamberg cathedral, and Cunegund founded a convent for Benedictine nuns at Kaufungen. Their generosity and loyalty to the church earned Henry and Cunegund the favor of the pope, who crowned them Holy Roman Emperor and Empress in 1014.

Predictably, Henry's borders were under continual attack from neighboring kings and rulers. He managed to reclaim Bohemia, but he was forced to give up minor territories to the count of Flanders and the king of Poland. Unlike other emperors, he was less interested in asserting his authority over foreign lands than in improving life for his people in Germany. As a result, at the time of his death Germany's economy was flourishing, the church in Germany was vigorous, and throughout the country government functions were carried out by honest, able administrators, all of whom had been appointed by the emperor.

After Henry's death, Cunegund became a nun at Kaufungen, where she divided her days between visiting the sick, praying, and studying. She would not permit anyone to treat her as a retired empress, but only as just another nun. After her death, she was buried beside Henry in the Bamberg cathedral. Both husband and wife are venerated as saints.

Tomb cover of Emperor Henry II and his wife Cunegund

ZOE

Empress of Byzantium (c. 978–1042)

Constantine VIII would never permit his daughters, Zoe and Theodora, to marry. On his deathbed, with no son to succeed him, Constantine finally consented for Zoe to marry Romanus, a patrician distantly related to the imperial family. Romanus was sixty years old, Zoe fifty, yet after years of waiting, she came to married life with a powerful sex drive. Romanus showed no interest in Zoe; he had only married her to become emperor. But Zoe did not remain lonely long—she began an affair with her handsome young chamberlain Michael the Paphlagonian, who was about nineteen years old. On April 11, 1034, servants found Romanus dead in his bath. Zoe and Michael married the same day.

With no hope of having a child, the couple adopted their nephew, also named Michael. When Michael senior died in 1041, young Michael inherited. Jealous of Zoe's influence in the government and her popularity with the people of Constantinople, Michael falsely accused her of trying to kill him and exiled her to a convent. This sparked a riot in the city, which led Michael to decide it might be prudent to bring Zoe back. That was not enough for the mob, who still wanted the young emperor's head. In their attack on the palace, three thousand died, but Michael escaped. As for Zoe, the insurgents carried her on their shoulders in triumph. She was proclaimed empress, and her sister, Theodora, co-empress.

Once calm had returned to the city, the sisters addressed their most pressing problem—disposing of the ex-emperor Michael. Custom decreed that an emperor must be a perfect physical specimen, so the sisters sent an executioner to blind Michael. He was permitted to retire to a monastery, where he died in 1042.

That same year Zoe married for the third time—Constantine IX Monomachus, a patrician who was as handsome as he was sophisticated. She and Theodora agreed that he should be crowned emperor and rule with them, which laid the foundation for a happy marriage. Constantine was grateful to Zoe for elevating him to the pinnacle of society; she was happy to have the attentions of another good-looking young man—so much so that she did not mind that he had a mistress. Zoe died in 1050, beloved by her husband and her people.

Mosaic portrait of Empress Zoe in the Hagia Sophia

OLAF II

King of Norway (c. 995–1030)

Olaf was only twelve when his father signed him up for a kind of apprenticeship with an experienced—and successful—Viking raider named Hrani. In the four years that followed, Olaf learned how to pillage, fight, and kill. He raided towns along the Baltic, then at age sixteen joined a Viking band that was raiding English towns, including Canterbury, where Olaf slaughtered innocent civilians and set fire to the town's castle. From England he sailed to Normandy, where, to everyone's surprise, Olaf converted to Christianity. He was eighteen at the time.

Two years later, Olaf returned home to Norway to secure his right to the Norwegian crown and to continue the establishment of Christianity begun by King Olaf Tryggvason. Like many other Christian Norsemen, he never entirely abandoned his Viking mind-set. It was Olaf's policy to convince Christian Europe that Norway was not a land of blood-crazed heathens, and the only way to accomplish this was to make his people Christian. His methods were not gentle, but they were persuasive. With his army, he marched through the countryside, destroying pagan temples, cutting down sacred groves, smashing idols of the Norse gods. He punished men who would not be baptized, blinding some, lopping off the hand or foot of others, even sentencing some to death. Olaf's method's worked—perhaps because the Vikings, who were brutal and violent by nature, respected brutality and violence in others.

In 1028 Canute, king of Denmark and England, invaded Norway with an enormous army to assert his claim to the crown. Outnumbered and taken by surprise, Olaf fled to Kiev; he left behind his wife, but took along his mistress—yet another indication that some of the finer points of Christian practice eluded Olaf.

During his two years of exile, Olaf collected an army, then he sailed back to Norway and met his enemies at a place called Stiklestad. After hours of brutal fighting, neither side had the upper hand. Then three of Canute's warriors attacked Olaf: one hacked at his leg with an axe while a second jammed a spear into the king's belly, and the third slit open his neck. Drenched in blood, Olaf slipped to the ground and died.

Some of Olaf's men claimed that when they touched the dead king's body, their wounds were instantly healed. Olaf's chaplain, Bishop Grimkell, declared these healings were miracles, and proclaimed Olaf a saint.

Olaf II known as 'The Saint'

CANUTE THE GREAT

King of Denmark and England (c. 995–1035)

The settlement Alfred the Great had made with the Vikings more than a century earlier made the English king Aethelred uneasy—he did not like sharing England with the Danes, nor did he trust them. In the year 1002, Aethelred ordered a massacre of all the Danes in England. The precise number of Danish men, women, and children killed is unknown—certainly hundreds, possibly thousands. In Oxford, the Danes sought sanctuary inside the Church of Saint Frideswide, but an English mob burned it down. Among the dead inside the church was King Svein of Denmark's sister, her husband, and their child.

Svein retaliated by attacking England, doing so much damage that Aethelred bought him off with vast amounts of silver—the tribute/bribe became known as Danegeld. But it was not enough. In 1013 Svein, with his eighteen-year-old son Canute, invaded England intent on conquering it. Svein died a year later, but Canute pushed on, until in 1016 he was king of all England. In the 1020s he claimed the crown of Norway, assumed control of portions of Sweden, and accepted the fealty of the Scots who were afraid he might conquer their country, too. Canute was lord over an empire.

It's ironic that the first king to rule over a united England was a Dane, but Canute respected his English subjects, preserved their laws and customs, encouraged trade and commerce, and fostered a new style of art that drew upon English and Scandinavian models. Like virtually all the Danes in England, Canute was a Christian, and he atoned for the depredations of ancestors by repairing and enriching churches and monasteries that had been damaged by the Vikings; and he built new ones as well. He established such good relations between English and Danes and created such a stable kingdom that in 1027, he felt sufficiently secure to make the trip to Rome to see the pope crown Conrad II Holy Roman Emperor.

At his death Canute was buried in Winchester Cathedral. In the seventeenth century, during England's civil war, antimonarchist troops broke open all the royal tombs—including Canute's—and scattered the bones.

Benoist sculp.

MACBETH

King of Scotland (c. 1005–1057)

Macbeth is best known as the bloody tyrant of Shakespeare's play who murders anyone he considers a threat to his power. It usually comes as a surprise to learn that there was a real king of Scotland named Macbeth. There was a Lady Macbeth, too—her name was Gruoch.

Macbeth did kill King Duncan, but not when the king was a guest in house. In fact, the real Duncan was not the wise, royal father figure of Shakespeare's play but a rash man, about thirty years old, whom Macbeth killed in battle. Duncan's queen and sons fled the country, and in 1040 Macbeth was proclaimed king. He still had a few political odds and ends to clear up: he killed in battle Duncan's father, who led an uprising against Macbeth, and he made a truce with Thorfinn the Mighty, the Viking earl of Orkney. The powerful Siward clan invaded the Scottish county of Lothian, but Macbeth drove them out. In 1050, he felt sufficiently confident of the stability of his kingdom that he and Thorfinn made the long pilgrimage to Rome, where, one chronicler reports, Macbeth "scattered alms like seed-corn."

In 1054, Duncan's son Malcolm, backed up by the Siwards and an English army, entered Scotland and fought Macbeth at Dunsinane. The battle appears to have been a draw, but for some reason, in order to make peace, Macbeth turned over to Malcolm the Scottish counties of Lothian, Cumbria, and Tayside. Three years later Malcolm made war on Macbeth again. At the Battle of Lumphanan, Macbeth fell in combat. Although the king was dead, Macbeth's army was victorious, and Macbeth was succeeded by his stepston, Lady Macbeth's boy, Lulach. Ironically, Macbeth was killed on the seventeenth anniversary of the day he killed Duncan.

Macbeth with his murderous henchmen lurking on the far right

HAROLD II GODWINSON

King of England (c. 1022–1066)

On January 5, 1066, Edward the Confessor, King of England, died. He had no child, and the question on everyone's mind was, "Had he named a successor?" The English said that on his deathbed Edward had chosen his brother-in-law, Harold Godwinson, to succeed him. This is plausible, not least because the Witan, an assembly of the most distinguished men in England (and a forerunner of Parliament) met within hours of Edward's death, recognized Harold as king, and arranged to have him crowned the very next day.

Harold had the makings of a great king. At forty-four years of age, he had political experience (his family had been the most skillful power brokers in England for more than fifty years), he was eloquent, and he inspired confidence in men. Furthermore, he had five sons which virtually assured that the English royal line would continue.

Across the English Channel was another politically savvy man who believed he should be king of England—William, Duke of Normandy, the illegitimate son of Edward the Confessor's first cousin. In 1064, Harold Godwinson had been shipwrecked on the coast of France, and William had come to his rescue. During Harold's stay in France, William pressured him to take an oath recognizing William's right to succeed Edward. Because the oath was made under duress, it was not valid. William did not care; if Harold ever acted contrary to the oath, it would give William an excuse to invade England. And in 1066, that is what he did.

Tragically, just at the moment when Harold should have been preparing to repulse the Normans, the Vikings invaded northern England. Harold and his entire army rode north and took the Viking army entirely by surprise, killing more than six thousand. Then they turned around and rode swiftly back to meet the invasion from Normandy.

On October 14, 1066, more than eight thousand Normans waded ashore at Hastings, where they were met by Harold's seventy-five hundred exhausted troops. Nonetheless, the English held their own, and it is believed they might have prevailed had Harold not been killed, struck in the eye by an arrow. At the death of their king, the English fled.

Harold was England's last Anglo-Saxon king, and his defeat and death also marked the end of Anglo-Saxon England. William and the Normans would introduce an entirely new culture that would transform England forever.

King Harold Godwinson makes his final stand against the Normans at the Battle of Hastings, October 14, 1066

William I the Conqueror

King of England, Duke of Normandy (1027–1087)

William was the child of Duke Robert of Normandy and Herleva, an undertaker's daughter. Robert never married Herleva, but he did acknowledge William as his son and heir. At Robert's death in 1035, seven-year-old William became duke of Normany, but with no authority, no allies, and not even a guardian to look after the boy-duke's interests, Normandy descended into chaos. Greedy knights and noblemen stole ducal property; several members of Robert's family were murdered; and in 1047 the Count of Brienne made an attempt to take over all of Normandy. By this time William was twenty years old, and with the help of the king of France, he defended what was left of his inheritance, then began the long, difficult job of restoring order to Normandy.

In 1053, William married Matilda of Flanders. They were an odd couple—he stood over six feet tall and would grow obese, while Matilda was less than five feet tall and remained petite all her life. They had ten children together.

Today, very few historians believe William's claim that his cousin Edward the Confessor promised him the crown of England. But William's army believed it, and after he killed King Harold and routed the English army at Hastings, he spent five brutal years subduing Anglo-Saxon England: when the people of Yorkshire rose against him, he devastated the countryside, ensuring that a huge percentage of the population would starve to death.

Almost overnight everything in England changed. William drove out the Anglo-Saxon aristocracy gave their lands and manor houses to his Norman followers. He deprived Anglo-Saxon bishops and abbots of their office and replaced them with Normans. He introduced feudalism to England, making the Anglo-Saxon peasantry little better than slaves. He sent out census takers to itemize the land of possessions of everyone in England—the better to know how to exploit the conquered country's resources. Even the language changed: French became the high-status language, English the language of the lower classes, a situation that endured for four hundred years.

William's conquest of England is of the most extraordinary events in history, because rarely has a monarch changed the course of a nation so completely.

The equestrian statue of William the Conqueror at his birthplace, Falaise

DAVID II THE BUILDER

King of Georgia (1073–1125)

"Restorer" might be the more accurate title for David II. From the time he was crowned king at age sixteen, he revitalized his country, which was in such a sad state that even the national capital had been in foreign hands for four hundred years.

Islam and the Byzantine Empire were the two greatest challenges to the existence of Georgia. They had the kingdom hemmed in, with Muslims in firm possession of the capital Tbilisi, and Muslim Turkish nomads wandering across the Georgian province of Kartli unopposed. But then Georgia's luck changed: in 1096 Pope Urban II, responding to appeals from the Byzantine emperor for military assistance against the armies of Islam, called for a crusade to save the Byzantine Empire, cut off any possible Muslim invasion of eastern Europe, and liberate the Holy Land.

With the Turks under pressure from the crusader armies, David saw his opportunity to push back the invaders and reclaim Tbilisi. The decisive battle came at Didgori, in which a force of crusaders helped the Georgians defeat their common enemy.

Incredibly, while securing his kingdom's borders, David also found time to be patron to the arts and scholarship in Georgia. At Gelati Monastery, he founded an academy where the most promising children in the realm—regardless of rank—were educated.

At the time of David's death, Tbilisi was Georgia's capital once again, defended by an impressive new fortress, Rustavi, that David had constructed on the south side of the city. And the kingdom of Georgia extended from the Black Sea to the Caspian Sea. Georgian Christians praised David as the savior of their nation, and even his Muslim subjects had good things to say about him—he granted them amnesty and tolerance. "He soothed their hearts," one Muslim contemporary of David wrote, "and left them alone in all goodness."

Georgian fresco of King David the Builder, right, holding a model of the church

ROGER II

King of Sicily, Calabria, and Apulia (1095–1145)

As the descendants of Viking settlers and the native French population of Normandy, the Normans were one of the finest warrior nations in western Europe. By 1017 Norman mercenaries, hired by Italian aristocrats, were fighting in southern Italy to drive out the country's Byzantine overlords. But when the war was over, the Normans stayed in southern Italy, conquering cities and towns until, by 1091, virtually all of southern Italy and Sicily were in Norman hands.

Out of this Norman patchwork of dukedoms and principalities, Roger II of Sicily created a unified kingdom by compelling the Norman lords of southern Italy to recognize him as their king. In 1130, he had the southern Italian provinces and the island of Sicily firmly under his control; on Christmas Day of that year he was crowned king of Sicily, Calabria, and Apulia.

In addition to Italians and Normans, Roger's kingdom included Arabs, Greeks, and Jews. He treated them all equally and adopted whatever he found most useful from their own civilizations. His civil service was modeled on that used in the Byzantine Empire. His treasury imitated the Arab method of controlling finances. His chancery was based on the French style of conducting the king's business. He issued all official documents in Latin, Greek, and Arabic so everyone in the kingdom could understand them. Roger was Catholic, but his subjects included Muslims, Jews, and Orthodox Christians; realizing that religious persecution or even religious favoritism would only serve to disrupt the country, he enforced a policy of religious tolerance.

Roger built spectacular Catholic churches in Sicily, including the Cappella Palatina in Palermo, which blended Norman architecture with Byzantine and Arabic decoration. More important, he created at his court an atmosphere where scholars from throughout the Mediterranean world, irrespective of their race or religion, could gather and exchange ideas.

Roger's system of government was unusual for its time, but it was so well founded that it survived him for another two generations. He is regarded as the greatest of the Norman kings.

Mosaic depicting King Roger II being crowned by Jesus Christ

MELISENDE

Queen of Jerusalem (1105–1161)

Melisende was the oldest of four sisters. Having no boys in the family did not trouble her father, Baldwin II, King of Jerusalem. He raised Melisende to be a queen.

The Kingdom of Jerusalem was an anomaly in the Middle East that had been founded in 1099 after the success of the First Crusade. In Melisende's day it stretched along the Mediterranean Sea from Gaza up through present-day Israel, Lebanon, and Syria to southern Turkey. Christian nobles and princes, almost all of them descended from crusaders who had come from France and Flanders, had carved out great estates for themselves around the cities of Tripoli, Antioch, and Edessa.

Melisende's father encouraged her to marry Count Fulk, a widely admired military commander. She consented, and the couple had a son, Baldwin III. A year after the prince was born, Melisende's father died and she and Fulk ruled Jerusalem together. But not for long; Fulk tried to elbow his wife out of the way and assume full royal authority. He even falsely accused her of adultery, but to his surprise the nobles and churchmen rallied around Melisende, then staged a palace coup that immobilized the king.

Even during times of family upheaval, Melisende was a generous patron of the arts and of the church. She gave generously to shrines and hospitals. And she supported a scriptorium in Jerusalem where artists turned out glorious manuscripts, including a prayer book for her, the famous *Melisende Psalter*.

In 1144, when a Turkish army captured the great city of Edessa, Melisende appealed to the pope for help; he responded by announcing a new crusade. The commanders of the crusade, Louis VII of France and Conrad III of Germany, convinced Melisende's son Baldwin, now sixteen years old, to attack Damascus. This was a wretched idea as there had been close ties between the kingdom of Jerusalem and the emirate of Damascus for years. By attacking Damascus the crusaders alienated the Christians' only Muslim ally in the Middle East. Worse, the crusaders failed to take Damascus or recapture Edessa.

When Melisende died in 1161, the historian William of Tyre wrote a eulogy that read in part, "Striving to emulate the glory of the best princes, Melisende ruled the kingdom with such ability that she was rightly considered to have equaled her predecessors."

Marriage of Queen Melisande of Jerusalem and Fulk V

le patriarche

Toujours venir d'amour meilleur

MANCO CAPAC

Emperor of the Incas (died c. 1107)

The story of Manco Capac, the first emperor of the Incas and founder of their civilization, is filled with the type of details and subplots one finds in mythologies all across the globe. Yet there is a general consensus among historians that Manco Capac was an actual historical figure, not just a mythical character.

The legends say that Manco, along with his three brothers and four sisters, lived in a cave in the Vilcamayu Valley. The cave was in a town called Paqari-tampu, "abode of the dawn." The name probably led to the belief that Manco and his siblings were all children of the Sun. They came to the scattered tribes who lived near Lake Titicaca and brought them civilization. Finding that the people went about naked, Manco's sister-wife, Mama-Ocllo Huaco taught the women how to weave wool and cotton into cloth, while Manco taught the men how to farm. Manco insisted that the tribes abandon human sacrifice and worship the Sun. He also outlawed the practice of marriage between brothers and sisters except for Inca ruling class.

The story is rooted in actual events. There is evidence that the Inca settled near Titicaca, where the Allcovisa tribe already was established, and that there was some cultural exchange between the two groups.

Another story claims that Manco founded the city of Cuzco, but that is truly a myth. The Killke people lived in the city during the 900s, and the Inca did not arrive until the 1200s.

Manco is generally described as the first emperor of the Inca, but he did not use that title—Sapa Inca. His title, Capac, means warlord.

Manco died in or around the year 1107, and was succeeded by his and Mama-Ocllo's son, Sinchi Roca. It was Sinchi who led the Inca into the Cuzco Valley, which would become the center of their empire.

MANCO CAPAC

FIRST ——— ——— INCA.

Enrico Dandolo

Doge of Venice (c. 1107–1205)

The Dandolos, a family of Venetian aristocrats, were famous for living into their seventies and eighties at a time when on average few adults lived past forty. Enrico served in Venice's diplomatic corps, but he was given no access to high office until his elders died—by that time Enrico was in his sixties.

In 1171, the Byzantines turned on all Venetians living in their empire, confiscated their property, and imprisoned them. In retaliation Doge Vitale II Michiel mounted a punitive expedition against Constantinople, but an epidemic struck the Venetian force, killing off so many men that the doge felt he had no option but to return home. Vitale's tactical withdrawal enraged the Venetian public, who attacked and killed him.

Unable to assemble another army quickly, the government sent Enrico Dandolo to Constantinople to resolve the crisis through diplomatic means. But the Byzantines refused to negotiate, and expressed their contempt for Venice and its ambassador by blinding Enrico. For the rest of his life, Enrico nurtured a deep-seated hatred of the Byzantines.

A man of iron will, Enrico rejected the idea that he must spend the rest of his life as an invalid. He remained in public service, and in 1193, when he was about eighty-four years old, he was elected doge of Venice.

In 1199, Europe launched the Fourth Crusade to recapture the Holy Land from the Saracens. The commanders arranged with the Venetians to provide the necessary ships, but in 1202, when the crusaders assembled in Venice, they hadn't the funds to pay their debt. Doge Enrico offered them a solution: he would forgive the debt if the crusaders made a detour and helped Venice reconquer the city of Zara, which had rebelled against Venetian rule. The crusaders agreed, but after taking Zara, there was another detour—to Constantinople, where the crusaders, directed by Enrico, became so caught up in Byzantine politics that on April 13, 1204, the soldiers of the cross stormed and ransacked the greatest Christian city in the east. It is thought that with the conquest of Constantinople, Enrico Dandolo had gotten his revenge at last. He died in the city in 1205 and was buried in Constantinople's greatest church, Hagia Sophia.

The Crusaders' entry into Constantinople by Eugene Delacroix

ALFONSO HENRIQUES I THE CONQUEROR

King of Portugal (1109–1185)

Alfonso Henriques I was the founder of Portugal, the man who turned a province into an independent kingdom, drove the Moors from Lisbon and Santarém, and kept the Spanish at bay. Interestingly, his greatest opponent was his own mother, Teresa, who wanted Portugal united to Galicia, the province in the northwest corner of Spain.

Alfonso had an independent frame of mind even as a boy; it is said that at age thirteen his arguments with his mother over the destiny of Portugal became so heated that she banished him.

The next year Alfonso became a knight and collected an army to take control of the lands he had received by inheritance from his late father. It took six years of fighting before Alfonso and Teresa's family feud was settled at last at the Battle of São Mamede. There Alfonso took his mother captive, and then imprisoned her for the rest of her life in a convent in Leon, Spain. After that victory Alfonso took a new title, prince of Portugal. Portugal had never had a prince before because it had never been an independent nation before.

Between 1129 and 1139 the prince was at war with the Moors who occupied southern Portugal. The decisive victory came at the Battle of Ourique, and his troops, who had been waiting a decade for this moment, proclaimed Alfonso king of Portugal. Without recognition from some great power outside Portugal, Alfonso's royal title was empty. No Spanish king would recognize Alfonso, so he went over their heads: he wrote to Pope Innocent II declaring that he was the devoted liegeman of the Holy Father and swearing to continue his campaign against the Moors until they were driven from Portugal. Meanwhile, Alfonso's agents were hammering out a treaty with the Spanish king of Leon that also recognized Portugal as an independent nation. The pope, ever cautious in international affairs, finally acknowledged Alfonso as king of Portugal in 1179—fifteen years after he had first written to Rome.

Alfonso's last heroic act before he died was to ride to the rescue of his son at Santarém, where he was surrounded by a Moorish army. Alfonso scattered the Moors and saved the city and the prince.

ERIK IX

King of Sweden (c. 1120–1160)

During the Middle Ages, all kings were expected to be warrior kings, skilled at keeping their people safe from invaders and perhaps strong enough to seize territory from their neighbors. By temperament, Erik IX preferred to focus on his kingdom's domestic issues, but outside forces often compelled him to act aggressively.

Erik came to the throne with two ambitions: to revise the Swedish law code and to strengthen Christianity in his country. Christianity had come late to Sweden, and while the royal family was devoutly Christian, a considerable portion of the nobles and the common people still worshipped the Norse gods. Violent anti-Christian uprisings had broken out in Sweden time and again in the twelfth century. Erik addressed this by implementing a new legal code that gave protection to the church in Sweden, recognized the rights of Swedish Christians, and outlawed pagan worship. For the rest of his reign, Erik's pagan subjects looked for an opportunity to avenge themselves.

Meanwhile, the Finns made repeated destructive raids into Swedish territory. Erik assembled an army and inflicted a crushing defeat against the Finns. Then, following the example of Charlemagne, he tried to neutralize Finnish aggression by bringing them into the European mainstream. In 1154 Erik sent a personal friend, Bishop Henry of Uppsala, to establish missions in Finland; two years later Henry was murdered by a Finnish soldier.

The next threat Erik faced came from Denmark when the king, Magnus, tried to conquer Sweden. The Danes, assisted by a force of rebellious anti-Christian Swedes, invaded the kingdom in 1160. Erik was at Mass in the church at Uppsala when he received word that invaders were closing in. He waited until the Mass was over, then armed himself in the churchyard, mounted his horse, and rode out with his men to meet the enemy. Several Danes attacked Erik simultaneously, wounding him and knocking him off his horse. They mocked the wounded king as he lay on the ground, jabbing him with their swords, until finally one man struck Erik in the neck, killing him.

The Swedes venerated Erik as a royal martyr and the patron saint of their country. The gold and silver shrine that holds Erik's remains is still on display at Uppsala cathedral.

This gold and silver casket contains the bones of Erik IX

S · ERICVS · REX · ET · MAR

Henry II and Eleanor of Aquitaine

King of England, Duke of Normandy, (1133–1189) and
Queen of England, Duchess of Aquitaine, Countess of Poitiers (1122–1204)

Henry and Eleanor were the most remarkable royal couple of the Middle Ages. Their partnership began as a passionate love match. On their wedding day Henry was nineteen, and Eleanor was thirty-one and formerly queen of France (her marriage to King Louis VII had been annulled). She was heiress to the wealthiest provinces in France; he was next in line to be king of England. Both were intelligent, sophisticated, impatient with conventional conduct, ambitious, and very good-looking.

Henry's quest for centralized power brought him into direct conflict with a man as willful as himself. Thomas Becket was Henry's lord chancellor and a close friend. In 1162, when the archbishop of Canterbury died, Henry appointed Becket, thinking that his friend would help him, or at least not hinder him, as he brought the church in England under his control. But Henry was wrong. Becket took his new office seriously and refused to let the king curtail the independence of the church. The quarrel ended when four of Henry's knights, at his instigation, rode to Canterbury and hacked Becket to death inside his own cathedral.

In the aftermath of the murder, Louis VII of France organized a coalition of Henry's rivals to make war on England and curb Henry's power. Eleanor joined the coalition, with the understanding that Henry would be removed and her easily manipulated eldest son Prince Henry installed as king. But Henry defeated his enemies and captured his wife, then kept her under house arrest in various castles around England. Why the couple fell out of love is uncertain; perhaps it was a result of Henry's infidelities, perhaps because he would not share power with his queen.

Henry died of an injury received in a jousting match, and Eleanor outlived him by fifteen years. When her son and Henry's successor, Richard the Lionheart went on crusade, he left the administration of the country to Eleanor. For the rest of her life, her sons treated her with the respect and deference she had longed to receive from Henry.

Henry and Eleanor enter Winchester en route to their coronation in London.

Jayavarman VII

King of the Khmer (1125–1215)

Jayavarman VII was a hero-king who liberated his country from invaders, a builder-king who erected sublime temples in the city of Angkor, and a champion of Buddhism—before Jayavarman's reign only one other Khmer king had been a Buddhist.

Jayavarman was fifty-two—an old man by the standards of his time—when a Cham army from modern-day Vietnam invaded the Khmer Empire (present-day Cambodia). Although he was a prince, the son of a Khmer king, he had never been aggressive in asserting his right to the throne. Perhaps his Buddhist principles encouraged him to remain passive; perhaps he was reluctant to start a civil war. But the Cham invasion of his country, their sacking of the capital, and their murder of the Khmer king Tribhuvanadityavarman finally convinced Jayavarman to act. He organized a resistance movement to the Cham occupation of his country, and in the span of five years, he had driven out the Cham. In 1181, at age sixty-one, Jayavarman was at last crowned king of the Khmer.

In old age he forgot the passivity of his youth. His military campaigns not only secured his empire's borders but they expanded his rule into portions of Laos, Burma, and the Malay Peninsula. In retaliation for the Cham invasion of his country, Jayavarman led an invasion of the Cham kingdom and sacked their capital city.

Among his own people, however, Jayavarman was not a warrior but a saint. He followed the Mahayana Buddhist movement, which emphasizes identification with those who are suffering. He built hospitals for the sick and hostels for travelers, and dug reservoirs to ensure a ready supply of fresh water for his people.

In his capital, Angkor, he erected magnificent temples in the memory of his parents. Preah Khan, built in honor of the king's father, was immense, requiring more than ninety-seven thousand servants to maintain it, and was staffed by a thousand teachers and a thousand sacred dancers. Ta Prohm, the temple built in honor of Jayavarman's mother, was splendid but smaller—only 80,000 thousand servants were necessary to maintain it, and it housed 18 priests and 615 sacred dancers.

For himself, Jayavarman constructed the Bayon temple, one of the world's most recognized Buddhist monuments, renowned for its soaring towers, on which are carved monumental stone faces. These beautiful temples are his most enduring monuments.

Monumental sculpture of the head of King Jayavarman VII

SALADIN

Sultan of Egypt and Syria (c. 1137–1193)

In Arabic his name was Salah al-Din; Saladin is the European form. He was a Kurd born in the town of Tikrit in what is now Iraq. His entire adult life was given over to reconquering the territory the Europeans had occupied in the Middle East since the First Crusade nearly 140 years earlier. Saladin represented himself to his fellow muslims as the champion of Islam who would drive out the crusaders.

In 1187, Saladin marched on Jerusalem. On the arid plain of Hattin he trapped a crusader army, slaughtering seventeen thousand crusaders and capturing hundreds, including the king of Jerusalem, Guy of Lusignan. Saladin spared Guy's life but ordered all the Templar and Hospitaller knights, the cream of the crusader forces, to be beheaded. The remaining crusader prisoners were sold as slaves. Three months later he captured Jerusalem. Rather than massacre the Christian inhabitants, he permitted them to leave in peace if they paid a ransom. Those who could not pay he sold into slavery.

Europeans responded to the fall of Jerusalem to Saladin with the Third Crusade, led by Richard the Lionheart of England, Philip II of France, and Frederick I of Germany. The war proved inconclusive—the crusaders weren't strong enough to retake Jerusalem, but Saladin was not strong enough to clear the crusaders from the country. The war ended with the Peace of Ramla, a treaty which stated that the Muslims would retain control of Jerusalem, and unarmed Christian pilgrims would be permitted to visit the holy city. A year after signing this treaty, Saladin died.

Saladin had a reputation among Christian historians of the time as a chivalrous man, and he did show mercy to some prisoners. Yet in balance, he could be as brutal as any other commander of his day, Muslim or Christian.

During his life he taught the Christians of Europe an important lesson: if they cherished any hope of holding the Holy Land, it would be enormously expensive and require the commitment of large numbers of fighting men. But he also taught the armies of Islam that only well-trained professional troops would keep the crusaders out of the region.

Eva Macmurrough

Princess of Leinster (1145–1188)

In 1854, the Irish artist Daniel Maclise unveiled his large history painting, *The Marriage of Strongbow and Aoife*. In the center of the painting stands Aoife, or Eva in English, downcast, dejected, the victim of unscrupulous men, while all around her are scenes of her fellow Irish suffering all manner of sorrows. Maclise has identified the grief of an Irish princess forced into an unhappy marriage with the Irish nation, forced to submit to seven hundred years of English rule.

While it is true that Eva's wedding took place amid scenes of death and destruction—Richard Strongbow stormed and captured the city of Waterford one day, and married Eva in the Waterford cathedral the next—exactly what she thought of her husband is not known.

It began with her father, Dermot, king of Leinster. Dermot's closest friend and ally was Murtagh Mac Lochlainn, high king of Ireland. In 1166, when Murtagh was killed in battle, all of his friends and allies became targets of ambitious Irishmen eager to become high king themselves. One of the contenders, the O'Rourke clan, attacked Leinster and defeated Dermot's army so thoroughly that the royal family barely escaped.

Dermot fled to Wales, then traveled to England, where he appealed to King Henry II to help him regain his throne. Henry gave Dermot permission to recruit an army, so the Irish king went back to Wales, where he gathered Welsh bowmen and Norman infantry, including the earl of Pembroke, Richard De Clare, known as Strongbow. To the earl Dermot promised his daughter Eva, along with the right to succeed him as king of Leinster.

Dermot and his Norman and Welsh allies quickly captured Waterford, Wexford, and Dublin. Then Strongbow began a series of raids in County Meath to expand his holdings in eastern Ireland. In 1171, Dermot died and Strongbow asserted his claim to the crown of Leinster, which set off a fresh war between Strongbow and various Irish nobles.

Now Strongbow appealed to King Henry for help, and in 1172 the English king landed with an army, established English authority over the region, and declared himself Lord of Ireland.

Strongbow died in 1176; Eva never remarried, which has suggested to some historians that in her widowhood she asserted her independence, refusing to be a political pawn again.

GUY OF LUSIGNAN
King of Jerusalem, King of Cyprus (c. 1150–1194)

Guy of Lusignan was a scoundrel who was largely responsible for the loss of the Christian kingdom of Jerusalem to Saladin. He had come to the Holy Land because he was no longer welcome in his homeland of France after he and his brothers ambushed and murdered Patrick, the earl of Salisbury.

The Holy Land was a snake pit with various lords intriguing to marry into the royal family and thereby become king of Jerusalem. The reigning king, Baldwin IV, suffered from an advanced case of leprosy and was expected to die any day. (Baldwin eventually died in 1185 at age twenty-four.) The man who married Baldwin's sister, Sibyl, had the best chance of becoming king, and by good luck or careful scheming, it was Guy who became Sibyl's husband. After Baldwin's death, Guy and Sibyl were crowned king and queen of Jerusalem.

The coronation coincided with Saladin's campaign to take back Palestine from the Europeans. When Saladin laid siege to the city of Tiberias, Guy rode out at the head of twenty thousand men to rescue the city and destroy Saladin. At a barren plain called Hattin, Saladin surrounded the crusader army, cutting them off from any supply of water. Employing his archers and sending repeated and devastating cavalry charges into the crusaders ranks, Saladin destroyed almost the entire army. Among the three thousand survivors taken prisoner were Guy, many nobles and distinguished knights. Saladin sent Guy to a prison in Damascus, then continued through Palestine, capturing every Christian city in his path, including Jerusalem—with no crusader army to defend her, Sibyl surrendered Jerusalem to Saladin.

By the time the Third Crusade reached the Holy Land, Guy had been ransomed, Sibyl had died, the nobles had refused to recognize Guy as king, and a new round of scheming for the crown of Jerusalem had begun. Regarding Guy as the man who had lost the holy city, Richard the Lionheart resolved to get the troublemaker out of the country. He sold to him the island of Cyprus, where, once again, Guy ruled as a king.

581

GUY DE LUSIGNAN,
ROI DE JÉRUSALEM ___ † 1192.

RICHARD I THE LIONHEART

King of England, Duke of Aquitaine (1157–1199)

Richard spent less than a year in England—he was very busy fighting wars in France and the Holy Land—yet from the day of his coronation in 1189, he has been one of the most popular English kings.

The year he was crowned, he took the crusader's vow, swearing to give his life to liberate the Holy Land from the Saracens. En route, part of his fleet was caught by a storm at sea and many of his men were shipwrecked on the island of Cyprus. Among the survivors were Richard's fiancée and one of his sisters. Instead of treating the shipwrecked men with kindness and the ladies with honor, Isaac Comnenus, the ruler of Cyprus, imprisoned them. When Richard, who was safe on the island of Rhodes, learned of the insult, he summoned the remnants of his fleet, invaded Cyprus, made Isaac a prisoner, and released the captives. It is said that Richard promised Isaac he would not put him in irons—instead he made him wear chains of silver.

Richard arrived in the Holy Land at Acre, where his reinforcements enabled the crusaders to capture the city. He went on to capture the city of Joppa fortresses in the southern part of the country, and he defeated Saladin at the Battle of Arsuf. But Jerusalem eluded the crusader king; the best he could do was make a truce with Saladin that guaranteed Christians the right to visit the holy places in peace.

On his way home Richard was shipwrecked in the territory of his nemesis, Leopold, Duke of Austria. He tried to escape in disguise but was recognized and imprisoned in Dürnstein Castle. Leopold demanded a ransom of 150,000 marks, the equivalent of 65,000 pounds of silver. It took two years for the English to raise such an enormous ransom.

In 1199 Richard was at war again, this time with the king of France. He had laid siege to a little circular castle, Chalus-Chabrol, and early in the evening of March 25 he strolled around, supervising the siege. On the battlements stood an archer with a crossbow. Spotting the English king, he fired; the arrow struck Richard in the shoulder, near the base of his neck. A surgeon cut out the arrowhead, but the wound became infected, and Richard died twelve days later.

Even in death he did not return to England: Richard's body lies buried at Fontevraud–l'Abbaye near Chinon and his heart in the cathedral of Rouen.

Tamar

Queen of Georgia (c. 1160–1213)

When she was eighteen Tamar's father, George III, named her his heir and made her his coruler. After her father's death in 1184, a large portion of the Georgian aristocracy rejected her rule, arguing that Georgia had never been and could not be governed by a queen. Thanks to the support of some of the leading military men in the country as well as the head of the Georgian Orthodox church, Patriarch Michael IV, Tamar survived this challenge to her authority. To mollify the nobles, she agreed to marry the man they had chosen for her, Prince Yuri from Kiev. The couple did not get along. To counteract Yuri's support among her more mutinous nobles, Tamar began promoting men who were loyal to her, and cultivating potential new allies. By 1187, Tamar was strong enough to insist on a divorce.

She chose her next husband herself—David Soslan, an experienced warrior who defeated the anti-Tamar nobles. Nonetheless, Tamar never permitted David to become king on equal terms with her. She was the supreme ruler, and he was her consort. The couple had two children, the future George IV and the princess Rusudan, who someday would reign as queen in her own right, just like her mother.

Under Tamar and David, Georgia expanded its territory from the Sea of Azov to the Caspian Sea. The queen also exercised significant influence over the Empire of Trebizond—technically Byzantine territory but located just across the border from Georgia.

Tamar was also concerned about Georgia's interests in far-off lands. She sent money to support the community of Georgian monks living on Mount Athos in Greece, and she negotiated with Saladin to ensure that the eight Georgian monasteries in Jerusalem would not be molested.

At home Tamar encouraged the arts, especially the art of book production and manuscript illumination. During Tamar's reign, Georgian artists developed an intricate new style of painting derived from Byzantine Christian and Persian Muslim models.

Tamar died suddenly after a brief, unexpected illness. She was buried in the Gelati Monastery, where her ancestor David IV had founded an academy. Over the centuries, the location of Tamar's grave was forgotten, and it still has not been rediscovered.

Fresco depicting Queen Tamar with her father, King George

GENGHIS KHAN

Emperor of the Mongols (c. 1162–1227)

It took the Romans four hundred years to build their empire. Genghis Khan forged a much larger empire in only twenty-five years. At the time of his death, he ruled from Sea of Japan to the Caspian Sea.

His given name was Temüjin, and he was the son of a Mongol chief. Temüjin was only eight years old when a rival tribe poisoned his father. The clans who had recognized Temüjin's father as their lord would not pledge the same allegiance to a child, so they abandoned him along with his mother, brothers, and sister. The family would have starved had Temüjin and his mother not been such resourceful, strong-willed individuals.

Throughout his teens and twenties Temüjin formed alliances and friendships with leaders of various Mongol clans and tribes until gradually he was recognized as a chief. With the help of these friends, he destroyed his rivals and united all the tribes into a single great Mongol nation. At a massive assembly, the Mongols acclaimed Temüjin as their "khan of all khans," and he took the name Genghis, derived from the Mongol word for strong.

In 1207, Genghis made his first move against a non-Mongolian enemy, attacking the Tangut people and forcing their king to pay an annual tribute to him. At the time Genghis was not thinking of building an empire; rather, he wanted to enrich his people by making surrounding kingdoms his vassals. But when the Jin emperor in northern China demanded that Genghis swear fealty to him, Genghis refused and invaded the country. The wealth and technological sophistication of China exceeded anything the Tanguts could offer, and it was there that the Mongol Empire was born. The Mongols swept westward, conquering territory that included the present-day nations of Kazakhstan, Pakistan, Afghanistan, Iran, Georgia, and Armenia, and they even raided Bulgaria and the southern regions of Russia and Ukraine.

Genghis's method was to leave the government of his conquered provinces in the hands of local officials—as long as they proved loyal. While he could be merciless to aristocrats, he cherished engineers, physicians, scholars, and craftsmen, some of whom he sent to Mongolia to teach their skills to his people. And because he was indifferent to what an individual believed, he tolerated all religions.

Genghis Khan seated in his tent by Rashid al-Din in 1318

LLYWELYN THE GREAT
Prince of Wales (c. 1173–1240)

The little country of Wales was ruled by several princely families, each of whom followed the Welsh custom of dividing up their land among all their sons—a tradition that weakened the country and made it an easy target for its much more powerful neighbor, England. Llywelyn ap Iorwerth was one of those young princes who saw his inheritance divided up piecemeal. He was determined to reconstruct Welsh political society along the lines of English and French traditions, where power and authority passed to the eldest son and the realm was ruled by one king.

Llywelyn inherited a slice of Gwynedd, Wales's northernmost principality. After a prolonged struggle, he obtained possession of the lands that had been parceled out to his uncles. Then, to defend his territory against the English, he erected a string of stone castles along the border—the first stone castles built by a Welshman. Soon, Llywelyn controlled the principalities of Powys and Ceredigion. Almost all of Wales was now under his rule.

Hoping to establish a mutually respectful relationship with King John of England, Llywelyn fought on the English side during their invasion of Scotland, and he married John's illegitimate daughter, Joan. But Llywelyn and John fell out over who should receive the fealty of the Welsh barons. Llywelyn maintained that in rank he was the equal of the king of England, but John replied that since Llywelyn's predecessors had sworn fealty to John's predecessors, the Welsh prince was, in fact, a vassal of the English king.

Llewelyn refused to be a vassal, so John struck back by invading and occupying part of northeastern Wales. Meanwhile, a separate conflict between the English king and his bishops and nobles ended in 1215 when they forced John to sign the Magna Carta, medieval England's Bill of Rights. Taking advantage of John's weakened position, Llewelyn attacked the Marches, the borderland between Wales and England, capturing the key fortresses Carmarthen, Cardigan, and Montgomery. In 1216, in recognition of Llewelyn's military successes, all the princes and leading men of Wales acknowledged Llewelyn as their lord.

Llywelyn is still recognized as the greatest of the Welsh princes, the one who was most successful in defending the independence of Wales.

Mosaics of Llywelyn in the college tower of modern day Cardigan

Andrew II

King of Hungary (c. 1177–1235)

The kings of Hungary enjoyed unlimited power and vast wealth. They were the largest landowners in the country, and no one came close to them in terms of income. Then, beginning in the twelfth century, the kings began granting portions of their lands to various noble families as a means of securing their loyalty. Andrew II followed this custom, but in ways that alienated his nobles.

Before he came to the throne, Andrew fought a string of wars to expand Hungary's borders. Many of the knights who fought for him were Germans, and as king he rewarded these men by giving them immense tracts of Hungarian land. Soon these German lords evolved into a separate class that enjoyed so much property and so much wealth as to earn the resentment of the less wealthy, less influential Hungarian nobles. Andrew was driving a wedge between the native-born and the foreign aristocracy. And then he made matters worse.

As expenses for his wars and his extravagant style spiraled out of control, Andrew raised the serfs' taxes, which meant the serfs had less to less to hand over to their lords. Once again, the Hungarian nobles felt that they were being robbed, and this time they rebelled.

In 1222, the nobles were in a position to make demands upon their king. They forced Andrew to sign the Golden Bull, Hungary's Magna Carta, which curtailed royal authority, made the lesser nobles equal to the greater nobles, and recognized the nobles' right to reject the act of any Hungarian king if it violated Hungarian law. In the aftermath of signing the Golden Bull, the king and the nobles agreed that there should be some formal group to hear the grievances of the nobility—this organization became the Diet, the Hungarian parliament.

Because he was so rash in his exercise of absolute power, Andrew undermined the authority of the Hungarian kings and was forced to give the country the beginnings of representative government.

Andrew II (far left) in Heroes Square in Budapest

FREDERICK II

Holy Roman Emperor (1194–1250)

Frederick's admirers called him *stupor mundi*, the wonder of the world. His detractors said that at the very least he was an atheist and perhaps even the Antichrist.

Frederick had been raised in Palermo, Sicily, a cosmopolitan city of Normans, Greeks, Arabs, and Jews. By the time he reached adulthood he was fluent in Arabic and Greek, he had read the Koran, and he was strongly attracted to the kind of luxuries found in Islamic courts—he wore the opulent robes of a sultan and kept a harem. His Islamic tastes combined with lifelong sparring with the pope persuaded his enemies that Frederick was no Catholic. They were mistaken; while Frederick was never a dutiful son of the papacy, he never gave up the religion in which he had been raised.

Throughout Frederick's life, he and the pope wrestled for preeminence. The popes had always asserted that since they crowned the Holy Roman Emperors, the emperors were subject to them. Frederick was willing to recognize the pope's spiritual authority (when it was convenient), but insisted that in political matters, no one outranked a Holy Roman Emperor. Other emperors had taken the same position, but none had attracted the same level of animosity as Frederick, because Frederick was much better at playing this game than his pro-papal opponents.

As lord of Germany, southern Italy, and Sicily, he had the Papal States, the pope's territory in central Italy, hemmed in. If he waged war against the Papal States, the pope would probably lose—a fact of which the pope was aware.

Thanks to his fluency in Arabic and his familiarity with Islamic culture, Frederick arranged a peace treaty between the crusaders in the Holy Land and the sultan of Egypt. To keep peace in Germany, he conceded to the host of German princelings' rights and privileges that they claimed had belonged to them since time immemorial. All kings were patrons of the arts, but Frederick also encouraged the sciences by founding the University of Naples and endowing the medical school at Salerno.

Frederick II was a man of supreme self-confidence who never doubted for a moment that God intended him to be the greatest power in Europe.

LOUIS IX

King of France (1214–1270)

The deepest desire of Louis IX of France was to be a model Christian king, and in many respects he succeeded—so much so that in 1297 he was canonized by the Catholic Church.

A series of calamities that befell Europe in the 1240s strongly affected Louis's international outlook. In the spring of 1241, the Mongols devastated Poland and Hungary, crushing every army sent against them. Then in 1244, the Christians in Palestine were overwhelmed by a Muslim army from Egypt.

Louis sought a diplomatic solution to the Mongol threat, sending ambassadors with rich gifts to the Great Khan, and receiving Mongol ambassadors in return. As for the Muslims in Egypt, he tried containment. For many years Egypt had been the launching point for Muslim invasions of the Holy Land and the Byzantine Empire. Louis's goal was to bottle up the Egyptians long enough to give the Christians of the Middle East time to regroup, so they would be strong enough to defend themselves without help from western Europe.

Louis and his army of crusaders captured Damietta in the Nile Delta, the gateway to Egypt, in 1249, but less than a year later a Muslim army defeated the crusaders and captured Louis. The price paid for his freedom was the surrender of Damietta and an enormous ransom for his life and the lives of the surviving crusaders.

Back in France, Louis instituted a new approach to law in which justice was strongly tempered by mercy: He commuted death sentences, even of rebels. He required even-handed application of the laws, abolishing the privileges that had let the aristocracy get away, literally, with murder. He was lavish in his gifts to the poor and the helpless. And he built that gem of Gothic architecture, Sainte-Chapelle, to enshrine Christ's Crown of Thorns.

When word reached Louis that a sultan had captured the cities of Caesarea and Joppa, he organized another crusade. En route he became so ill that his ship had to drop anchor in Tunis in northern Africa. There, far from home and far from the Holy Land, King Louis died.

Saint Louis IX by El Greco

KUBLAI KHAN

Emperor of China, Great Khan of the Mongols (1215–1294)

Kublai Khan's reign marked a departure from the traditional life of a Mongol ruler: he virtually gave up conquest and devoted himself to administering his vast empire, which stretched from Korea to eastern Hungary and Poland. His policy was to grant the countries within his empire as much self-government as was practical, and to stop pillaging once a land or city had come under Mongol dominion.

He established himself in northern China, where he assembled a team of learned Chinese to help him gain the confidence of his Chinese subjects and rule them in a way that would neither frighten nor antagonize. He adopted the style of Chinese rulers. When he built a summer residence for himself in Inner Mongolia, he designed it along Chinese lines with a marble palace, Buddhist temples, and beautiful parklands; Kublai named this place Shangdu, which the English poet Samuel Taylor Coleridge rendered "Xanadu" in his poem "Kubla Khan."

In China, Kublai founded a new dynasty, which he named Yuan, and he lived and ruled as a Chinese emperor, complete with the performance of traditional Confucian rituals. He encouraged foreign trade (the Polo family was among the European merchants Kublai welcomed to his capital). He was a patron of Chinese painting, calligraphy, and drama, and he encouraged advances in Chinese medicine.

In the administration of his empire, he wanted the best men, and so his bureaucracy included Muslim financial advisors, European merchants, and Daoist soothsayers.

But Kublai's peace-loving policy irritated Mongol traditionalists. They believed Great Khans should be conquerors and that if this khan had no interest in fighting and expanding the empire, perhaps he did not deserve the highest office. So Kublai invaded southern China, defeating the Song dynasty emperor. He forced Burma and Champa (present-day South Vietnam) to submit to him. He attempted a naval invasion of Japan, but a typhoon destroyed his fleet.

The last years of Kublai's life were filled with trouble. The Japan campaign had almost emptied the treasury. His favorite wife and his son and heir both died. To comfort himself, he turned to consuming large quantities of food and drink. He died terribly obese, his once great mind clouded by alcohol.

ALEXANDER NEVSKY

Prince of Novgorod, Grand Duke of Vladimir (1221–1284)

In 1938, when the Soviet Union lived under the threat of an invasion from Nazi Germany, the great Russian director Sergei Eisenstein released a film that spoke directly to his comrades' anxieties. *Alexander Nevsky* told the story of another German invasion, in 1242, and how the Russian people triumphed over it.

Alexander Nevsky, the hero of the film, was a Russian prince who was raised to fight. At age sixteen he went to war with his father against the Mongols. At age eighteen he scored his first great victory, driving back the Swedes at the Neva River (he took the surname Nevsky to recall that battle). In 1242, when Alexander was twenty-two years old, he met his greatest challenge. The Teutonic Order, a German military order, invaded Russia in an attempt to seize Russian territory and occupy Russian ports on the Baltic Sea.

On April 5, 1242, an army of approximately one thousand knights of the Teutonic Order and their mercenaries met Alexander's army of five thousand men at Lake Peipus north of Pskov. It was still winter, and the lake was frozen solid—or at least it looked that way. Leading with their heavy cavalry, the order charged the Russian ranks, which broke apart under the assault. But Alexander's men regrouped and surrounded the order. Attacked on all sides, many of the order and their infantry retreated across the lake. As they reached a place where the ice was thin, it cracked open, and men and horses tumbled into the frigid water, where their armor dragged them under.

Alexander enjoyed other successes, most notably persuading the Mongol khans to withdraw their tax collectors from Russian soil and stop impressing Russian men into the Mongol army, but the "Battle of the Ice" made the prince's reputation. Tsar Peter the Great revered Alexander, the Russian Orthodox Church declared him a saint, and Stalin identified with him. In a 2008 poll, more than 2 million Russians voted Alexander Nevsky as the greatest hero in their nation's history.

ALFONSO X THE WISE

King of Castile and Leon (1221–1284)

Alfonso was a man of many rare gifts: he was a poet, a musician, a composer, an astronomer, and a patron of historians, painters, and sculptors. He is best known today for his *Cantigas de Santa María*, (Songs of Saint Mary), a collection of dozens of popular songs and liturgical hymns in praise of the Virgin Mary.

Alfonso came to the throne of the Spanish provinces of Castile and Leon at a time when the Spaniards were gaining the upper hand over the Moorish occupation of southern Spain. Alfonso consolidated Spanish gains in Andalusia, the Moors' greatest province, while at the same time trying, unsuccessfully, to acquire the French provinces of Navarre and Gascony and to establish a foothold in Morocco.

In 1264, Muslims living under Castilian rule rebelled against Alfonso. It took two years to put down the revolt, and when he subdued the Muslims, the king expelled them from their homes and gave their property to Spanish Christians.

Alfonso faced a revolt from his nobles when he tried to implement a new legal code that would have made the nobles answerable to an ordinary court rather than to a panel of their peers. Then ordinary townspeople rebelled when the king demanded new taxes from them. In both instances Alfonso backed down. The nobles felt vindicated in defending their ancient privileges, but the townspeople, who appear to have been more patriotic, agreed to pay to the king a new annual tax to defray the costs of operating the kingdom.

The last years of Alfonso's life were full of trouble. The Moors invaded Castile; his eldest son died; and his second son, Sancho IV, persuaded a national assembly to name him king and strip his father of all authority, leaving Alfonso with only the title of king. Before he died, Alfonso disinherited Sancho.

One of the greatest Spanish kings of the Middle Ages, a man of so many accomplishments, died wretched and disappointed.

DINIS AND ELIZABETH

King (1261–1325) and Queen (1271–1336) of Portugal

Dinis and Elizabeth's marriage got off to a bad start. On their wedding day she was twelve, he was twenty. He showed no interest in his child bride and spent his nights with one or another of his mistresses. When Elizabeth was in her late teens, they began to live as husband and wife, and in 1291 she gave birth to a son whom they named Alfonso. Dinis never gave up his mistresses, and when he died he left seven (or perhaps nine) illegitimate children, all of whom he had recognized as his own and all of whom he had brought to the palace, ordering Elizabeth to raise them.

Although he was a thoughtless husband, Dinis was a conscientious king. With the Moorish threat to Portugal virtually neutralized, he could devote himself to domestic issues. He encouraged foreign trade and navigation; he confiscated uncultivated land from the church and the nobles and gave it to families who would farm it. He planted pine forests near the coast to stop erosion. He had swamps drained so even more arable land would be available. He had the laws of Portugal translated into Portuguese. And with Elizabeth, he founded the University of Coimbra.

Dinis's home life, however, was becoming nasty. He made no effort to hide his preference for one of his illegitimate sons, Alfonso Sanchez, a state of affairs that deeply wounded his heir, Prince Alfonso. Angry and resentful, the prince became convinced that his right to succeed was in jeopardy, so he conceived an elaborate plot to murder his half brother, depose his father, and become king. Dinis discovered the plot and was ready to punish Alfonso severely, but Elizabeth pleaded with him to forgive their son.

Twice more Alfonso tried to overthrow his father, and each time Elizabeth managed to defuse the volatile situation. On one occasion, however, her powers of persuasion failed, and Dinis and Alfonso prepared for dynastic war. Before the battle began, Elizabeth rode out between the two armies and refused to leave the field until father and son made peace.

After Dinis died, Alfonso, in spite of all his fears, became king. Elizabeth left the court for Coimbra, where she built a small house beside a hospital; the queen worked in the wards every day until her death eleven years later.

PHILIP IV THE FAIR

King of France (1268–1314)

Conflicts between kings and popes were commonplace during the Middle Ages, but few kings were as aggressive as Philip in trying to assert authority over the church. His nemesis was Pope Boniface VIII, who responded to the interference of men like Philip into church affairs with a proclamation that a man would not be saved if he were not subject to the pope. Philip responded by declaring Boniface a heretic and calling for an international council of bishops to depose him. To get the council started, Philip sent a delegation to Italy, where his men attacked Boniface, beating him so severely that he died of his injuries a month later.

Philip had another target: the Knights Templar. Founded in 1118 in the Holy Land to safeguard Christian pilgrims and defend Christian territory, the Templars were respected for their utter fearlessness in battle and for the holiness of their lives. They were also immensely rich, the result of countless gifts and bequests as well as their own good investments. Jealous of their wealth, Philip accused the Templars of vile hypocrisy, charging that they spat and trod upon the crucifix in their secret rituals, and that the older knights sodomized the younger. In a carefully orchestrated plot, Philip had all the Templars throughout his realm arrested on the same day, October 13, 1307. In prison the knights were subjected to such hideous tortures that many, including their grand master, confessed to Philip's outrageous charges. When they retracted the confessions, saying they had made them under terrible duress, Philip had the Templars burned at the stake.

He was equally merciless with his own family. He presided at a trial of two knights who were charged with committing adultery with his daughters-in-law. Once again torture was employed, and Philip found the two men guilty and sentenced them to hideous deaths. What appears not to have occurred to him was that by staging this trial he had exposed his own grandchildren to the suspicion that they were illegitimate.

Yet in spite of all these things, Philip declared that he was a defender of Catholic orthodoxy and Christian morality. His deepest wish was that he would be compared favorably with his grandfather, Saint Louis IX. This wish went unfulfilled.

The Templars are arraigned before Philip IV and Pope Clement V

ROBERT I THE BRUCE

King of Scotland (1274–1329)

Robert is the valiant king who won for Scotland its independence from England. But he was not always a gallant hero. In the first place, his family's claim to the Scottish crown was tenuous. In the second place, when the English king, Edward I, invaded the country, Robert and his father threw their support behind the English.

Robert redeemed himself during the uprising led by Sir William Wallace (of *Braveheart* fame) by siding with the rebels, but his troubles were not over because there were still rival claimants to the Scottish throne. In 1306 he met one of them, a man named John Comyn, in a church in Dumfries on the pretext that both men would be on their best behavior on holy ground. But in an act of unforgivable treachery, Robert drew his dagger and murdered Comyn (actually he was still alive when Robert ran out of the church, but two of Robert's supporters hurried inside and finished Comyn off). Edward I declared him an outlaw, and Pope Clement V excommunicated him for sacrilege; nonetheless, Robert proclaimed himself king and was crowned at Scone, Scotland's traditional coronation site.

In 1307, the English invaded Scotland again and defeated Robert at Methven. He fled Scotland, and while he was in hiding on Rathlin Island off the coast of Ireland, the English captured and imprisoned his wife, daughter, and sister, and killed three of his brothers. Incredibly, Robert came back, raised another army, and in 1314 at Bannockburn scattered the English army led by Edward I's ineffectual son, Edward II.

Seeking moral support as well as international recognition for their king, in 1320 the Scottish nobility wrote the Declaration of Arbroath, in which they traced the antiquity of the Scottish monarchy and petitioned the pope to acknowledge Scotland's independence and Robert's right to rule. The pope granted the Scots' request.

Edward II still maintained that he was king of Scotland, but in 1327 his wife led a coup that deposed and murdered him. Then the English queen made peace with Robert.

Robert I lies buried in Dunfermline Abbey. He had asked that his heart be buried in the Holy Land, but it never got any farther than Spain; eventually it was brought back to Scotland for burial in Melrose Abbey.

The charge of Sir Henry de Bohun against the Scottish King Robert the Bruce during the Battle of Bannockburn, 1314

Stefan IV Dusan the Mighty

Emperor of the Serbs, Greeks, and Albanians (c. 1308–1355)

Stefan's family was a contentious lot: the kings were jealous of one another's power, and the princes were impatient to succeed to the crown. Consequently, in the first half of the fourteenth century, Serbia suffered through two civil wars between two sets of fathers and sons. Stefan's father rebelled against his own father, King Milutin, but the revolt failed, Stefan's father was captured, and Milutin punished his disloyal son by having him blinded. In 1331, Stefan followed in the family tradition by rising up against his father—but Stefan was a lucky rebel who succeeded in deposing the old man.

Stefan was a decisive king. He made peace with Serbia's nemesis, Bulgaria, and married a Bulgarian princess, Helen. He stripped the Serbian nobles of the power and privileges they had grabbed while the royal family was trying to slit one another's throats. Then he embarked on a string of conquests that transformed Serbia from a little kingdom into an empire. He captured the fortresses of the Byzantine Empire that stood along his border. He conquered a portion of northern Greece, most of Macedonia, and all of Albania. In 1346, he celebrated his victories by having himself recrowned as emperor of the Serbs, Greeks, and Albanians. Yet he still was not content and went to war again, this time conquering the Greek provinces of Epirus and Thessaly. He had hoped to reconquer Herzegovina, formerly a Serbian province, and he dreamed of capturing Constantinople, too, but he never achieved either of these goals.

By Stefan's day the schism between the Catholic and the Orthodox churches was nearly 350 years old, yet he surprised, perhaps even shocked, his countrymen when he opened discussion with the pope regarding the possibility of bringing the Serbian Orthodox church back into union with Rome. Both Catholic and Orthodox clergy in Serbia were so outspoken against the plan that ultimately Stefan was obliged to abandon it. Nonetheless, when the Turks invaded eastern Europe, Stefan expected the pope would ask him to lead a crusade in defense of Christendom. Before the pope could make such an offer, Stefan died unexpectedly.

He was right about the threat presented by the Turks: in the years after his death, they pressured Stefan's son into relinquishing almost all the land his father conquered.

FRANCESCO GRIMALDI

Prince of Monaco (died 1309)

On Monaco's coat of arms are two brown-robed Franciscan friars, each bearing a sword. The unusual figures commemorate the man who was the founder of the Grimaldi dynasty, the family that has ruled Monaco without interruption for more than seven hundred years.

In the thirteenth century there was a castle on the rocky outcrop of Monaco. The garrison protected a stretch of the Riviera from marauding Saracen pirates. At the same time much of Europe was split between two rival political factions—one that declared that the Holy Roman Emperor had supreme authority in Europe, and another that said such authority belonged properly to the pope. By 1297, the Monaco castle was in the hands of pro-imperial troops.

Not far away was the Italian city of Genoa, a wealthy commercial capital that supported the pope's cause. One of the leading families of Genoa were the Grimaldis, a clan that produced shrewd merchants and bankers but also cunning warriors. Francesco (some histories refer to him by the French form of his name, François) was one of the fighting Grimaldis. He believed that the imperial garrison at Monaco was a threat to Genoese shipping. On January 8, 1297, he led a small band of armed men to the castle gates. He was dressed in the brown habit of a Franciscan priest, but under the robe he wore armor and carried weapons. While his companions concealed themselves in the shadows, Grimaldi pounded on the gate. What he said to the guards is unknown—perhaps he asked for shelter for the night, or perhaps he said he had been called to bring last rites to a dying man—but the soldiers let him in. The gate was lightly guarded, and once inside, Grimaldi threw off the robes, drew his sword, and killed the guards. Then he opened the gate, and his men crept inside, fanned out through the castle, and took the entire garrison prisoner.

The Prince's Palace of Monaco, the home of the Grimaldi family, occupies the site of the fortress captured by their ancestor Francesco.

Francesco Grimaldi in the robes of a Franciscan friar

John II the Good
King of France (1319–1364)

On the battlefield John was brave and chivalrous, but in the council chamber he was a fool. Anyone with a loud voice and a domineering personality could sway his decisions, and once he had made a decision—even if it was obviously a bad one—John clung to it stubbornly.

France at this time was locked in a life-or-death struggle against England in what has become known as the Hundred Years' War. In 1354, John attempted to buy off the English by ceding to their king, Edward III, virtually all of the southwestern provinces of France. Many of the leading nobles of the realm—including John's own son, the dauphin Charles V—considered the treaty a national disgrace. Together with Charles II, the king of Navarre, the dauphin plotted to depose his father, but John learned of the plot. He pardoned the conspirators, but four months later changed his mind, had Navarre arrested, and ordered summary executions of several of Navarre's supporters in France. These rash acts set off a civil war. And things became much worse five months later when the English, commanded by Edward, the Black Prince of Wales and son of Edward III, smashed the French army at Poitiers and took John prisoner.

With the country humiliated and the king a captive, France descended into anarchy. Bands of ex-soldiers wandered the countryside thieving and murdering. Angry peasants known as the Jacquerie attacked and killed noblemen and looted their castles. And in Paris, the influential bourgeoisie expelled the dauphin from the city.

After four years of negotiation, France agreed to an exorbitant ransom of three million gold pieces for their king. He returned home and began to rule as a reformed king. John dismissed or no longer consulted the men who had given him bad advice, thereby winning back the confidence of the nobles and the well-to-do men of Paris. And he organized a new army to put down disturbances in the countryside. When the French treasury could no longer afford to make the ransom payments, John returned voluntarily to England to negotiate a new arrangement or, if was the will of the English king, to accept imprisonment again. Such nobility of character impressed the French and the English. Sadly, John died in London, still negotiating the terms of his release.

Jehan Rey de France

EDWARD

The Black Prince of Wales (1330–1376)

Arguably the most popular prince of Wales England has ever known, Edward was hailed throughout his life as a model of chivalry who moved easily from victory to victory. His greatest triumph was the Battle of Poitiers, where he not only defeated the French but captured their king, John II.

In his own day, no one called him the Black Prince—that name popped up in the sixteenth century, perhaps as a reference to his black armor or his black shield. When he was thirty-two he married Joan, the Fair Maid of Kent ("fair" meaning lovely in this context) and from his palace in Bordeaux—Edward's father had made him duke of Aquitaine—they presided over a court where intelligence and courage were prized, and music and poetry flourished.

Edward's military career began when he was sixteen and fought in the Battle of Crécy, another famous English victory over the French. Technically, he was in command of the English center, but the teenager had the modesty and good sense to be directed by older, experienced fighting men.

In spite of his reputation for chivalry, Edward could be ruthless. In 1355, he adopted a scorched-earth policy—his army pillaged then burned five hundred towns and villages in southern France. He led a second scorched-earth campaign through France the next year, culminating with his victory at Poitiers and his capture of King John.

By 1369, Edward was chronically ill, perhaps with an incurable strain of dysentery, or possibly with undiagnosed cancer. In 1370, he announced his determination to retake the city of Limoges, which had just fallen to the French. Too ill to ride a horse, he traveled there in a litter. When Limoges fell, Edward unleashed his men. The city was sacked, then burned, and hundreds of the inhabitants were massacred.

In 1371, Edward returned to England, where he lingered on for another five years before dying at age forty-six. He had asked to be buried humbly in the crypt of Canterbury Cathedral; instead, his family and his country laid him to rest in a splendid tomb beside the shrine of Saint Thomas Becket. It can still be seen there today.

John

Duke of Berry (1340–1416)

In the midst of the Hundred Years' War, John, the son of King John the Good and younger brother of King Charles V of France, proved to be a hopeless soldier and an even worse mediator, even between the squabbling factions within his own family. Unfortunately, the mental incapacity of his nephew King Charles VI obliged John to step in as regent and attempt to restore order. Of course, there were other royal princes and dukes—all of them John's brothers or nephews—each of whom believed he would be better suited to the task than the duke of Berry. They may have been right—John had no gift for administration. As a result, England invaded again to take advantage of strife among the French and to scoop up whatever cities and provinces they could.

As a politician John was a disaster, but as a connoisseur and collector of art his judgment was flawless. He was attracted to anything beautiful, from architecturally sublime castles to exquisite little jewels. He commissioned the finest goldsmiths to create beautiful receptacles in which he displayed his impressive collection of holy relics. He had entire workshops of weavers who turned out superb tapestries to decorate the walls of his private apartments. And he worked very closely with the Limbourgs, three Flemish brothers who were among the best painters of their day. The Limbourgs designed and painted for the duke magnificent prayer books, known as books of hours. The finest of these is the legendary *Très Riches Heures de duc de Berry*, famous for its full-page paintings of the work and pleasures of each month of the year, along with a portrait of John, opulently dressed and surrounded by his treasures.

By a strange coincidence, all three of the Limbourgs and Duke John died in 1416, probably in an epidemic.

Manuscript illustration of the Duke of Berry (seen in the dark robe)

Wladyslaw II Jagiello
King of Lithuania and Poland (c. 1351–1434)

The Teutonic Order was one of several military groups founded during the Crusades. Its members were knights, but they took the same vows as monks—poverty, chastity, and obedience. They were, in other words, monks in armor. In northern Europe, the knights claimed that their mission was to defend Christian lands against invasions by the pagan Prussians and Lithuanians, yet the knights also attacked Catholic Poland and Orthodox Russia, which led many northern Europeans to believe that the knights' ambitions were more political than religious.

By the late fourteenth century, Lithuania was no longer the easy target it had been for the knights. Grand Duke Jagiello was a fearless warrior who ruled a vast territory that encompassed modern-day Lithuania, Ukraine, Belarus, and portions of western Russia. The Teutonic Order could not push Lithuania around anymore.

Meanwhile, across the border in Poland, an eleven-year-old girl, Jadwiga, was ruling as "king." Poland and Lithuania both had been victims of raids by the Teutonic Order. In 1385, Jadwiga's representatives approached Jagiello with an interesting offer: marry Jadwiga, become king of Poland (she would revert to the title of queen), and thereby unite the two countries against any encroachment from the Teutonic Order. In exchange, Jagiello and all his people would convert to the Catholic faith. Jagiello agreed.

After a three-day crash course in Catholicism, Jagiello was baptized; three days after that, he and Jadwiga married. He took the name Wladyslaw and ruled as King Wladyslaw II Jagiello. As king, he respected Poland's political traditions, sought the advice of Polish nobles, and rewarded his Polish and Lithuanian supporters by distributing land. Then he returned to Lithuania to begin the conversion of his country. It is said that because so few Polish priests could speak Lithuanian, Jagiello did missionary work himself, teaching his people how to say the Apostles' Creed and the Lord's Prayer.

Jadwiga's gamble that the union of Poland and Lithuania would trump the Teutonic Order was proved correct in July 1410, when Jagiello and his cousin Vytautas led an army of nearly fifty thousand Poles, Lithuanians, and mercenaries against the Teutonic Order. The Battle of Grunwald was a bloodbath in which Jagiello and Vytautas's forces all but annihilated the knights of the Teutonic Order, breaking their power in northern Europe forever.

Wladyslaw Jagiello before the battle of Tannenburg

Margaret I

Regent of Denmark, Norway, and Sweden (1353–1412)

An extraordinary set of circumstances led this amazing woman to become queen of three Scandinavian countries. She was a princess of Denmark who had spent most of her adolescence in Sweden, and then married the king of Norway. In 1375, her father died, leaving no male heir. Margaret lobbied the nobles and leading men of Denmark to recognize her five-year-old son, Olaf, as king, with herself as regent until he came of age. In 1387, her husband died, and once again Margaret put to use her persuasive powers, having the Norwegian royal council recognize Olaf as king and herself as regent.

Meanwhile, the king of Sweden died, and the Swedish lords elected Margaret's nephew Albert as king. When Albert died in 1389, the Swedes turned to Margaret and Olaf. Now she was regent of three Scandinavian countries, with her son ready to inherit all of them. Representatives from Denmark, Norway, and Sweden issued a formal declaration acclaiming Margaret as their "fulmaegtig frue og husbond," their all-powerful lady and master.

Tragically, by this time Olaf had died, too. With no husband and no son, Margaret was in a vulnerable position, particularly since the German princes to the south and the politically influential Hanseatic League of German merchants wanted the Scandinavian countries weak and easy to manipulate. She persuaded the three kingdoms to recognize her grandnephew Erik of Pomerania, as the heir. The Danes, Norwegians, and Swedes consented, and Margaret had the fourteen-year-old boy crowned at Kalmar.

For the next fifteen years, Erik watched as Margaret ruled. She drove from office anyone who opposed her and replaced them with new men loyal to her. But she gave Scandinavia twenty years of peace, during which time cultural and economic life flourished. Unfortunately, after Margaret died, Erik could not hold together his great aunt's grand Nordic union.

OWEN GLENDOWER

Prince of Wales (c. 1354–1416)

Owen was descended from or related to most of the princely families of Wales. But by the mid-fourteenth century, ambitious Welshmen eager to advance their political careers had little choice other than to go to England. As a young man, Owen lived in London and was connected to the royal court. He fought for Richard II during England's invasions of Scotland in 1385 and 1387. But in his house Owen lived as a Welshman who welcomed Welsh visitors, especially poets.

In 1400, he was back in Wales and over the next five years he led an uprising to drive the English out of his country and reclaim Wales's independence. It was a struggle the Welsh could not successfully complete on their own, so Owen turned to dissatisfied English lords for help. He married Catherine, the daughter of Lord Mortimer, and formed an alliance with Henry "Hotspur" Percy, the most formidable fighter in the most prominent family in northern England. The high-water mark of Owen's uprising came in 1404 when he was master of all of western Wales, made a treaty with the French, and won the tacit agreement of the Scots to help him shake off English rule. And he assumed the title Prince of Wales. His plans included establishing a Welsh parliament and perhaps even a Welsh church independent of Rome.

Owen's success did not last. In 1405, he lost a decisive battle to Henry IV at Worcester, and over the next three years saw the English take back virtually everything he had won.

He fled into the mountains, striking out from time to time to defend his home territory or to make a raid across the border into England. But after 1412, the historical record falls silent and we learn no more of Owen. It is believed that he died in 1416, at the home of his daughter Alice in Herefordshire in western England.

Bayezid I

Sultan of the Ottoman Empire (c. 1354–1403)

The Battle of Kosovo, June 15, 1389, ended in triumph for the Ottoman Turks, disaster for the Serbs, and murder for Sultan Murad, who was assassinated by a Serbian prisoner.

Word of the murder was taken at once to the sultan's eldest son, Bayezid, who upon hearing the news had himself proclaimed sultan at once, in the midst of the army. Then he sent men to his brother Yacub with orders to strangle the young man. Bayezid would tolerate no rivals.

Bayezid became sultan at a time when the Byzantine Empire was dying—thanks in large part to the successful conquests of the Ottomans. In the 1390's, a call went out across Europe to come to the aid of Byzantium. In 1396, 120,000 princes, noblemen, knights, and common soldiers—the flower of chivalry collected from Scotland to Poland—met the Turks outside the city of Nicopolis in Bulgaria. Bayezid crushed the European coalition, driving the few thousand survivors back across the Danube, and ordering the immediate execution of perhaps as many as ten thousand prisoners.

In 1401, Bayezid was poised to capture Constantinople when a messenger brought word that Tamerlane had invaded Ottoman territory with an army of about 140,000 Mongols. Reluctantly, the sultan changed his plans and marched east across Anatolia to meet the invader. Near modern-day Sivas in Turkey, Tamerlane scored a great victory over the Ottomans by attacking their flanks and their center simultaneously and capturing Bayezid.

Tamerlane mocked Bayezid, inviting him to a banquet where the meal was served by the women of the sultan's harem—all of them naked. For a year Bayezid endured one humiliation after another: Tamerlane exhibited the sultan in a cage, used him as a footstool, and put him in horse harness to pull a chariot. Before the year was out, Sultan Bayezid was dead, still a captive of Tamerlane.

Had it not been for Tamerlane's untimely invasion, Bayezid would have gone down in history as the conqueror of Constantinople. But he left a legacy nonetheless: for centuries, new Ottoman sultans followed his example and murdered their brothers and other members of their family who might prove to be rivals.

Bayezid I brought before Tamerlane

JADWIGA
Queen of Poland and Lithuania (1374–1399)

Jadwiga was only a year old when her parents betrothed her to Wilhelm, future grand duke of Austria. Such early betrothals were commonplace among royal families, who used their children to cement political alliances. Nonetheless, such betrothals did not always end in a marriage.

In 1382, Jadwiga's father died, and two years later the Polish nobles chose the ten-year-old to rule as their "king." They suggested to Jadwiga that she should marry the grand duke of Lithuania, Jagiello, one of the most powerful monarchs in northern Europe. She agreed and cancelled the agreement her parents had made in her name to marry Wilhelm. The young suitor took the trouble of traveling to Cracow to try to persuade Jadwiga to honor their betrothal, but she had made up her mind to unite Poland and Lithuania by marrying Jagiello.

In 1386, Jagiello, now known as Wladyslaw Jagiello, married Jadwiga in the cathedral of Cracow. She was twelve; he was thirty-six.

Wilhelm's family, the Habsburgs, lashed back at Jadwiga by spreading malicious gossip: Wilhlem and Jadwiga were secretly married, the Hapsburgs said, and by marrying Jagiello, Jadwiga was committing bigamy.

It is difficult to tell if Jadwiga's marriage to Jagiello was a happy one. The age difference was significant, of course. We know they cooperated in refounding the university in Cracow—now known as the Jagiellonian University—and that they were generous in their gifts of sacred vessels, vestments, and works of art to the churches that were springing up all over Lithuania. When the Teutonic Order raided Lithuania, Jagiello prepared for war while Jadwiga sued for peace, but that may have been a case of the royal couple playing "good cop/bad cop."

In 1398, Jadwiga announced that she was expecting a child. Her Polish and Lithuanian subjects rejoiced, but the pregnancy did not go well. Jadwiga gave birth prematurely to a daughter who lived only three weeks. Jadwiga died four days later of complications from the delivery.

The Poles especially mourned her: Jadwiga had brought new strength to their country, revived its intellectual life, and tried to make peace with the Teutonic Order. To this day, Jadwiga is revered as a national heroine and one of Poland's patron saints.

HENRY V

King of England (1387–1422)

Shakespeare portrays the young Henry as a rake who was perfectly at ease in taverns and brothels, carousing with thieves, whores, and other rascals. It's a colorful picture, but not a probable one. In fact, Henry was an energetic, dependable prince who governed the country well during his father's illness in 1410–1411. Perhaps he governed too well, because when King Henry IV was well enough to rule again, he removed his son from the royal council. For two years Prince Henry had nothing to do but wait for his ailing father to die.

In 1413, Henry IV died and his son was crowned Henry V. His first crisis was religious: an old friend, Sir John Oldcastle, had joined the Lollards, a proto-Protestant sect, and conspired to assassinate Henry and seize the throne. Someone betrayed the plot and the king's life was saved, but it took three years before Oldcastle was tracked down, tried, and executed for treason.

A second plot, this one political, led by three noblemen, was exposed in 1415. Again, Henry acted swiftly, executing the conspirators.

Once he had settled domestic disturbances, Henry turned to foreign adventure; he was determined to reassert England's claim to the crown of France. In 1415, he sailed to France, captured Harfleur, and was on his way to Calais when he encountered a large French force. Henry's army numbered six thousand men, many of them sick with dysentery. The French, led by the dauphin, the marshal of France, and many other high-ranking nobles, numbered twenty thousand men. The armies faced off across a sodden, muddy field. The English began the fight when Henry ordered his archers to fire, thus decimating the French infantry. As the French cavalry charged, their heavy war horses got bogged down in the mud, and the English archers picked them off as English men-at-arms attacked the French with axes, swords, and daggers. The French lost 10,000 men at Agincourt—including 132 noblemen and 1,500 knights. The English lost 300.

In 1420, through a combination of warfare and negotiation, Henry forced the king of France to disinherit his own son and recognize the English king as regent. To seal the bargain Henry married the French princess Catherine. Henry was pursuing his conquests in the south of France when he was stricken with dysentery. He died in France, leaving behind an infant son, the new king of England and France.

HENRY THE NAVIGATOR
Prince of Portugal (1394–1460)

At age thirty-nine, Prince Henry, the third son of the king of Portugal, still had not found his calling. He had tried conquest of Moorish territories in Spain and Morocco, but failed. He had tried to establish his own court, but too many of his courtiers turned out to be criminals—murderers, rapists, even a few pirates. He dreamed of becoming lord of the Canary Islands, but never managed to control them. Then, in 1433, an astrologer charted the prince's horoscope and declared that Henry was about to discover a talent that would suddenly shine forth.

Among the other privileges Henry enjoyed as a royal prince, he had an exclusive right to authorize voyages of trade and/or exploration to Madeira, the Azores Islands, and along the western coast of Africa. He also had at his disposal an enormous income derived from his many estates and a monopoly on fishing rights and soap manufacturing, among other things. Drawing upon these rights and riches, Henry sponsored a series of voyages that began as reconnoitering missions for a projected invasion of the Canaries, segued into a trade venture that brought back African gold and slaves to Portugal, and then became a full-fledged voyage of discovery, with Henry's ships navigating the Senegal and Gambia rivers and exploring the Cape Verde Islands.

The Portuguese explorers who came later would build upon these early achievements until Vasco da Gama, in a ship flying the flag of Portugal, sailed around Africa and reached the coast of India. Henry initiated what has become known as the Age of Discovery.

PRINCE HENRY OF PORTUGALL

HONI · SOIT · QVI · MAL · PENSE

CEUT

SEJONG THE GREAT

King of Korea (1397–1450)

It is rare for absolute monarchs to be humane, yet Sejong the Great genuinely had the well-being of his people at heart.

He came to throne in 1418, when he was twenty-one years old. The coastal areas of Korea were being harassed by Japanese pirates, and the border lands were being raided by China and Manchuria. In 1419, Sejong attacked a Japanese pirate fleet, killing 700 and taking 110 captive. In the aftermath of his victory, Sejong negotiated a treaty with Japan that put an end to piracy in Korean waters. To repel Chinese and Manchurian raiders, the king erected new fortresses along the border, and sponsored the manufacture of more artillery as well as experiments in new forms of weaponry.

With the kingdom secure, Sejong initiated an astonishing array of domestic programs. He founded the Chipyonjon, or Hall of Worthies, a research institute where the best scholars produced new works on topics that ranged from astronomy to geography, from medicine to agriculture. He also sponsored a new compilation of all medical techniques drawn from the experience of skilled Chinese and Korean physicians.

As an author and poet, Sejong wanted to increase literacy among his people. He introduced Hangul, a new phonetically based Korean alphabet to replace the much more difficult writing system based on Chinese characters.

Sejong was also a compassionate man. During periods of poor harvests, he sent government officials out into the countryside with carts piled high with sacks of rice, beans, and salt to feed the starving.

He revised the criminal code, replacing harsh physical punishments for misdemeanors with fines. Sejong also created a new prison system in which men and women prisoners lived apart, the cells were kept clean, the prisoners were permitted to bathe weekly, and the prison buildings were constructed so they would not be oppressively hot in the summer or freezing cold in the winter.

Typically, conquerors and warlords are given the title "the Great." Sejong is one of the few monarchs whose greatness lay in his benevolence.

Example of Sejong's alphabet still used today

HIAWATHA

Chief of the Five Nations (c. 1450)

There are several schools of thought regarding when Hiawatha lived—the 1100s, the 1400s, and the 1500s. Seventeenth-century texts written by European settlers in North America refer to Hiawatha, but the earliest full-scale account of his life was not written until the nineteenth century by the Mohawk chief Joseph Brant. Although Henry Wadsworth Longfellow's poem, "The Song of Hiawatha," popularized this historical figure, the story line of the poem has almost nothing to do with the real Hiawatha.

Hiawatha lived in what is now New York State at a time when the five great tribes that dominated the region—the Mohawks, Oneidas, Onondagas, Cayugas, and Senecas—were locked in a relentless cycle of violence, from full-scale wars against other tribes to bloody feuds within families or clans. Hiawatha urged the tribes to unite into a single great nation, known collectively as the Iroquois. As the symbol of their union he created a belt of wampum made of purple and white shells. The chain of shells bound together in a single belt represented the union of the clans and tribes.

One of Hiawatha's greatest challenges was to eliminate the tradition of revenge killing. Hiawatha offered at least three possibilities: a ten-day period of active mourning when the family or clan withdrew from community life and was consoled by feasts and gifts offered by their neighbors; the adoption of a captive to take the place of the dead family member; or the ritual torturing to death of a captive to permit the family to vent their grief and anger.

According to an Iroquois legend, Hiawatha was inspired and led by a spirit named Deganawida, who first appeared to him when Hiawatha was a murderous young man who survived by ambushing and devouring his enemies. It was the constant presence of Deganawida that gave Hiawatha the wisdom, courage, and persistence to unite the Five Nations and bring peace to the Iroquois.

Hiawatha departing down the river

ITZCÓATL

Emperor of the Aztecs (c. 1400–1440)

Itzcóatl means "the Obsidian Serpent." Obsidian is a hard black volcanic glass the Aztecs used for household cutting tools as well as for arrowheads, daggers, and sharp blades embedded in war clubs. As a renowned warrior, Itzcóatl would have known the more deadly uses of obsidian.

His reign began during a period of upheaval in the Valley of Mexico. The Aztecs were already settled in their capital city, Tenochtitlán, built on an island in the center of a large lake. (Present-day Mexico City was built over the site of Tenochtitlán.) Already they had conquered some neighboring tribes, but they were eager to expand their conquests. One of the Aztecs' chief rivals, the Tepanec Empire, was in chaos: the king had died, his son had been assassinated, and the assassin had usurped the crown. The princes who governed the Tepanec cities were acting independently of the usurper, making the empire disunited and weak. In 1428, Itzcóatl approached the kings of Texcoco and Tlacopan—city-states located on the shore of the lake where the Aztecs had their capital—and suggested that they unite and attack the Tepanecs together. Confronted with such a large, well-organized force, the disorganized Tepanecs surrendered. They acknowledged Itzcóatl as their emperor and swore to send him tribute.

After this initial success, the three rulers, now known as the Triple Alliance, launched a military campaign and within four years conquered five more kingdoms. Itzcóatl emerged as the dominant figure in the alliance and the Aztecs as the greatest power.

After the war, Itzcóatl began an ambitious building program, erecting temples on the island and laying down a causeway that linked Tenochtitlán to the mainland.

By the time of his death, Itzcóatl had firmly established the Aztec Empire in the Valley of Mexico. His successor would build upon his achievement. By the time the Spanish arrived in Mexico in 1519, the Aztec emperor ruled more than 20 million people.

The conquest and rules of Itzcóatl from the *Codex Mendoza*

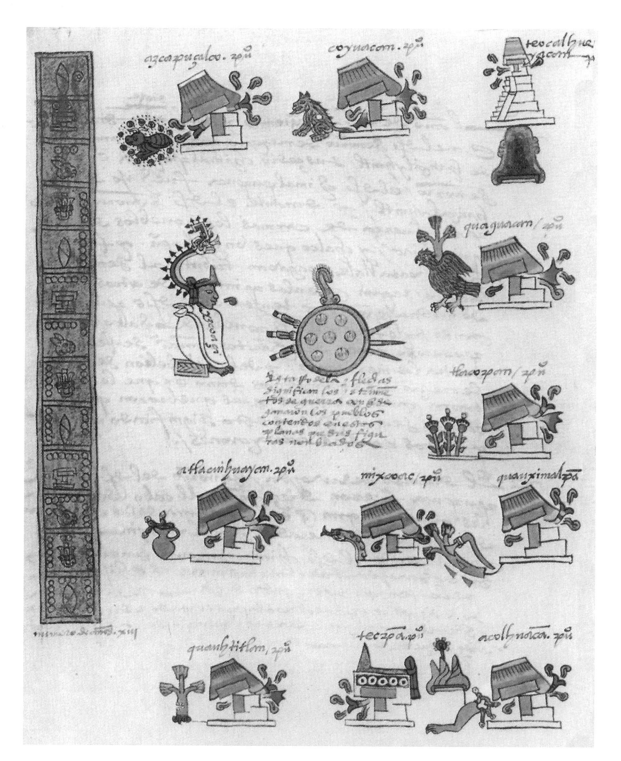

CHARLES VII
King of France (1403–1461)

Charles VII is notorious for being the king who abandoned Joan of Arc, the shepherd-girl-turned-warrior whose religious visions and military victories inspired the French and cleared the way for Charles to be crowned king.

The Hundred Years' War had been raging on and off in France since 1337. During Charles's boyhood, it appeared likely that the English would be the victors—they occupied most of the country, including the city of Paris.

In 1429 Charles, twenty-six years old, still had not been crowned king because the English held the territory around Rheims, the traditional coronation site of the kings of France. That year he met Joan, who told him with complete conviction that the King of Heaven had sent her to drive the English from France and see Charles crowned king. Charles was a nervous, hesitant man, painfully thin, knock-kneed, and strapped for cash besides. Joan saw none of these disadvantages; to her, he was the king.

Joan's complete confidence in her mission revived Charles's courage. He gave her thirty-five hundred fighting men and sent them to lift the English siege of Orléans. Incredibly, she succeeded in liberating the city. Then Joan moved into the Loire Valley, where she captured every English stronghold so Charles could travel safely to Rheims. Five months after they first met, Charles knelt in the Rheims cathedral to be crowned, while Joan stood at his side.

After the coronation, Charles received a letter from the duke of Burgundy, offering a truce. Perhaps because he did not wish to be indebted to a peasant girl, perhaps because he hated the expense and uncertainty of war with England, Charles agreed to the truce. A few months later, Burgundian troops captured Joan outside Compiègne. The duke of Burgundy set a ransom of ten thousand livres, but Charles made no attempt to raise the funds that would save Joan's life. The Burgundians passed her to the English, who charged her with witchcraft and burned her at the stake.

Twenty-five years after Joan's death, her mother and brothers petitioned the pope to reconsider the case with a view to nullifying the verdict and rehabilitating Joan's image. Charles, knowing that many of his subjects believed he was complicit in Joan's death, supported the review as a way to clear his own name.

Charles VII by Jean Fouquet

Constantine XI Palaeologus

Emperor of Byzantium (1404–1453)

By 1449, the year Constantine was crowned emperor, the once-great Byzantine Empire had shrunk to the Peloponnese in Greece, a slice of land along the southeastern shore of the Black Sea, and the city of Constantinople. Everything else had fallen to the Ottoman Turks, and now they were closing in. In 1452, the Ottomans built a fortress on the Bosphorus, the narrow strait that separates Europe from Asia, mounted three heavy cannons on the battlements, and gave orders that every ship that sailed into the strait must stop so that its cargo could be examined. The point was to prevent supplies or reinforcements from reaching Constantinople. One Venetian ship bearing food for the city had tried to slip past the castle; the Ottoman cannons sank the vessel. The surviving crew were executed, and the ship's captain impaled.

Realizing that time was running out, Constantine ordered the citizens of Constantinople to join him in repairing and reinforcing the city's defenses, stockpiling food and weapons, and mixing up batches of Greek fire, the deadly flaming liquid that for centuries had been the Byzantines' secret weapon. Most kings in western Europe ignored Constantine's appeals for troops, but some reinforcements trickled in: fourteen hundred Italian soldiers and a handful of Spanish sailors came to help the five thousand Greek troops defend the city. Arrayed against them was an Ottoman army that numbered between eighty thousand and two hundred thousand (depending on which source you care to believe). And the Ottomans had artillery.

On April 6, 1453, the Ottomans began bombarding the city walls, but the defenders drove back every attempt of the Ottoman troops to climb over the rubble and enter the city. In spite of such courage, Constantinople had no hope of repelling the Ottomans.

The final assault came on May 29, 1453. As tens of thousands of Ottoman troops stormed the walls, Constantine left his palace to fight and die with his men. As the Ottomans surged toward him, the emperor, his cousin, and a Spanish knight who had come to fight in defense of Constantinople charged the enemy. The three men were never seen again.

RENÉ D'ANJOU
King of Naples (1409–1480)

Although he was one of the most cultivated and well-connected men of his time, René d'Anjou has been virtually forgotten by everyone except historians. He fought with Joan of Arc outside Orléans, gave a young man named Christopher Columbus his first commission as a sailor, and persuaded his friends the Medicis and the Sforzas to collect and preserve rare manuscripts and books. Legend says that René was a pupil of the Flemish Renaissance master, Jan van Eyck, and it is true that René was a talented artist, but there is no solid evidence that he studied under the great painter.

As duke of Anjou, René ranked among the greatest nobles in France, but he was also closely related to the king and queen of Naples—they were his brother and sister-in-law. When the royal couple died within a year of each other, they bequeathed their kingdom to René.

René had a passion for chivalry and the romantic tales of King Arthur, Roland, Tristan, and the other literary heroes of his age. His favorite residence, the Château de Saumur, was a fairy tale castle of towers and turrets. Here, René staged many tournaments—they were his favorite activity—and he lavished such attention on the planning and execution of these jousts that ultimately he wrote a book on how to plan the perfect tournament. René's finished copy of the text, sumptuously illustrated, is on display in Paris's *Bibliothèque nationale*.

The king also wrote poetry: a satire of courtly love (for all his love of chivalry, he could not abide such artificial conventions) and a debate between a shepherd and a shepherdess on the nature of true love. The poem ran on for ten thousand verses, which prompted René's contemporary, the poet François Villon, to say that, generally, shepherdesses got to the point much quicker.

René spent the final years of his life living quietly in Provence, writing and painting illustrations for his books.

Portraits of Duke Anjou and his wife, Jeanne of Lavai

Vlad III Tepes Dracula

Prince of Wallachia (1431–1476)

Prince Vlad Dracula was not one of the undead, neither did he suck the lifeblood of his victims, neither is he regarded as a monster in his native country—what is now Romania. If anything, the Romanians regard Vlad as a national hero.

His father was known as Dracul, meaning "the Dragon," a reference to the military Order of the Dragon to which many knights and lords of the region belonged in the fifteenth century. Vlad's nickname, Dracula, means "son of the Dragon." Vlad lived during a brutal, dangerous time, when Hungarians, Bulgarians, and Ottoman Turks were all striving to conquer his homeland, Wallachia. While Vlad was still a boy, his father was compelled to become the vassal of the Ottoman sultan, Murad II; as a pledge of his good behavior, he surrendered his two youngest sons, Vlad and Radu, as hostages. Vlad nursed a deep hatred for the Ottomans, but living among them he learned their mind-set and their way of waging war. Meanwhile, a gang of rebellious boyars, or nobles, assassinated Vlad's father and murdered Vlad's older brother (one version says the young man was blinded, then buried alive).

After Mehmet, Murad's successor, conquered Constantinople, he pushed into eastern Europe. When the sultan led his army of ninety thousand troops into Wallachia in 1462, he was met by a horrific sight: an entire field planted with sharp stakes, and a Turk impaled on each one. It is said that to terrify the invaders, Vlad had rounded up and executed in this cruel way twenty thousand Turks. In spite of this horror, the Turks continued their invasion of Wallachia. Unable to meet such a massive force head-on, Vlad resorted to guerrilla tactics.

While Vlad fought for the freedom of his people from Turkish rule, his younger brother Radu, believing that resistance was futile, went over to the Turks. In 1462, Radu led a Turkish army against his brother's castle. Vlad was not there, but his wife was. Afraid of what would happen to her if she were taken captive by the Turks, the princess threw herself out of a tower window.

To get his brother out of the way, Radu made a truce with the king of Hungary, who promised to arrest and imprison Vlad. While Vlad sat in prison, the Turks completed their conquest of Wallachia. But in 1474, when he was a free man again, Vlad raised another army. He died battling the Turks in 1476.

Vlad dining in the midst of impaled bodies

MEHMET II THE CONQUEROR

Sultan of the Ottoman Empire (1432–1481)

When Mehmet II became sultan at age nineteen, no European ruler considered him a threat. As the youngest and least favorite son of the late sultan, Murad II, Mehmet had very little government experience and was so careless about military matters that he ignored insurgencies that broke out among the empires' Greek and Albanian subjects. During the first month of his reign, he made peace with Hungary, Serbia, Venice, and swore eternal friendship to Emperor Constantine XI in Constantinople. Mehmet's meekness may have gulled every other prince in Europe, but Constantine sensed the young sultan was a cunning and dangerous character.

One year later, 1452, Constantine's suspicions were proven to be correct: on Byzantine territory overlooking the Bosphorus, Mehmet built a fortress that threatened every ship that sailed the narrow strait. When Constantine sent emissaries to protest this violation of his territory, Mehmet had the ambassadors executed.

Another year passed and Mehmet was encamped outside the walls of Constantinople with an immense army and batteries of artillery. It was the dream of his life to capture the greatest Christian city in Asia, the last bastion of a once mighty empire. Constantine and his garrison of approximately six thousand men put up a valiant defense, but everyone inside and outside the city knew how the siege would end. The cannons battered down the walls of Constantinople, then tens of thousands of Turks surged into the city, slaughtering, raping, and pillaging so brutally that after a few hours, Mehmet called a halt to the orgy. Then he rode to the great church of Hagia Sophia, where he knelt on the marble floor and prayed—the traditional signal of Muslim conquerors that a church was about to be converted into a mosque.

In the weeks after the conquest, Mehmet resolved to be gracious to his Byzantine subjects. He gave them some degree of self-government, and appointed a monk named Gennadius to be their patriarch and the guarantor of their good behavior—any rebellion among the Greeks, and Gennadius would be the first to die.

In the years that followed, Mehmet conquered Serbia and Bosnia, consolidated the Muslim states in Turkey, and in 1480 terrified Europe by invading Italy. His Italian campaign ended abruptly when Mehmet died, poisoned, some said, by his physician.

QVI RESIDES SOLIO TANTI MAHOMETE PARÊTIS,
ET SVBIECTA TIBI TOT TVA REGNA VIDES

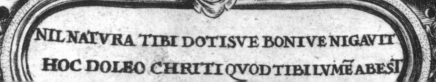

NIL NATVRA TIBI DOTISVE BONIVE NIGAVIT
HOC DOLEO CHRITI QVOD TIBI LVMÊ ABEST

MATTHIAS CORVINUS

King of Hungary (1443–1490)

Matthias was ten years old and his elder brother, László, fifteen when their father, governor of the Kingdom of Hungary, János Hunyadi, died. In the wake of János's death, Hungary was almost torn apart by plots and conspiracies as the Habsburg dynasty in Austria, the governor of Bohemia, and various Hungarian barons all contended to have their candidate seize the throne. In the upheaval, László's enemies beheaded him and Matthias was carried off as a hostage to Prague. Matthias might have remained in Prague for the rest of his life had not one of his uncles, backed up by an army of fifteen thousand men, convinced the Diet, the Hungarian parliament, to elect his nephew king.

As the tussle over the succession proved, Hungary was a troubled kingdom. The Germans, the Turks, the Austrians, the Poles, the Bohemians, and even the Venetians were all eager to swallow up, or at least carve up, Hungary. Even the Hungarian crown was no longer in the kingdom—the German emperor had carried it off. It took Matthias six years of virtually nonstop warfare to make Hungary secure, and it cost him sixty thousand ducats to ransom his crown from the emperor.

Within the borders of his realm, Matthias still had trouble with his unruly nobles. To keep them in line, Matthias introduced something Europe had not seen since the days of the Roman legions—a standing army of professional troops who received a regular salary. The troops, mostly fighting men from Poland, Germany, and Bohemia, were outfitted in black armor in tribute to their commander, "Black John" Haugwitz. Initially there were never fewer than eight thousand men serving in Matthias army; later he raised the number to thirty thousand.

The Renaissance was flourishing in Italy during Matthias's reign, and he longed to bring it to Hungary. He invited Italian artists and scholars to his court, founded a university at Bratislava, founded the Corviniana Library and filled the shelves with works of history, science, and philosophy. But all these things cost money, and maintaining the Black Army was also a drain on the treasury; to finance all these projects Matthias burdened his people with high taxes. Today, Hungarians regard Matthias as an enlightened monarch and a national hero, but at the time of his death, his discontented subjects were happy to see him go.

FERDINAND II OF ARAGON AND ISABELLA OF CASTILE

King (1452–1516) and Queen (1451–1504) of Spain

Spain in the 15th century was divided into several kingdoms—Aragon, Castile, Catalonia, Navarre. In addition, there was the kingdom of Granada in the south, the last outpost of the Moorish occupation of Spain. With their marriage in 1469, Ferdinand and Isabella began the unification of Spain. Part of that goal was the conquest of Granada, which they achieved in the momentous year of 1492.

For centuries Spain had been a religiously diverse country with Catholics, Jews, and Muslims generally living in peace together. But Ferdinand and Isabella envisioned a religiously and racially pure kingdom; if the Jews wished to stay in Spain, they must convert to Catholicism, otherwise they would be expelled from the country. This idea was not unique to Ferdinand and Isabella—virtually European ruler believed that religious unity was an essential component of national unity.

The deadline for the Jews was July 30, 1492. On that day 200,000 Jewish men, women, and children crowded on to ships and sailed for lands where they would be tolerated—North Africa, Turkey, and Italy.

Under the terms of the Treaty of Granada, Ferdinand and Isabella pledged themselves to permitting the Muslim community to stay in their homes and practice their religion—the king and queen were convinced that given time, the Muslims would convert. But the Muslims of Granada did not become Christians, and in frustration, officials of the Church and the State began to harass them. In 1499, the Muslims of Granada rebelled, and that gave the Spanish authorities the excuse to begin the expulsion of the Moors.

The loss of its Jewish and Muslim population was a severe blow to Spain: these people were often experts in medicine, finance, mathematics, and engineering. But the loss of such a large talent pool may have been dulled by what Spain gained from an unexpected quarter. In 1492, Christopher Columbus, with the support of Isabella, sailed three ships westward across the Atlantic expecting to find a short route to Asia. Instead, he ran into the Americas. For more than 300 years, Spain's fortunes would be linked to its wealthy American colonies.

Ferdinand and Isabella at the Surrender of Granada

RICHARD III

King of England (1452–1485)

For a king who reigned only two years, it is remarkable how much ink has been spilled over Richard III's character, beginning with Thomas More and William Shakespeare, both of whom portrayed Richard as a murderous tyrant (although Shakespeare's portrait is much more vivid than More's).

Richard was the last Plantagenet king of England, the dynasty that was founded some three hundred years earlier by Henry II. He may not have murdered his way to the throne, but he most certainly usurped it. When Richard's brother Edward IV died in 1483, Richard was named guardian of twelve-year-old Edward V and his ten-year-old brother, Richard. Almost immediately, Richard seized the crown from the new young king and imprisoned his two nephews in the Tower of London, where, at some unknown date, the boys were presumably murdered, most likely on Richard's order. To give his usurpation the appearance of legitimacy, Richard had spread a rumor that the two princes were illegitimate because their father's marriage to their mother had been bigamous and therefore invalid. A great number of the nobility, who did not like the arriviste pretensions of the queen's family, were willing to swallow this absurd story and throw their support behind Richard. Parliament followed suit.

Shortly after Richard's coronation his closest friend, Henry Stafford, duke of Buckingham, led an uprising against Richard in favor of Henry Tudor, the earl of Richmond. The uprising failed, and Stafford was captured, found guilty of treason, and beheaded.

Buckingham's execution frightened a great many of the nobles who had supported Richard and sent them scurrying to France, where they offered their services to the exiled Henry Tudor.

In 1485, Henry sailed across the English Channel with an army to unseat Richard. The king's army outnumbered Tudor's two-to-one, but in the middle of the battle several noblemen deserted the king and took their men over to Henry Tudor's side. Yet Richard—the last English king to go personally into battle—fought ferociously. He got close to Tudor but was immediately surrounded and killed by Henry's men. According to legend, he died shouting, "Treason! Treason! Treason!"

CATHERINE CORNARO

1454–1510

The Cornaro family, or Corner as they were called in the Venetian dialect, were one of the grandest noble houses in Venice, whose interests extended to the island of Cyprus where Catherine's father owned extensive estates. When James, the king of Cyprus, asked to marry Catherine, the Cornaros were delighted.

The marriage was held by proxy. A grand procession escorted 14-year-old Catherine from her family's palace to the Doge's Palace where Cyprus' ambassador to Venice stood in for his sovereign. No doubt because she was so young, Catherine remained with her parents in Venice for another four years before setting out for Cyprus. She and James had one year together before he died, unexpectedly, at age 33. At the time of his death, Catherine was pregnant.

To protect Venice's interests in Cyprus and safeguard the Venetian queen against a potential invasion from the kingdom of Naples (which had had its eye on the island for years), Captain-General Pietro Mocenigo brought a fleet to the island and reinforced all the fortresses of Cyprus with his own men.

There was a faction on the island that did not like Venice's interference in Cypriot affairs. Before dawn on November 13, 1473, a small group of armed men, led by the archbishop of Nicosia, forced their way into Catherine's palace, murdered her uncle, her cousin, her chamberlain, and her doctor, then demanded that she pass over her infant son and grant the right to succession to Alfonso of Naples.

In response to the coup, Mocenigo hanged the ringleaders and threw the rest of the conspirators in prison. Venice sent two councillors to administer Cyprus, while Catherine remained as a powerless figurehead. The next year, her little son died. After 16 miserable years of living under virtual house arrest, Catherine negotiated to return home to Venice; in exchange for her freedom she abdicated and handed over her kingdom to the doge.

As a token of appreciation, the doge gave her the fief of Asolo, a hill town on the mainland. There, to relieve her tedium, she established a cultivated court of poets, musicians, and scholars. Visitors found the court's sophisticated atmosphere delightful, but Catherine was bored senseless; yet, having no other option, she endured it for the last 20 years of her life.

Portrait of Catherine Cornaro attributed to Titian

ANDREA GRITTI

Doge of Venice (1455–1538)

Andrea Gritti was raised by his grandfather, Triadano, one of Venice's most trusted diplomats. Consequently, Gritti spent his boyhood and adolescence accompanying his grandfather on sensitive missions to the royal courts of Europe.

After the fall of Constantinople to the Ottoman Turks, Venice was the first western power to establish commercial and diplomatic ties with the sultan. At age 30, Gritti tried his hand at commerce and settled in Constantinople. He became friendly with Sultan Bayezid II and served as the liaison between the European merchants in the city and the Ottoman government. In the meantime, he collected intelligence about the Turks and passed it back to the government in Venice. The Ottomans must have suspected Gritti was interested in more than good trade relations, because when war broke out between Venice and the Ottoman Empire, Gritti was thrown into a Turkish prison. Yet even in jail he still managed to get information to Venice.

After four years of warfare, the sultan sent a message to the Venetians, suing for peace. He suggested that one of the peace commissioners representing Venice's interests should be Gritti—whom the sultan had ordered released from prison.

By 1505, Gritti was back home—just in time for a fresh war, this time against the warrior pope, Julius II. Venice had been seizing territory on the Italian mainland, and the papal forces were part of a military league sworn to take this territory back. In battle after battle the league defeated the Venetians. In 1509, Gritti was appointed Captain General of the Venetian forces and he recaptured virtually all of Venice's newly acquired dominions on the mainland. In recognition of his services to Venice, Gritti was elected to the Procuratoria of St. Mark, an exclusive association restricted to members of the noblest families in the city.

The crowning honor of his career came in 1523 when Andrea Gritti was elected doge, or duke, of Venice. He was 68—a very old man for his time, yet during his 15-year-reign he proved an able administrator. He withdrew Venice from the wars that were tearing Italy apart. He tried to avoid further conflicts by persuading Francis I of France and Charles V of Spain that the real enemy was the Ottoman Empire, which was preparing to invade Hungary. He died as doge in 1538.

Andrea Gritti by Titian

Maximilian I

Holy Roman Emperor (1459–1519)

Maximilian's father, Frederick III, was the first member of the Hapsburg family to become Holy Roman Emperor. After him, the family held on to the title until 1740.

For most of its history, the Hapsburg dynasty had ruled in German-speaking lands: Germany, Austria, Bohemia. Maximilian made the Hapsburgs players on a much broader international stage, primarily through the marriage of his son Philip the Handsome to Juana la Loca, daughter of Ferdinand and Isabella of Spain. By this marriage, the Hapsburgs became heirs to the Low Countries, Burgundy, Spain, and Spain's colonies in the New World. It was one of the greatest dynastic coups since Henry of England married Eleanor of Aquitaine.

Maximilian was more successful at the bargaining table hammering out the details of an advantageous marriage for his children than on the battlefield. Although he recovered Austrian territory that had been occupied by the Hungarians, and pushed back a Turkish invasion at Villach in southern Austria, he was compelled to grant Switzerland its independence. His incursions into northern Italy ended in failure—he captured Milan and Verona, but then lost them again. In fact, there was a couplet at the time on this very subject, "Let others wage war, but thou, O happy Austria, marry; / For those kingdoms which Mars gives to others, Venus gives to thee."

Maximilian was the first Holy Roman Emperor to break a tradition that stretched back to Charlemagne: he did not go to Rome to be crowned by the pope. With the permission of Pope Julius II, he called himself "Elected Roman Emperor," a distinction that satisfied the Holy Father.

In imitation of the great families of Italy who were enthusiastic patrons of the Renaissance, Maximilian invited all types of scholars to his court—mathematicians, astronomers, linguists, theologians. And he became an avid patron of German Renaissance artists, most notably Albrecht Durer and Albrecht Altdorfer.

Thanks to Maximilian's matrimonial form of diplomacy, the Hapsburgs would influence the course of Europe history into the 20th century.

Maximilian with his wife Mary, his son Philip the Handsome, and his three grandsons

PHAS FRATER CARNALIS IO·
· MARITI DIVAE VIRG MARIE

JACOBVS MINOR EPVS· MARIA CLEOPHÆ· SOR·
HIEROSOLIMITANVS· VIRG MAR PVTATIVA M
TERTERA D N·

IOSEPH IVSTVS SIMON ZELOTES CONSO·

Montezuma

(c. 1466–1520)

There was a legend among the Aztecs that their god, Quetzalcoatl, had sailed away to dwell with the sun god. His return in the form of a pale-skinned, bearded man would portend the fall of the Aztec Empire.

If the Aztec Emperor Montezuma initially took Hernan Cortes for Quetzalcoatl, he realized his mistake soon enough: by their actions Cortes and his men showed they were very human.

In 1502, Montezuma became the ninth tlatoani, or emperor, of the Aztecs. They were an aggressive, warlike people, and Montezuma expanded his empire by conquering the territory known today as Chiapas in southern Mexico. Bernal Diaz del Castillo, one of the conquistadors who accompanied Cortes, described Montezuma as "about forty years old, of good height, well proportioned, spare and slight, and not very dark…. He did not wear his hair long but just over his ears, and he had a short black beard, well-shaped and thin. His face was rather long and cheerful, he had fine eyes."

Initially, Montezuma was not afraid of the Spaniards—there were pathetically few of them compared to his own vast army. In 1519, he met Cortes at a causeway that led into the Aztecs' capital city, Tenochtitlan, the site of present-day Mexico City. He gave Cortes gifts of gold and silver, and invited the Spaniards to live in his palace as honored guests.

In May 1520, Cortes left Tenochtitlan with some of his men to confront a rival conquistador. In his absence the Spaniards left behind in Tenochtitlan attacked the Aztecs during a religious festival, slaughtering perhaps as many as 600. As the entire city rose up against them, the Spaniards seized Montezuma. When Cortes returned a few weeks later, the palace was still besieged by the Aztecs. He fought his way inside, then forced Montezuma to stand on a balcony and order his people to fall back. Instead the Aztecs stoned their emperor.

That night Montezuma died. The Spanish account says Montezuma succumbed to the injuries he suffered from his own people. The Aztec account says Montezuma, no longer useful to the Spanish, was stabbed to death and his body dumped in the street.

EDWARD V
King of England (1470–1483?)

On April 9, 1483, King Edward IV died. The coronation of Edward V was set for June 22. It was a longstanding custom among English royalty for a new king to stay in the royal apartments at the Tower of London for several days before being crowned. In fact, the traditional processional route to Westminster Abbey began at the Tower, so there was nothing ominous when 13-year-old Edward and his 10-year-old brother Richard were escorted there.

As a child, Edward could not rule in his own right; his uncle, Richard, Duke of Gloucester, had been appointed his protector, or guardian; until the king came of age, Duke Richard would run the country. But then a story began to circulate that the princes were not legitimate. Robert Stillington, the bishop of Bath and Wells and Lord Chancellor of England, declared in Parliament that in 1464, when Edward IV married Elizabeth Woodville (the princes' mother), he was already married to a woman named Eleanor Talbot. If this were true, the king had committed bigamy, thus invalidating his marriage to Elizabeth and making his son ineligible to succeed to the crown of England.

Eleanor Talbot had died in 1468, and aside from the word of Bishop Stillington there was no other evidence. Nonetheless, overnight the coronation of Edward V was cancelled. On June 25, Parliament issued a decree that the sons of Edward IV were illegitimate, and declared that the true king was Richard, Duke of Gloucester. On July 6, it was the duke who followed the traditional route to Westminster Abbey where he was crowned King Richard III.

After the summer of 1483, the princes vanished. In all likelihood Richard III ordered them killed, but there is no solid evidence of his responsibility. This set of circumstances set off more than 500 years of legends, conspiracy theories, and sometimes ferocious partisanship among amateur and professional historians.

In 1674, the skeletons of two children were discovered under a staircase in the Tower. King Charles II assumed they must be the lost princes, and ordered the bones buried in Westminster Abbey. The remains were exhumed for study in 1933, but given the forensics of the time neither the age nor even the sex of the skeletons could be determined. The mystery lives on.

Edward V and Richard, Duke of York, in the Tower

Margaret Pole

Countess of Salisbury (1473–1541)

What an unhappy life Margaret had. She was three when her mother died in child-birth. At age five Margaret's father, George, Duke of Clarence, was arrested for plotting against his brother, King Edward IV, and secretly executed in the Tower of London. Then her younger brother Edward was beheaded on a trumped up charge of treason.

As for Margaret, in 1491 she married Sir Richard Pole, a knight whose courage during the wars in Scotland had won the favor of King Henry. The couple had four sons and a daughter. In 1505, Richard died.

When Henry VIII came to the throne it appeared that Margaret's misfortunes had come to end. The new king returned all her estates which his father had confiscated, exonerated her late brother, asked Margaret to be godmother to his daughter Princess Mary, and appointed her governess of the princess' household.

During the Anne Boleyn crisis, Margaret tried to find a middle way between obedience to the king and loyalty to Mary and her mother, Catherine of Aragon. But Henry and Anne demanded full consent to the legitimacy of their marriage and of the king's new title, Supreme Head of the Church in England. When Margaret hedged, Henry dismissed her from Mary's household.

Then in 1536, one of Margaret's sons, Reginald, a Catholic priest living in Europe, published a book in which he was intensely critical of Henry's claim to supremacy in religious matters and his persecution of faithful Catholics. The book outraged the king, who swore to wipe out the Pole family. In 1539, Henry ordered the execution of Margaret's son Geoffrey, his wife, and ten other Pole relatives. Margaret was arrested in 1539; no evidence of treason could be found against her, yet she was kept locked up for more than two years. On the morning of May 28, 1541, the lord lieutenant of the Tower of London informed her she would be executed within the hour. Margaret protested that she had not been convicted of any crime; it did not matter—the king wanted her dead.

As a person of royal blood she was executed in private. The executioner was inexperienced; his first blow of the axe missed the neck, striking Margaret's shoulder. It took several blows to behead her. She was 68 at the time of her death.

ANNE

Duchess of Brittany (1477–1514)

Throughout the Middle Ages there were large sections of what is now France that were independent of the French king. Navarre, in the south along the Pyrenees was one such state, and Brittany on the Atlantic coast was another. Over the centuries, the French kings attempted to absorb these independent realms into their kingdom.

In 1488, Charles VIII of France defeated Francis II, Duke of Brittany, in battle at the little Breton town of Saint-Aubin-du-Cormier. Under the terms of surrender, Francis declared that he was a vassal of the king of France. It appeared that this was the end of an independent Brittany.

Weeks after signing the treaty, Francis fell off his horse and died of his injuries. His eleven-year-old daughter Anne succeeded him. Almost immediately Anne and her advisors began looking around for a monarch for her to marry, someone strong enough to enable Brittany to regain its independence. The most likely candidate was the Holy Roman Emperor, Maximilian I. Anne married him by proxy in 1490, but before she could meet her husband and consummate the marriage, Charles VIII of France invaded Brittany and forced Anne to marry him.

Seven years later, Charles died but Anne was still not free—under the terms of the treaty she signed at the time of her marriage to Charles, if he died first and they did not have a son she must marry his successor, Louis XII. By this time Anne was a grown woman who had learned how to govern and how to bargain. She insisted that her title, Duchess of Brittany, and her right to govern her province be confirmed by Louis. Louis agreed, and even accepted the secondary title, duke consort, which meant in Brittany Anne outranked him. It was a modest concession on Louis' part, and it must have been obvious to everyone that the days of Brittany's autonomy were over. Nonetheless, even the appearance of independence meant a great deal to Anne.

In addition to being devoted to Brittany, Anne loved music and works of art, especially tapestries. It is likely that the famous Unicorn Tapestries displayed in The Cloisters museum in New York were made for her.

Before she died, Anne left instructions that at her death her heart was to be removed, placed in a gold shrine, and buried in her parents tomb in Nantes, among the tombs of all the other independent dukes of Brittany.

The Dominican friar Antoine Dufour presents Anne with a copy of his book praising famous women.

JUANA LA LOCA

Queen of Castile and Aragon, Count of Flanders (1479–1555)

It was love at first sight. Juana, princess of Spain, daughter of Ferdinand and Isabella, possessed exotic looks—dark complexion, dark hair, and eyes an unusual shade of sea-green. She was quiet, restrained, and intensely pious. Philip, count of Flanders, by contrast was fair skinned, fair haired, very handsome, very athletic, and very outgoing. He found his princess so enchanting he insisted on being married to her that day. After her wedding night with Philip, Juana fell so wildly in love with her husband that he became the center of her universe.

The honeymoon ended quickly. Juana did not enjoy banquets, dancing, hunting—all the pursuits Philip loved. Seeing him flirt with other women sent her into terrible rages. When Juana had a tantrum, Philip struck back by refusing to sleep with her.

The couple had six children, four girls and two boys, but Juana took no interest in them. In 1501, when she and Philip traveled to Spain for a formal visit, Ferdinand and Isabella noticed that their daughter's seriousness had changed into deep melancholy. After a few weeks Philip declared he could not bear the Spanish weather and was going home to the Low Countries; because she was in an advanced state of pregnancy Juana could not travel. This separation from her husband further depressed her spirits. In Spain she had an episode, running out one night in a terrible storm, she ordered the guards to open the castle gates so she could rejoin her husband. The guards refused, and Juana sank down on the ground where she stayed all night and all the next day, refusing all help and even dry clothes.

Back in Brussels she had another episode. Juana was convinced that Philip was having an affair with a beautiful fair-haired young woman of the court. Armed with a pair of scissors she attacked the woman, cut off her hair, then slashed her face. Philip locked his wife in her apartments.

In summer 1506, Philip was struck with a mysterious illness; after six days, he died. Juana, wild with grief, could not bear to be separated from the body. She decided to take Philip's body to Granada for burial in the royal vault. She insisted on traveling only at night, by torchlight. When at last the procession arrived in Spain, King Ferdinand, seeing the state of his daughter, had her kept under lock and key in the castle of Tordesillas, where she died 49 years later.

Henry VIII

King of England (1491–1547)

The best-known of all England's monarchs, Henry VIII was not a great king, nor even a good man, but he did transform England radically.   At 18 years of age when he became king, Henry stood six feet tall, was strikingly handsome, athletic, well-educated, quick-witted, and charming. After the final gloomy, penny-pinching years of his father's reign, young Henry was greeted enthusiastically by his subjects. In their euphoria, many people missed, or overlooked, the new king's less attractive qualities: egotism, obstinacy, rage whenever his will was obstructed.

Henry married Catherine of Aragon, a Spanish princess six years his senior. They had a daughter, Mary, but Henry wanted a son; it was his unshakable opinion that a woman could not rule England. Tragically, all of Henry and Catherine's sons came into the world stillborn, or died when they were only a few weeks old. By 1526, Henry was growing tired of his queen and anxious about the succession; he wanted to marry Anne Boleyn.

For seven years, Henry's envoys negotiated with the pope for an annulment of his marriage to Catherine, but the pope dragged his feet. When Anne announced that she was pregnant, Henry broke with Rome, declared his marriage to Catherine invalid, married Anne, and demanded that the entire nation recognize his new marriage and his new title, Supreme Head of the Church in England.

When Anne failed to provide Henry with a son, he had her executed on false charges of adultery, incest, and witchcraft. Of the four wives who followed Anne, only one gave the king a son, Jane Seymour, and she died shortly after giving birth.

In his fifties, Henry became morbidly obese and required assistance just to walk across a room. His mood varied from depression to bitterness to wrath, only his sixth and last wife, Catherine Parr, was able to calm him. In spite of the trauma he had inflicted upon his country, many of the common people still loved him, convinced that the king had been the victim of bad advice from wicked councilors.

His son Edward reigned only six years, dying at age sixteen. He was followed by Catherine of Aragon's daughter, Mary, who ruled for five years. It was Anne Boleyn's child, Elizabeth, who enjoyed a full reign of 45 years, thereby proving that her father had been wrong—England could be ruled successfully by a woman.

Portrait of Henry VIII by Hans Holbein the Younger

·TATIS· ·SVÆ·XLIX·

SULEIMAN I THE MAGNIFICENT

Sultan of the Ottoman Empire (1494–1566)

Suleiman I brought the Ottoman Empire to the zenith of its political and cultural splendor. He took the city of Belgrade, wrested the island of Rhodes from the crusader Knights of St. John, conquered Hungary, and marched his army to the gates of Vienna, threatening all of Western Europe. His navy seized all the major ports in North Africa. His army overran modern-day Iraq. The Mediterranean, the Red Sea, and the Persian Gulf became, essentially, Ottoman lakes where the sultan's fleet sailed unopposed.

Suleiman cast his wars in a religious light, truly believing that God intended him to make the whole world submit to Islam. Suleiman's near invincibility so distressed Martin Luther that the reformer called upon all Europeans, Protestants and Catholics alike, to join in a crusade to defeat the sultan, whom he described as "the very devil incarnate."

In terms of art and architecture, the sultan commissioned hundreds of new buildings from his favorite architect, the brilliant Sinan. He is most famous for designing the Suleymaniye Mosque in Constantinople, but Sinan also built mosques, schools, and even bridges and soup kitchens throughout the empire. He enriched the cities of Damascus and Baghdad, as well as Islam's most sacred cities, Mecca and Medina, with splendid new monuments.

Like other sultans, Suleiman had troublesome sons. In 1553, bands of Turks in Asia Minor who were unhappy with Suleiman's rule urged the sultan's eldest son, Mustafa, to depose his father. Before the young man could act, Suleiman had him executed. In 1559–1561, two of Suleiman's younger sons, Selim and Bayezid, squabbled over who would became sultan at their father's death. This quarrel turned into open warfare in which Bayezid was defeated and executed.

By the time of his death 1566, Suleiman had made the Ottoman Empire the greatest power in the Western Hemisphere. After studying the military might and tremendous wealth of the Ottomans, the Austrian diplomat Ogier Ghislain de Busbecq lamented, "When the Turks have settled [their war with Persia], they will fly at our throats supported by the might of the whole East; how unprepared we are I dare not say."

Suleiman riding through the ruins of the Hippodrome in Constantinople

CHARLES V

King of Spain and Holy Roman Emperor (1500–1558)

Charles V's life corresponded with the rise of the Reformation, the conquest of Mexico and Peru, the first European contact with Japan, and the publication of Nicholas Copernicus' theory that the Earth and all the other planets revolve around the Sun. Any one of these events would have been enough to shake up European society, yet they all occurred within a matter of 50 years.

He was just 21 years old and only recently had been crowned Holy Roman Emperor when he presided at the assembly where Martin Luther defended his unorthodox religious opinions. Luther refused to back down and the pope's representative condemned him as a heretic. From that moment Christianity in Europe was split into two camps, Catholic and Protestant—and Charles had been a witness to the rift.

But 16th-century politics made strange bedfellows. Pious Catholic though he was, Charles wanted to possess Italy—most of which was papal territory. In 1527, during the war between the emperor and the pope, an army of Spaniards, Italian mercenaries, and German Lutherans captured Rome. The pope locked himself inside his fortress, Castel Sant'Angelo, while outside, Charles' troops raped nuns and laywomen, tortured monks and noblemen, murdered anyone who got in their way, and committed countless crimes of vandalism and sacrilege in the churches of Rome. Charles had not been at the head of these troops, but they were his men and he was held responsible.

Thanks to his empire in the Americas, Charles was the wealthiest monarch in Europe. The treasure of the Aztecs and the Incas—tons of it—flowed across the sea into Spain. The gold funded Charles' wars, but also his building projects such as his grand palace in Granada, his patronage of great masters such as Titian, and his sponsorship of explorers such as Magellan.

He tried to bring order and justice out of the disorderly times in which he lived. He wanted to restrain the violence directed at the native population in the Americas, but at the same time he endorsed the death penalty for anyone convicted of heresy.

In 1556, Charles, exhausted from the demands of his empire, abdicated. Then he retired to a monastery where, two years later, he died.

The entrance of Emperor Charles V into Antwerp

ATAHUALPA
(1502-1533)

In 1527, Atahuala's father divided the Inca Empire in two—the northern half he bequeathed to Atahualpa, his illegitimate son, the southern half he gave to his legitimate son Huascar. Civil war was inevitable, and the bloody, destructive conflict dragged on until 1532, by which time the population of the empire was depleted, its cities battered, its economy in ruins. But Atahualpa won; he took Huascar and all his family prisoner and ordered their execution.

In the aftermath of the war Atahualpa retired to a small spa town, Cajamarca, to relax. There he received word that a Spanish "army" of about 180 men, led by Francisco Pizzaro, had marched into Cuzco, the Inca capital. On November 15, the emperor of the Incas met the Spanish conquistador. Pizzaro invited the emperor to a feast in his honor the next day. Atahualpa accepted.

The next day, Atahualpa arrived, borne in on a litter, attended by thousands of unarmed courtiers. One of Pizarro's chaplains, Father Vicente de Valverde, approached and gave the emperor an overview of the Christian faith, then asked him to accept baptism. The priest handed Atahualpa a copy of the gospels; the emperor flipped through the pages, then tossed the book to the ground. As Father Valverde walked back to the ranks, Pizzaro gave the signal and his men opened fire with their muskets and their cannon, then the cavalry charged. The Inca had never seen firearms, artillery, or horses before; they panicked, and being defenseless, were cut down by the thousands.

Atahualpa, now Spaniards' prisoner, promised to fill a room with treasure if Pizarro would set him free. Pizarro agreed. It took 24 tons of gold and silver to fill the room—the greatest ransom in history—but Pizarro went back on his word. Instead of freeing Atahualpa, he put him on trial for killing his brother and worshipping pagan gods; the court found the emperor guilty and condemned him to be burned at the stake. On August 29, 1533, just before the fire was lit, Father Valverde approached Atahualpa one last time—if he accepted baptism, he could die quickly by the garrote. Atahualpa consented; after the priest baptized the emperor, the executor strangled him, then burned his body.

Father Vicente de Valverde attempts to explain the Christian faith to Atahualpa

Hurrem Sultan

(1510–1558)

The Koran permits a Muslim man four wives, and sultans usually had many more, yet Suleiman the Magnificent married only one woman—Hurrem Sultan.

She was born in the town of Rohatyn in the Ukraine. Her father was a Ukrainian Orthodox priest, and her Christian name was Anastasia. When she was in her early teens, a band of Crimean Tartars raided Rohatyn; Anastasia was one of the captives carried off to the slave market at Kaffa. She was taken with a shipment of other slaves to Constantinople where she was purchased for Sultan Suleiman's harem.

We do not know anything about her appearance or her personality, but she made an impression on Suleiman, who began to spend time with her. In a jealous rage, the sultan's favorite, Mahidevran, attacked Anastasia, beating her badly. When Suleiman learned of it, he banished Mahidevran and their son, Mustafa, to Manisa on Turkey's Aegean coast. Once Mahidevran was gone, Suleiman devoted himself to Anastasia.

At some point, Anastasia converted to Islam and acquired the name Hurrem, which comes from the Arabic word for "noble" or the Persian word for "cheerful." Her nickname was Roxelana, probably derived from the Turkish name for her homeland, Ruslana.

Hurrem and Suleiman had five children, but Mahidevran's son Mustafa was the sultan's acknowledged heir. When Mustafa toyed with the idea of deposing his father, Hurrem seized the opportunity and persuaded Suleiman to have his rebellious son strangled. This cleared the way for one of her sons to become sultan.

As a sign of his esteem, Suleiman freed Hurrem (as a woman of the harem, she was still a slave), then married her. She advised him on matters of state, and even corresponded with foreign monarchs—two of her letters to Sigismund II, King of Poland, have survived.

As the sultan's wife, she had a large income, part of which she used for charitable purposes. She built a mosque and religious schools, but also a public fountain, a public bath, a hospital for women, and a soup kitchen.

Hurrem outlived Suleiman and saw her son, Selim, become sultan.

A public bath, Haseki Hurrem Sultan Hamami, commissioned by Hurrem.

CATHERINE DE MEDICI

Queen of France (1519–1589)

The Medici family of Florence were not royalty or even nobility—they were bankers. But they were also shrewd politicians who used their money and their contacts to marry into the nobility, become rulers of Florence, and even get several of their sons elected pope. It was one of these Medici popes, Clement VII, Catherine's uncle, who arranged for her to marry the French Dauphin, or prince, Henry.

Catherine was educated, clever, well-spoken, and had a natural curiosity, yet the French nobility, and even the French common people, never warmed to Catherine—she was not royal, and she was a foreigner. Her marriage to Henry was also not a success—he was more devoted to his mistress, Diane de Poitiers, than to his wife. The royal couple were not completely estranged, however—they had ten children.

In 1559, Henry died from a wound received in a tournament. The following year, his heir, Francis II died. Next in line came the prince Charles, but he was only ten years old; Catherine was named regent. Now that she had power, she used it. The politically ambitious, devoutly Catholic Guise family was trying to elbow their way into the royal family; as a counterbalancing measure, Catherine tried to rally French Protestants, the Huguenots, around the throne. The Duke de Guise responded by attacking a group of Huguenots while they were at worship, killing 74 and wounding more than 100. The outrage set off a religious war in France that lasted a decade. To bring the bloody, destructive war to a close, Catherine agreed to grant toleration to the Huguenots.

Two years later, one of the leaders of the Huguenots, Admiral Gaspard de Coligny, was wounded in an assassination attempt. Fearing that the Huguenots would rise up to avenge the admiral, King Charles IX called upon French Catholics to kill all the Huguenots. Catherine almost certainly participated in and approved of what has become known as the St. Bartholomew Day Massacre, in which French Catholics killed thousands of French Protestants.

Catherine was overwhelmed by the madness of the time. Two days before Christmas 1588, her son Henry had eight prisoners, all members of the Guise family, hacked to death. Catherine, already sick with pleurisy, gave up, took to her bed, and died 13 days later.

LAPU-LAPU

King of Mactan (c. 1521)

Ferdinand Magellan was a Portuguese navigator and explorer who convinced the king of Spain that, in spite of the presence of the Americas, there was indeed a direct route westward across the Atlantic to the Spice Islands (by which he meant present-day Indonesia). His route took him, unexpectedly, around the southernmost tip of South America, through what is now known as the Strait of Magellan, and then across the Pacific to another surprise—the Philippine Islands, which were entirely unknown to Europeans.

In April 1521, Magellan and his men landed at Cebu where they were welcomed by the king, Rajah Humabon. Magellan had a Malay servant who understood most of what Humabon said, and so the Filipinos and the Spanish were able to communicate. Seeing how eager Magellan was to establish Christianity in the islands, Humabon, his queen, and 400 of their people asked to be baptized. Then Humabon asked Magellan to do him a favor—sail to Mactan and kill his enemy, Rajah Lapu-Lapu.

We know nothing about Lapu-Lapu, not even his age, but he must have had an excellent intelligence system in the islands. As 49 Spaniards waded ashore at Mactan, they were confronted by 1,500 of his warriors arrayed in three divisions. As Lapu-Lapu led his men in a charge, the Spaniards opened fire with their muskets and crossbows, but the weapons failed to terrify the enemy.

Hoping to distract some of the warriors away from the battlefield, Magellan sent a few men to set fire to the village. But the sight of their homes burning only further enraged the Filipinos. A poisoned arrow struck Magellan in the right leg, and he called for a retreat. Many warriors closed in around Magellan; as he fell face down in the sand, the warriors stabbed him again and again with their spears and hacked him with their swords. A member of Magellan's crew who wrote an account of the battle, said, "Thereupon, beholding him dead, we, wounded, retreated, as best we could, to the boats, which were already pulling off."

Lapu-Lapu had won a victory over his rival Humabon and over a foreign power. He has gone down in Filipino history as a hero who resisted the occupation of the Philippines.

Lapu-Lapu (in feather headdress) and warriors attack Ferdinand Magellan

Rani Durgavati

Queen of the Gond Kingdom (1524–1564)

As the Moghal emperor Akbar pushed into Central India as part of his campaign to conquer the entire country, he offered terms to Rani Durgavati: put up no struggle, accept vassal status, and Akbar would permit her to continue to exercise some autonomy in Gond. Her councilors suggested that she accept the emperor's offer, but Rani is said to have replied, "Better to die free than live as a slave!"

Rani Durgavati descended from a line of warrior kings. Her ancestor, Vidyadhar, had fought off a Muslim invasion of India in the 12th century. By the time Akbar stood poised to invade her country, Rani had ruled for 14 years, ever since the death of her husband, Dalpatshah. The couple had a son, Vir Narayan, and Rani was determined to pass on to him a kingdom independent of the Mughals.

Gond had no professional army. Fighting men were farmers and craftsmen pressed into service in times of national emergency. To support these barely trained troops, Rani had perhaps 1,000 cavalrymen and a few hundred battle elephants.

Akbar, on the other hand, had trained fighting men. He invaded Gond with tens of thousands of infantry, 50,000 cavalry, and 1,000 battle elephants.

Rani and the Mughal invaders met at the Narrai Valley, where Rani positioned her army on narrow ground between hills on one side and two rivers on the other. The terrain gave her the advantage, and she drove back the Moghal army. Her 19-year-old son, Vir Narayan, led three successful charges against the Mughals, but then he was badly wounded by an arrow and forced to leave the battlefield.

Rani, mounted on her battle elephant, took full command of the Hindu forces. Then she, too, was wounded by arrows: one pierced her jaw, another buried itself in her neck. She fell unconscious, and when she regained her senses, her mahout, who drove her elephant, pleaded with her to let him take her to safety—the battle was lost. Rather than live to see her people defeated, Rani drew her dagger and killed herself.

For centuries, Rani was a tragic figure in India's history. During the independence movement early in the 20th century, she was recast as a heroine who resisted foreign occupation of India.

Rani Durgavati seated under a canopy, listens to music.

Philip II

King of Spain (1527–1598)

Philip II saw himself as the defender of Catholic Europe against the Protestants and the Ottoman Turks. By casting himself in this role, he was almost constantly at war and his treasury, in spite of the immense revenue that poured in from Spain's colonies in the New World, was almost always empty.

It must have been a frustrating life for the king. Everywhere he turned, he was met by rebellion. In 1567, in an attempt to force the Moriscos, the descendants of the Moors living in Granada, to assimilate completely into Spanish society, Philip issued a decree that banned Moorish dress, forbade anyone to speak Arabic or Berber, and required all Moriscos to take Christian Spanish names. The Moriscos rebelled, and it took three years of hard fighting to subdue them.

In the Low Countries, the situation was worse. These were Philip's ancestral lands, inherited from his grandfather Philip the Handsome. Anger over Philip's high taxes, combined with the emergence of fiery Calvinist preachers, led to a revolution in which both sides were guilty of the worst atrocities. Ultimately it ended in partition: what is now Belgium and Luxemburg remained under Spanish control, while what is today the Netherlands became independent.

A far greater disaster was Philip's war with England, a land over which he had once been king (he had married Mary I, Henry VIII's eldest child). In 1588, to depose Elizabeth I, restore Catholic rule, and avenge the judicial murder of Mary, Queen of Scots, Philip sent his Armada of 130 ships to invade England. The Spanish fleet was defeated by the English at sea, then destroyed by violent storms.

One of his major victories, however, occurred at another naval battle, Lepanto in 1571. Here Spain joined with other European powers and destroyed an Ottoman fleet, ending the Turks' dream of complete naval supremacy in the Mediterranean.

Although constantly dealing with conflict, Philip insisted on hearing the details of virtually every aspect of his administration. He believed it was his duty to listen to the appeals of even the humblest subject in his empire.

IVAN IV THE TERRIBLE

Tsar of All Russia (1530–1584)

In balance, Ivan the Terrible was not all bad. To defend Russia, he created a standing army. To handle disputes among the peasants, he established a council known as the Zemsky Sobor. To increase trade with Western Europe, he opened the port of Archangel on the White Sea to English merchants known as the Muscovy Company. He welcomed into his country German craftsmen who could teach new skills to the Russians. He subdued the Mongol khans of Kazan and Astrakhan, and pushed into Siberia. In thanksgiving for his victory at Kazan, he commissioned the Cathedral of St. Basil, arguably Russia's greatest architectural treasure.

Ivan's terrible period began in 1553, when he fell deathly ill. He called to his bedside the *boyars*, the noblemen of the country, to hear them swear allegiance to his son, who was still an infant. Many boyars refused, believing that with Ivan's death, the crown would be up for grabs. But Ivan recovered, and ever afterwards was suspicious of his nobles. A worse blow came in 1560 when Ivan's beloved wife, Anastasia, died. Ivan was convinced some boyars had poisoned her, and his grief and rage unleashed a bloodbath on those he perceived as his enemies. He had thousands rounded up, tortured, and murdered. Ivan executed not only the guilty, but also their families, so that no one would remain alive to pray for their souls. He was carrying his vendetta into the next world.

A fresh wave of terror began in 1565 with the creation of the Oprichnina, a fearsome, violent squad of "enforcers," who fanned out across the countryside, wrapped in black cowls, riding black horses, with the heads of dogs mounted on the pommels of their saddles. The Oprichnina hunted down suspected traitors—boyars as well as peasants. Precisely how many they killed is unknown, certainly hundreds.

In 1581, Ivan struck his daughter-in-law for dressing immodestly. The blow was so severe that she miscarried. When her husband, Ivan's son, came to her defense, the tsar struck the young man in the head with his heavy metal walking stick. To Ivan's horror, the prince died from the blow.

In 1584, Ivan died suddenly while playing chess. Poison was suspected, and in the 1960s, when his tomb was opened, his body was found to contain a lethal level of mercury.

WILLIAM THE SILENT

Prince of Orange (1533–1584)

William was born into a Lutheran family but was raised a Catholic as a condition for inheriting the title Prince of Orange. As a young man, he became one of Charles V's favorites; during the ceremony in which the gout-afflicted king of Spain abdicated, he leaned on William's shoulder for support.

In 1559, as Calvinism gained ground among the people of the Low Countries, King Philip established the Inquisition there. The persecution of his Protestant subjects disturbed William and led him to consider, probably for the first time in his life, opposing the policies of his king. The Protestants of the Low Countries reacted with a wave of iconoclasm. From August to October 1566, Calvinist mobs attacked Catholic churches and monasteries, smashing statues and stained glass windows, destroying paintings, and committing acts of sacrilege that shocked and infuriated Catholics. The governor of the entire region, Margaret of Parma, asked several noblemen, including William, to intervene to restore order, but Philip II believed stronger measures were called for. He sent Fernando Alvarez de Toledo, duke of Alba, to the Low Countries. In response, William (who was said to be named "the Silent" because of his refusal to weigh in on controversial topics) resigned his offices and raised a rebel army.

His first success was capturing the town of Brielle. Soon he captured almost every other city and town in Holland and Zeeland. In 1579, the northern provinces united and in 1584 renounced their allegiance to Spain. But the union was not as perfect as William would have liked: neither Calvinists nor Catholics were willing to grant each other tolerance in cities or provinces where one religion or the other was dominant. (William, by this time, had become a Calvinist).

Philip II declared William a traitor and set a price of 25,000 crowns on his head. Balthasar Gerard, a 27-year-old French Catholic, despised William as a renegade to his king and his faith. He made an appointment to call on William at his home in Delft on July 10, 1584. As William descended a flight of stairs to meet him, Gerard drew a pistol, shot William in the chest and killed him.

William the Silent is not only the Father of The Netherlands, he is also the first statesman to be assassinated with a handgun.

A satirical painting that shows Philip II of Spain riding The Netherlands cow, Elizabeth I of England feeding it, and William the Silent holding it steady by the horns

ELIZABETH I

Queen of England (1533–1603)

The two issues that dominated Elizabeth's reign were religion and whom she should marry. By choosing Protestantism as England's state religion, she antagonized her Catholic subjects and made England a target for Catholic powers, such as France and Spain, who might try to depose her. She lifted the anti-heresy laws, but persecuted Catholics under the guise that they were politically disloyal because they would not recognize her title, Supreme Governor of the Church of England.

Time and again Elizabeth's advisors and even Parliament pleaded with her to marry to provide the kingdom with an heir, but Elizabeth always feared that a husband would try to dominate her. She toyed with the idea of marrying her childhood friend and close confidant, Robert Dudley, or the French prince, Francois, Duke of Anjou, but nothing came of these flirtations. She liked the company of handsome young men and over the years she had several favorites—Dudley, Robert, Earl of Essex, and Sir Walter Raleigh.

The greatest threat to Elizabeth was her cousin, Mary, Queen of Scots. If Elizabeth were to die, Mary would become queen of England, and since Mary was a Catholic, she would try to lead England back to union with Rome. Furthermore, Mary had a son, so her line would continue. Sadly, Mary had none of Elizabeth's political savvy; she became entangled in civil unrest in Scotland until she was forced to ride to England to ask for Elizabeth's protection. Elizabeth gave it—by imprisoning her cousin for 21 years. In the end, she had Mary beheaded on a charge of plotting with English Catholic conspirators to murder Elizabeth and become queen of England.

Elizabeth's reign was graced with a literary renaissance, particularly in drama and poetry. William Shakespeare and Christopher Marlowe dominated the stage, while sharing the limelight with such poets as Sir Philip Sidney, Edmund Spenser, and John Donne.

In 1601, two years before her death, Elizabeth delivered a kind of valedictory speech to Parliament. "There is no jewel, be it of never so rich a price, which I set before this jewel; I mean your love," she said. "You may have many a wiser prince sitting in this seat, but you never have had, or shall have, any who loves you better."

Portrait of Elizabeth I toward the end of her reign

TUSKALOOSA

Chief of the Mississippian Tribes (died c. 1542)

In 1539, the governor of Cuba, Hernan de Soto, with 800 men, called upon Chief Tuskaloosa at his village, Atahachi, in what is now central Alabama. A member of de Soto's expedition, described Tuskaloosa as, "tall of person, muscular, lean, and symmetrical. He was the suzerian of many territories, and of numerous people, being equally feared by his vassals and the neighboring nations."

The Spaniards held a little tournament to entertain/impress the Indians; several times, the riders, their lances leveled, charged the chief, but Tuskaloosa did not flinch, in fact he seemed barely interested in the joust. After the Indians and the Spanish dined together, de Soto asked the chief to provide men to carry the Spaniards baggage and women to cook and provide sexual favors. Tuskaloosa refused, so the Spanish took him prisoner, with the understanding that his life depended on the good behavior of his tribe.

Nonetheless, the Indians were not cooperative. They would not provide canoes for the Spanish to cross the Alabama River; two of de Sotos men were captured by the Indians and the porters and women never arrived.

The Spanish pushed on to the town of Mabilia where they found hundreds of well-armed young warriors behind a wooden stockade. Tuskaloosa told de Soto he was tired of traveling with the Spanish, he would stay in Mabilia. It was a thinly veiled way of saying it was time for the Spanish to leave. But de Soto did not take the hint. As the Spanish tried to force Tuskaloosa outside the palisade, another chief intervened; in a scuffle, a Spaniard drew his sword and cut off the chief's arm. At this, the warriors attacked, and the Spanish ran outside the town.

For eight or nine hours, a battle raged around Mabilia. Then the Spanish breached the walls, set fire to the houses, and massacred the warriors. Among the dead were Tuskaloosa's son, but the chief's body was never found. He may have escaped.

As for de Soto, he lost 200 men and 148 were wounded. All of his supplies had been carried inside Mabilia, and all were destroyed in the fire. In addition, 45 horses were killed. They were in a far worse state than before they took Tuskaloosa prisoner. Yet they continued the expedition further into the country.

De Soto "discovering" the Mississippi

MARY I

Queen of Scots (1542–1587)

Mary's life would have been so much happier if she could have remained queen of France. At age five, she had been sent there to be raised by her future in-laws (Mary was betrothed to the French Dauphin, Francis). But their marriage and reign were brief—in December 1560, after only two years, Francis died and Mary went home.

Her homeland, which she had not seen in fourteen years, had become a dangerous place. The country was split between the dominant Protestant faction that had led a violent Reformation in the country, and the minority Catholic faction.

Mary adopted a policy of religious toleration, attending Mass privately in her palace chapel. In 1565, she married Henry, Lord Darnley, an Englishman and a Catholic. They had a child, James, but the marriage was not a success. Darnley wanted a share of royal power; Mary, who had come to think him a fool, refused. In retaliation, Darnley schemed with some Scottish lords to murder Mary's closest advisor, David Rizzio. They burst into Mary's private apartments, dragged Rizzio into the next room, and stabbed him to death. A year later a second plot, fomented by no-one-knows-who, blew up a house at Kirk o'Field where Darnley was confined to a sickbed. His body was found in the garden and it is uncertain if he was killed in the explosion or finished off by someone afterward. It was widely believed in Scotland that Mary was involved in the plot. Her hasty marriage three months later to James, Earl of Bothwell, did nothing to improve her reputation.

Within weeks, the Scottish lords rebelled against her, imprisoned Bothwell, forced her to abdicate, and separated her from her son. Mary fled to England, hoping Elizabeth would give her an army to retake her kingdom. Instead, Elizabeth kept her under house arrest for 21 years. During those years, she became the focus of Catholic plots in England and abroad. In 1587, she was charged with conspiring against Elizabeth, and although she argued that no English court had any right to try her, she was convicted and sentenced to death. At her execution, she wore a blood-red chemise, the Catholic liturgical color of martyrs. She was buried a year after her death in Peterborough Cathedral. When her son, James, became king of England, he moved Mary's body to Westminster Abbey, where it lies in a magnificent white marble tomb.

Mary tries to intervene as Scottish lords murder David Rizzio

AKBAR THE GREAT
Mughal Emperor (1542–1605)

Throughout his reign, Akbar's relationship with his Hindu subjects was ambiguous. At one point, he eliminated two hated symbols of Muslim oppression—the *jizya*, a tax all non-Muslims had been obliged to pay for the right to continue to practice their own religion, and a second tax assessed on all Hindus who traveled to Hindu shrines. Then he reinstated the *jizya*. Then he abolished it again. Furthermore, he lifted the obligation that Hindus were answerable to *shari'a*, Islamic law, and restored to them their own law code and their own courts. He gave the Hindu states some degree of autonomy. He permitted Hindus to build new temples, but only if they received his express permission first: a Hindu general who began construction of a temple without permission was forced to convert it to a mosque. As a result, Akbar's reputation among Indian Hindus is mixed.

Akbar was a man who loved beauty. In his quest for a perfect dwelling place, he built Fatehpur Sikri, a magnificent complex that includes a palace, a mosque, an immense garden, and a worship hall. It is an architectural marvel, but Akbar's engineers constructed it too far from any source of water, and so after Akbar's death, his successors abandoned it.

His conquests included the states of Bengal, Gujarat, Kashmir, and Kabul. Much as he loved Fatehpur Sikri, the water problem made it difficult for him to live there full time. Akbar spent part of each year traveling throughout his realm observing how the vassal princes and his own officials were governing the empire.

European visitors to his court described Akbar as pale, tall, broad shouldered, and having very long arms. To enhance his greatness, stories circulated that at age 19 he killed an attacking tiger with a single blow of his sword, and on another occasion, forced a wild elephant to kneel before him.

Akbar's reputation is a complicated one. He left behind him a greater empire; he attempted, not very successfully, to unite his subjects, but his own worldview got in the way of his good intentions.

Abkar (center) among his people

Tokugawa Ieyasu

Shogun of Japan (1543–1616)

There was an emperor in Japan in the 16th century but he was a figurehead. Real power lay in the hands of the great samurai families, a class of aristocratic warriors. For at least a century, the families had been fighting among themselves for absolute power in Japan. Tokugawa was caught up in the turmoil early—at age four, his father was obliged to hand him over as a hostage to an enemy clan.

Tokugawa was 17 when he became the leader of his clan. His domain and his army were small, but he made the best of it, putting down rebellions among his subjects and reviving military discipline among his troops. Since he was relatively weak, Tokugawa always looked for an opportunity to ally himself with a powerful lord. But life was not all warfare: Tokugawa married and started a family, and he developed a passion for falconry that would last throughout his life. And all the while, he continued to build his army.

By 1600, Tokugawa had one of the largest fighting forces in Japan. At Sekigahara, 50 miles northeast of Kyoto, he met his chief rival and defeated him. Tokugawa was now the most powerful man in Japan. In 1603, the emperor issued a proclamation recognizing Tokugawa as shogun, a kind of military dictator.

The Portuguese, Dutch, and English were all clamoring for the right to trade with Japan; Tokugawa welcomed them all since international commerce would enrich his country. He was especially interested in acquiring European firearms. Catholic missionaries from Portugal and Spain had been permitted to teach their religion in Japan and they were having great success, with tens of thousands of converts. Tokugawa regarded these Japanese Catholics as persons of uncertain loyalty—in a showdown between Japan and the European powers, would they side with their homeland or with their fellow Christians? Tokugawa instigated an anti-Christian policy that would be enforced brutally by his successors.

Tokugawa established himself at Edo, modern-day Tokyo, where he built the largest castle complex in the world.

Tokugawa put an end to civil war and brought unity, peace, and new wealth to Japan. He welcomed foreign trade but resisted foreign ideas. He insisted that Japan must remain Japanese, but he was not an isolationist like later shoguns.

DON JUAN OF AUSTRIA

Governor-General of the Low Countries (1547–1578)

This dashing military man crammed tremendous accomplishments into a short life. As the illegitimate son of Charles V, he was kept out of the way, but when Philip II became king, he recognized his half-brother, gave him a large income and the title "Don Juan of Austria."

Juan longed for a military career, and in 1568, he had his first experience, fighting Moorish pirates in the Mediterranean. The next year, Philip ordered Juan to put down the Moriscos Uprising in Granada.

At age 24, Juan received his greatest commission: the Ottoman Turks were preparing an enormous fleet to dominate the Mediterranean; a Holy League comprised of Spain, Venice, Genoa, Savoy, the Papal States, and the Knights Hospitaller were assembling a navy to defeat the Turks. Philip named Juan commander of the Holy League's fleet. Young, handsome, energetic, and with a track record of victories, Don Juan inspired loyalty and confidence among his men and his fellow officers. On October 7, 1571, the Holy League and the Turks met at Lepanto in the Gulf of Patras off the coast of Greece. It was a stunning victory in which the Holy League sank 50 Turkish galleys, captured 137 more, liberated 10,000 Christian galley slaves, and killed, wounded, or captured 20,000 Turks. Don Juan became the hero of Europe.

Next, Philip named Juan governor-general of the Low Countries where the provinces were in open rebellion against Spain. It was a difficult assignment, but Juan comforted himself with a romantic notion of using the Low Countries as a launching place for a raid on England to free Mary, Queen of Scots. Once she was free, he would marry her.

He did enjoy one major success in the Low Countries—the Perpetual Edict of 1577 in which he promised to withdraw Spanish troops from the region if the people recognized his authority and returned to the Catholic religion. The seven northern provinces—modern-day The Netherlands—rejected the offer, but the ten southern provinces—present-day Belgium, Luxemburg, and Nord-Pas de Calais in France signed the edict.

Don Juan died a year later of typhus. In spite of his illegitimacy, Philip buried him with the Spanish royal family in the crypt beneath the Escorial palace.

The naval battle of Lepanto

Boris Godunov

Tsar of All Russia (c. 1551–1605)

If it is true, as the forensic evidence gathered in the 1960s suggests, that Ivan the Terrible died of mercury poisoning, Boris Gudunov was probably one of the men who plotted his death. It's also likely that Boris' agents slit the throat of Ivan's 10-year-old son, Dmitri, to eliminate any possibility of the boy growing up to be a rival.

Boris had no solid claim to the crown except that he was one of three men named by the dying Ivan the Terrible to a council to rule Russia on behalf of his feeble son, Feodor. From 1584 until 1598, Boris served on this council, but he was soon acting as sole regent. He devised various strategies to keep Russia out of war: rather than confront the Ottomans directly, he sent funds to anti-Turkish forces in the Crimea. To reduce Tartar and Finnish raids, he built new towns along the borders. To keep Siberia in Russian hands, he colonized it, founding new cities such as Tobolsk.

In 1598 Feodor died. The patriarch of Moscow urged the *boyars*, or nobles, to elect Boris tsar. Boris preferred to be elected by a national assembly which would give the appearance that the Russian people had elected him. Such an assembly was called and the vote in his favor was unanimous. Weeks later, Boris was crowned tsar.

Boris genuinely wanted to improve life in Russia. He invited foreign scholars to open schools, and sent some of the most promising Russian boys to be educated at universities abroad. But he always remained a suspicious man, fearful of plots and rivals. In the last years of his life, a man appeared claiming to be Dmitri who, miraculously, had escaped his assassins. He gathered followers and an army and, soon after Boris died in 1605, this pretender had himself crowned tsar. False Dmitri, as he came to be known, ruled for ten months before he was exposed as a fraud, murdered, and his body burned.

RUDOLF II

Holy Roman Emperor, King of Hungary and Bohemia (1552–1612)

Rudolf was a king-emperor who had no interest in governing. His passions were art—commissioning it and collecting it—and scientific studies, although in this case, his interest in science spilled over into a fascination with the occult.

He made his capital at Prague, and invited painters, architects, philosophers, and astronomers to enrich his court and his city. He built a new town hall for the city, a new palace for the archbishop, and several new churches. His taste could run to the fanciful, even the grotesque, which explains why one of his favorite artists was Giuseppe Archimboldo who painted many bizarre portraits of Rudolf, using fruits, vegetables, and tree roots for the components of the emperor's face and body.

His collection had a grab-bag quality: fine books, ancient coins, exquisitely cut jewels, fine scientific instruments. He also purchased the best fine art on the market—works by Leonardo da Vinci, Albrecht Durer, Pieter Breughel the Elder, and Paolo Veronese.

The astronomers, Tycho Brahe and Johannes Kepler, worked at Rudolf's court, but so did Edward Kelley, a medium, and John Dee, an alchemist said to dabble in sorcery, who worked with the emperor trying to find the process that would turn base metals into gold.

When Rudolf did attempt to govern, he made a mess of things. For 11 years, he fought a war with the Turks, most of it battled out in Hungary. His Hungarian subjects, sick of the bloodshed and devastation, revolted. Rudolf's family stepped in and forced him to hand over his authority to his brother Matthias, who made peace with the rebels and the Turks. But Rudolf, who had caused all the trouble to begin with, thought Matthias had made too many concessions and tried to start a new war with the Turks. This time his family insisted that he abdicate in Matthias' favor.

Rudolf died angry and frustrated, but surrounded by lovely things.

HENRY IV

King of France (1553–1610)

The notorious St. Bartholomew Day Massacre, August 24, 1575, took place during the festivities celebrating Henry's marriage to the French princess Margaret of Valois (daughter of Catherine de Medici and sister of King Charles IX). While virtually every other leading Huguenot was murdered, Henry escaped by pretending to abjure Protestantism and making a false confession of faith as a Catholic. His in-laws never trusted his opportune conversion, and kept him a virtual prisoner. He escaped in February 1576, rejoined his Protestant friends, and led a new war of religion against the French king.

Over the years, one by one, all of Catherine de Medici's sons died. The French royal family had no more male heirs, and the next in line was Henry. But the French establishment would not accept a Huguenot king. In 1593, Henry solved the problem by becoming Catholic again. At the time of his conversion, he is said to have quipped, "Paris is worth a Mass."

After decades of war, France was in a near-disastrous condition. Henry believed that, if he was to revive his realm, he must be an absolute monarch: he consolidated all power in himself, ignored the Estates General (the national assembly), and interfered in the administration of cities and towns. But he also encouraged agriculture, industry, and new ventures such as silk-making. He made peace with England and Spain, and founded a military academy to train officers for the French army. He adorned Paris with the Tuilleries, the Pont Neuf, the Hotel-de-Ville, and the Place Royale. And he sent the explorer Samuel de Champlain to Canada to evaluate the resources there and the feasibility of establishing French colonies in the wilderness.

Henry had the common touch; he was at ease with anyone of any rank. The common people loved his wit and candor, the upper classes came to respect his ability to read character.

On May 14, 1610, Henry was riding in his coach through Paris when a Catholic fanatic named Francois Ravaillac (who believed the king was planning to make war on the pope) lunged at the king, stabbing him to death with a dagger.

The marriage of Henry IV and Margaret of Valois

JAMES I AND VI
King of England and Scotland (1566–1625)

England's Elizabeth I died childless and without appointing a successor, although her councilors stood around her deathbed, pleading with her name to someone. The logical choice was her closest surviving relative, James VI of Scotland, son of the tragic Mary, Queen of Scots.

James' mother had abdicated and fled the country when he was a year old, after which he was raised by stern Scottish nobles and even sterner Calvinist tutors. The lesson they forced on James—which he always rejected—was that the king ruled at the sufferance of the nobles and the people. James was freed from such limitations when he became king of England; beginning with Henry VII, the English had grown accustomed to the centralized authority of the monarch. But James took it one step further, declaring his belief in the divine right of kings, in other words, that he had been chosen by God, and any dissent was rebellion against the Lord. The Scots despised this doctrine, and even the English thought it went too far.

At his accession, James hinted to England's Catholics that he might be more tolerant of their religion than Elizabeth had been. When he reneged, a band of angry Catholic gentlemen planted barrels of gunpowder under the Houses of Parliament to blow it up when the Lords, the Commons, and the king and royal family were all in attendance. A Catholic nobleman named Monteagle received an anonymous tip to stay away from Parliament on November 5, 1605. Suspicious of the warning, he passed it along to the king, who ordered a search of the Parliament complex. In the cellars, guards found the gunpowder and one of the conspirators, Guy Fawkes, about to light the fuse.

The two most enduring achievements of James' reign was the English colonization of Virginia and his sponsorship of a new English translation of the Bible, known as the King James Version. The first settlement was named Jamestown, for the king. As for the Bible, produced at the height of England's literary renaissance, the King James Version is a masterpiece of English literature. And James deserves credit for one thing more—at no point during his reign did he lead England into war.

Nzinga Mbande

Queen of Ndongo and Matamba (c. 1583–1663)

By the mid-16th century, the Spanish and Portuguese colonies in the Americas were clamoring for slaves. To fill the demand, slave traders—both Europeans and Africans—raided West Africa, shipping tens of thousands of men, women, and children across the Atlantic. Any African tribe or kingdom that attempted to interfere risked destruction.

In 1624, Nzinga Mbande became queen of the Ndongo people, whose lands lay east of Luanda in present-day Angola. To put an end to her own people being carried off as slaves, Nzinga made a treaty with the Portuguese. They agreed to stop raiding in Ndongo lands and Nzinga and her people would serve as expediters, helping the Portuguese transport their slaves from the interior of Africa to the coast for shipment. To seal the bargain, Nzinga agreed to be baptized and took the Christian name Ana.

In two years, the Portuguese had reneged on the treaty. Angola's location was ideal for the slave trade, and they wanted it as part of their empire. Nzinga gathered her people and fled into the interior where they established a new kingdom called Matamba. Nzinga let it be known that runaway slaves and Africans trained in the use of European weapons were welcome.

To strike at the Portuguese, she created a professional warrior class, the *kilombo*, in which teenage boys severed their ties to their families and moved into a kind of military academy where they were trained to fight; their only loyalty was to Nzinga and their fellow warriors.

In 1641, Nzinga formed an alliance with the Dutch, fomented rebellion in Ndongo, then attacked with her kilombo. They captured Luanda but they could not hold it—the Portuguese were too strong. She was forced to retreat back to Matamba. The war dragged on sporadically for another 16 years until Nzinga and the Portuguese agreed to a truce. Once again, she set up her kingdom as a commercial intermediary state that carried trade goods from central Africa to the ports along the coast.

A host of legends grew up around her—that she had a harem of male lovers, that she was a cannibal. The stories were not true, but they titillated European audiences. Nzinga died peacefully in her bed at age 80.

This European portrait of Nzinga Mbande emphasizes her beauty and her savagery

GUSTAVUS ADOLPHUS

King of Sweden (1594–1632)

Only sixteen when he became king of Sweden, Gustavus Adolphus spent the first years of his reign at war, first with Denmark, then with Russia. These early conflicts gave him hands-on military experience and began his formation as one of the great generals of the 17th century.

Sweden had a small population, but Gustavus found that if he drafted 10 percent of all men over 15, he would have an army of 30,000. To this he added mercenaries hired from the Protestant states in Germany. He developed a new T-shaped battle formation for his infantry that made them more effective than the straight-line formation popular in other lands, and he revived the cavalry charge that had gone out of fashion with military strategists.

His adult life was consumed by the Thirty Years War, the most destructive of the wars of religion yet seen in Europe. Gustavus' astonishing victories made him a champion of the Protestant cause. He defeated Johann Tserclaes von Tilly, the commander of the armies of the Holy Roman Emperor, at Breitenfeld in 1631, and in a battle at the River Lech, defeated the imperial troops again and killed Tilly.

Gustavus' luck changed after the emperor appointed a new commander, Albrecht von Wallenstein, a man whose military talents were equal to that of the Swedish king. Gustavus attacked Wallenstein's camp outside Nuremberg, but the imperial general drove him off. A few weeks later outside Lutzen, the armies met again. Gustavus was still trying to recover from his heavy losses at Nuremberg, but he would not back away from this fight. Gustavus would not put on his steel breastplate—he had grown so fat that it did not fit comfortably, furthermore it chafed some old war wounds. He decided to lead one of his famous cavalry charges himself. The battlefield was shrouded in mist, and somehow Gustavus became separated from his men. Some imperial troops spotted him and shot the king dead.

The loss of Gustavus Adolphus unnerved the Protestant army initially, but his second-in-command, Bernhard of Saxe-Weimar, rallied the men. Shouting, "Avenge the king!" they attacked the imperial forces and won the battle.

Gustavus Adolphus is mortally wounded while leading a cavalry charge at the Battle of Lutzen

POCAHONTAS

Princess of the Powhatans (c. 1596–1617)

When English settlers founded Jamestown in Virginia in 1607, Pocahontas was between ten and twelve years old. This engaging young girl was fascinated by the strangers and spent a good deal of time visiting them.

The most famous incident in her life came in December, 1607. Powhatan warriors had captured Captain John Smith and taken him to their capital, Werowocomoco, on the York River. The captive Englishman was thrown to the ground at the feet of the chief, Pocahontas' father, and, as a warrior raised a war club over his head, Pocahontas rushed forward, and threw herself over Smith's body. In recent years, historians have come to believe that the rescue-from-execution was actually an elaborate adoption ceremony. Smith would not have understood this, just as the Powhatans did not understand that, although the chief had adopted Smith, Smith would never be subservient to him.

While her role in saving John Smith is not clear, Pocahontas did help the English colonists: she brought them food when they were starving; kept the peace between them and her people; and negotiated with the English to release all the Powhatans they were holding hostage.

Yet the tensions between the two nations kept mounting until the First Anglo-Powhatan War broke out in 1610. Even during the fighting Pocahontas continued to visit her friends at the settlement. In 1613, the English insisted that she remain with them as a hostage. In fact, they treated her like a guest, and within a year, she had converted to the Anglican faith, taken the name Rebecca, and become engaged to a colonist named John Rolfe. In 1614 they married.

Two years later, Rolfe, Pocahontas, and their infant son Thomas sailed to England where she was presented to King James I. One courtier marveled that Pocahontas "carried herself as the daughter of a King, and was accordingly respected... by persons of Honor." In 1617, the family planned to return to Virginia when Pocahontas fell ill and died in Gravesend.

Although she is often portrayed as a romantic figure, Pocahontas was a great deal more—the guardian of the first successful English settlement in America, and the first Native American to attempt to bring about a harmonious existence between Europeans and Indians.

Pocahontas in the dress of an English gentlewoman

Ætatis suæ 21. A°. 1616.

…toaks als Rebecka daughter to the mighty Prince
…whatan Emperour of Attanoughkomouck als Virgin…
…verted and baptized in the Christian faith, a…
…Wife to the …wor… Mr Tho: Rolff.

CHARLES I

King of England and Scotland (1600–1649)

Thanks to portraits by Anthony van Dyck, we have an image of Charles I as the most stylish of English kings. His precisely trimmed goatee and mustache, his wavy hair falling halfway down his back, his broad-brimmed hat set at a rakish angle, his silken tunic trimmed with a thick band of exquisite lace, King Charles looked the part of a self-confident gentleman.

He had his flaws, of course. Raised by his father, James I, to believe in his God-given to rule, Charles displayed disdain for the sensitivities of his subjects. At a time when the religious mood in the country was increasingly puritanical, Charles encouraged the Church of England to adopt certain Catholic practices, such as placing a gold crucifix or at least a cross on the altar. His wife, the French Catholic princess, Henrietta Maria, brought a throng of her friends over from France and persuaded the king to show particular favoritism to these French Catholics. Charles' inattentiveness to the temper of the times put him at odds with the Parliament, who struck back at the king by refusing to vote him any money. At the urging of his queen, Charles issued arrest warrants for five members of Parliament. Incensed, the Puritans and Parliamentarians in the country called for a revolution.

Charles sent his wife and children out of the country, established his headquarters at Oxford, and set about recovering his authority. He was a courageous, decisive commander, but the Parliamentarian army was not only magnificently equipped but also dominated by Puritans who regarded their war against the king as a heaven-sent mission. The Royalists could not match their supplies or fanatical commitment.

In 1648, Charles surrendered to a Scottish army, perhaps hoping they would keep him safe from the Parliamentarians; instead, they handed him over. In December 1648, a tribunal of Puritans and Parliamentarians sat in judgment on their king. There was no precedent for such a thing under English law, but the men of the tribunal were undeterred. Charles, however, refused to recognize the tribunal and would not enter a plea. The verdict was a foregone conclusion—guilty of high treason. But the sentence was not so easy to obtain: in the end, the vote was 68 to 67 to behead the king. He was executed publicly on January 30, 1649, an event that shocked Europe.

Charles I kneeling on scaffold at his execution

MURAD IV

Sultan of the Ottoman Empire (1612–1640)

The two greatest challenges at the beginning of Murad's reign were two elite units within his army—the Spahis, who were cavalrymen, and the Janissaries, who exercised Spartan-like discipline on the battlefield. The decisive moment came in 1632 when a band of Spahis and Janissaries intruded into the sultan's palace and demanded the execution of his grand vizier and 16 other leading men of the imperial court. The unfortunate men were executed, but after these members of the elite forces had withdrawn, Murad began plotting his revenge.

He sent loyal troops to attack and kill many of the Spahis and Janissaries. Next, under the guise of restoring religious purity, he shut down Constantinople's wineshops (Muslims were forbidden to drink alcohol), as well as the coffee houses—the sultan was convinced, with reason, that political dissenters met at these places. Murad also banned tobacco.

Murad was a tall, powerful man whose favorite weapon was a mace that weighed 132 pounds. After dark he would dress as a civilian and wander the streets; if he saw anyone smoking, or drinking wine or coffee, he would crush his skull with a single blow of his mace.

Murad's courage matched his physical strength; he was the last Ottoman sultan personally to lead his men into battle. In the war against Persia, he captured Azerbaijan, Yerevan, Tabriz, and Hamadan. He also recaptured Baghdad, which an earlier Ottoman sultan had lost. But after the conquest, he admitted to feeling a sense of let-down. "I guess trying to capture Baghdad was better than Baghdad itself," he said.

In the final years of his short life, he began to act erratically. At night he would charge out of the harem, barefooted and wearing a loose dressing gown; with his sword drawn, he charged through the streets, killing any pedestrian who crossed his path. Murad died at age 27 of cirrhosis of the liver—in defiance of his own law, he had taken to drinking wine and had become an alcoholic.

POWHATAN

Chief of the Powhatans (died 1618)

Wahunsunacock was his given name; Powhatan was the name he took when he became supreme chief of the 30 tribes that populated eastern Virginia. Very little is known about the early years of his reign: he defeated the Kecoughtan tribe and forced them to pay tribute to him; as punishment for some unrecorded slight, he annihilated the Chesapeakes who lived at present-day Virginia Beach; but he had no success forcing the Chickahominy tribe to submit to his rule. In 1608, Captain John Smith noted that every Indian tribe in the James and York river valleys paid homage to Powhatan, except the Chickahominies.

The decisive moment in Powhatan's life and that of his people was the arrival of the English in 1607. In their first encounters with one another, the English were impressed that Powhatan acted like a king, speaking proudly and showing no fear. As for Powhatan, he thought the English with their remarkable weapons were exactly the allies he needed to subdue the Monacan tribe. The famous episode in which Pocahontas, Powhatan's daughter, saved the life of captive John Smith may in fact have been an adoption ritual intended to make Smith a member of the tribe who would be obliged to fight for Powhatan against Monacans.

Powhatan's policy toward the English was a combination of pity and anxiety. In a land filled with wildlife, the hapless English could not feed themselves, so at the urging of his daughter Pocahontas, the chief sent gifts of food. But the English did not limit themselves to their fort—bit by bit they encroached onto Indian land. In 1609, regular shipments of supplies began arriving from England, Smith returned home, and the colonists began moving out of the Jamestown fort and establishing farms. An inconclusive war broke out, after which Powhatan remained supreme chief but real authority passed to his brother, Opechancanough, who had an aggressive anti-English policy.

In 1617, Uttamatomakkin, one of the Powhatans who had accompanied Rolfe and Pocahontas to England, brought Powhatan word that his daughter had died overseas. And he had more bad news: there were many more Englishmen than the Indians had imagined—their island across the Atlantic was filled with them. Powhatan retired from office, sank into a profound depression, and died the following year.

English colonist Christopher Newport presents Powhatan with a crown

CHRISTINA

Queen of Sweden (1626–1689)

Christina was only six years old when her father, King Gustavus Adolphus, was killed in battle. Her regent was Axel Oxenstierna, an intelligent, imaginative, utterly loyal man who continued Gustavus Adolphus' policy of making Sweden a major power in northern Europe. Oxenstierna also directed Christina's education, bringing in tutors so that she acquired mastery in the sciences, humanities, and languages. When she was 16, Oxenstierna began the princess' political education by inviting her to attend meetings of the Regency Council.

At age 18, Christina was crowned and began ruling in her own right. She embarked on a spending spree, buying and commissioning works of art, starting lavish building projects, and rewarding Swedish veterans of the Thirty Years War with generous gifts of land. Oxenstierna tried to control her profligacy, but the young queen ignored him.

The queen's advisors were eager for her to marry and have children who would preserve the dynasty, but Christina put them off. Then, in 1651, she shocked her court and the country when she announced that she would abdicate in favor of her cousin, Charles. The cries of dismay dissuaded her temporarily, but in 1654, she went through with the abdication and left Sweden forever. While staying at Innsbruck in Austria, she revealed that she had converted to Catholicism. This caused even more grief in Sweden, given that her father had been a champion of Protestantism during the Thirty Years War.

She continued to Rome, where she decided to settle. There she shocked the pope by appearing at her audience dressed in red, the color of Roman prostitutes.

Her palace in Rome became a salon where scholars, aristocrats, and cardinals gathered for stimulating conversation. But in addition to being a hostess, Christina was also an inveterate schemer. Having given up a crown in Sweden, she tried to become queen of Naples, and later queen of Poland. When one of her own household frustrated her Naples scheme by warning the Spanish envoy there of an impending invasion, Christina had the man's throat cut—while she watched. The murder infuriated the pope—he did not appreciate having the Church embarrassed by its most prominent convert. Yet 30 years later when Christina died, the scandal was forgotten, and she was buried in St. Peter's Basilica—one of only two women buried there.

Shah Jahan
Mughal Emperor (1628–1666)

Shah Jahan is remembered as the heartbroken husband who immortalized his love for his wife, Mamtaz Mahal, by erecting one of the world's loveliest monuments to house her tomb—the Taj Mahal. Less well-known are his wars against the Hindus and Christians of his empire. In 1632, he ordered that all recently erected Hindu temples, or temples that were currently under construction, must be torn down. He also ordered leveled Christian churches in the cities of Agra and Lahore.

Next he turned his attention to a Portuguese settlement outside Calcutta. Jahan made absurd claims that the Portuguese were pirates who were kidnapping Muslims. He sent an army that destroyed the town and massacred all the Christian inhabitants. In this regard, Shah Jahan was no different than many other monarchs who took it upon themselves to ensure the religious purity of their realms.

Paradoxically, although Jahan had nothing but contempt for the Hindu religion, he was an avid admirer of Hindu poetry and Hindu music. Gifted Hindi poets and musicians were always welcome in his court, and he spoke to them fluently in their own language.

The Taj Mahal is Jahan's masterpiece: he demanded absolute perfection from the architects, sculptors, and mosaic artists, and that is what he got. Every detail is exquisite, and although the tomb is enriched with onyx, jasper, lapis lazuli, malachite, and other precious and semi-precious stones, the result is harmonious.

The Taj is not the shah's only magnum opus: he built the beautiful Jama Mosque in Delhi and Pearl Mosque in Agra. Outside Old Delhi, he built the Red Fort where he installed in the grand audience hall the Peacock Throne, which stood on four golden legs while twelve emerald pillars supported the canopy overhead. Jahan's desire for exquisite jewelry was so well known that jewelers came from as far as Europe to sell him their finest (and most expensive) stones.

Jahan's final years were tragic: his son Aurangzeb killed his three brothers, deposed his father, and had himself proclaimed shah. For eight years, Jahan lived a virtual prisoner in the Agra Fort, attended by his daughter Jahanara. At his death, he was buried beside his wife Mumtaz in the Taj Mahal.

Jan III Sobieski

King of Poland (1629–1696)

At age 47, Jan Sobieski, commander-in-chief of the army of Poland, was elected king. To assuage the disappointment of the Holy Roman Emperor, Leopold I, who had expected he would be elected king of Poland, Jan signed a mutual defense pact in the event that either realm was attacked by the Turks.

Seven years later, the pact came into effect. Kara Mustafa Pasha, the Ottoman sultan's grand vizier, marched 150,000 men to the gates of Vienna. The city was defended by only 10,000 troops, and the call went out to Jan, as well as German and Austrian princes, to come to Vienna's aid. Jan, with 37,000 men, brought the largest contingent.

The walls of Vienna were stronger than the Turks had expected, so they began digging tunnels beneath and planting mines to bring the battlements down. They succeeded in blowing up three bastions, and, on September 8, the Turks occupied a portion of the wall. The city's commander, Ernst Rudgier, Count von Starhemberg, warned his men to prepare to fight the Turks street by street and house by house.

Meanwhile, the rescuers had arrived. Before dawn, the combined armies of Poles, Austrians, and Germans arrayed themselves for battle. For 12 hours the fight raged on the plain outside Vienna. Then, at 5pm, Jan led a cavalry charge of 20,000 horsemen—one of the largest cavalry charges in history. As they smashed the Ottomans' ranks, a large detachment of the Viennese garrison poured out of the city to join the melee. The Turks fled, leaving behind 15,000 dead and wounded, 5,000 prisoners, all their artillery, their entire camp and all their supplies. The victory at Vienna marked the end of Ottoman invasions into Eastern Europe. In the years that followed they were pushed out of Hungary and Transylvania.

A euphoric Count von Starhemberg embraced and kissed King Jan, calling him a savior. Jan, modestly, replied, "Venimus. Vidimus. Deus vicit." We came. We saw. God conquered.

For the rest of his life, Jan Sobieski was celebrated as the hero of Western Europe. The pope assigned a new holy day to the anniversary of the battle, and an astronomer named a constellation after the king, *Scutum Sobiescianum*.

CHARLES II
King of England and Scotland (1630–1685)

At age sixteen, Charles was evacuated from England along with his mother Queen Henrietta Maria, and all his brothers and sisters, to the Continent while his father King Charles I, stayed behind to fight for his crown. Three years later, Charles I was beheaded by his own subjects, and there was nothing the prince could do to prevent it or rescue his father.

For the next 11 years, Charles lived like an unwelcome poor relation of Europe's royal families. He had no money to support himself or his tiny handful of followers; no army to retake England and very little hope of ever returning to England at all, let alone as king.

But in 1658, the leader of the Commonwealth, Oliver Cromwell, died. The English, tired of more than a decade of a puritanical military dictatorship, were ready to welcome their exiled king. After his coronation, he rounded up the regicides. Of the 59 who had signed Charles I's death warrant, 12 were already dead; 13 were executed; 19 were sentenced to life in prison, and the rest escaped overseas. Oliver Cromwell's corpse was dug up, his body hung in chains, and his head mounted on a stake.

Now that he had the love of the English people, Charles was determined not to lose it. He acted through his ministers, so if a policy proved unpopular, the ministers took the brunt of public displeasure while the king sat above the fray.

After the dour years of Puritan rule when even Christmas had been outlawed, Charles introduced music, dances, and spectacular entertainments on an epic scale. He also overturned an old prohibition and permitted women to perform in plays (previously the parts had been played by boys in women's costumes). Nell Gwynn, his favorite mistress was an actress.

Charles and his queen Catherine of Braganza never managed to have a child—all of Catherine's pregnancies ended in miscarriage. But he had at least 14 illegitimate children by his various mistresses.

Charles had tried to introduce religious tolerance in England, but the antagonisms between Puritans and Anglicans and Protestants and Catholics were too deeply rooted. The king's religious opinions were a mystery, until on his deathbed, he converted to Catholicism.

The King's gardener presenting Charles II with a pineapple

LOUIS XIV

King of France (1638–1715)

Louis XIV reigned for an astonishing 72 years. When he became king at age five, his mother, Anne of Austria, and his minister, Cardinal Jules Mazarin, ruled for him. When Mazarin died in 1661, 23-year-old Louis refused to appoint another first minister; henceforth, all power would be in his hands.

The 17th century was the age of absolute monarchs in Europe, and no one played the part more adeptly, with more certitude, or with a greater sense of glory than Louis. He adopted the sun as his personal emblem—an immodest choice, but one that was accurate since he outshone all other European monarchs.

During Louis' reign, the French military experienced triumph after triumph on the battlefield. To ensure that he would never be defeated, Louis increased the size of his army to an astonishing 340,000 men (some sources say 400,000). He hired the ablest administrators he could find to ensure that the soldiers received the food, supplies, and, most importantly, their pay on time. An unhappy army of that size was a recipe for revolution.

He won victories and new territory in his wars against the Dutch and against the Germans, but the costs in terms of gold and human lives outweighed the gains. Toward the end of his life, Louis confessed that he had found going to war irresistible.

In terms of artistic achievement, Louis confined himself almost exclusively to the construction, decoration, and furnishing of Versailles, his spectacular palace and gardens outside Paris. It took 42 years to complete and cost 82 million livres. Rather than try to control his nobles, Louis' policy was to inspire a spirit of cooperation between the monarchy and the aristocracy. And so he invited his nobles to attend him at Versailles, where they all vied with each other to appear in the most sumptuous dress, offer the most gallant gesture, or make the wittiest comment.

The France he left at his death represented the pinnacle of European culture, and it was at peace. But its economy had been ruined by the king's expenditures, and Louis' absolutist model of monarchy would lead to the French Revolution.

Fame presenting a portrait of Lous XIV

KING PHILIP (METACOM)

Sachem of the Wampanoags (1640–1676)

Metacom's life traced the tragic collapse of friendly relations between the English settlers and the native tribes of Massachusetts.

His father was Massasoit, the Pilgrims' first ally and dearest friend. Yet only two years after Massasoit's death, the colonists kidnapped his son Wamsutta (also known as Alexander) because he had been selling Indian land to other colonies. Within days of his kidnapping, Wamsutta fell ill and died. Metacom (better known as King Philip) became sachem of the Wampanoags.

Almost immediately Philip was deluged with troubles. His territory bordered three colonies—Plymouth, Rhode Island, and Massachusetts Bay—each of which was jealous of the other and eager to acquire more Indian land. In this tug-of-war for real estate, the colonial courts often ruled in a manner that chipped away at Indian lands. Meanwhile, English traders were selling rum to the Indians, while colonists permitted their cattle and other livestock to wander into the Indians' fields and destroy the crops. When Philip, by a show of force, tried to intimidate the colonists into policing themselves, he was compelled at gunpoint to sign a treaty that made him subject to the authority of the colonial governments.

War was inevitable, and it broke out at Swansea, when Indian raiders killed some cattle in the fields outside the town. In response, an English boy raised a rifle and shot and killed one of the warriors. Soon Massachusetts, Rhode Island, and Connecticut were plunged into war, with both sides guilty of unspeakable atrocities. In addition to the massacres and torture, the English brought a new outrage—in August 1675, several hundred Indians surrendered at Plymouth with the understanding that they would be given amnesty; instead the governor, Josiah Winslow, shipped them off to be sold at the slave market of Cadiz, Spain. No one knows how many Indians were sold into slavery during King Philip's War, but among them were Philip's wife and son.

The cost of the war was horrific: out of a population of 50,000, approximately 2,000 colonists—men, women, and children—died. The casualty rate among Indians was even worse—perhaps as high as 6,000 out of population of 20,000. Among the dead was Philip. The English hacked off Philip's head and displayed it in the fort at Plymouth for the next 20 years.

Death of King Philip

ANNE

Queen of the Pamunkey (c. 1650–1715)

Anne's difficult task was to preserve her tribe's cultural integrity and what was left of the tribal lands in Virginia. The Pamunkey had been part of the thirty tribes once ruled by Powhatan (it is possible that Powhatan was a Pamunkey).

By the time Anne became queen of the tribe (queen was the term by which her white neighbors referred to her), most of the Pamunkeys' ancestral lands were owned by the colonists and what remained in the tribe's hands was not big enough to support them. Most of the wild games was gone, already killed by the Indians and the colonists, or run off deeper into the forest. Yet the colonial government demanded an annual tribute payment that the tribe could not afford.

To buy food, supplies, and to pay the tribute, Anne authorized the sale of some of the tribe's precious land, yet the surveyors cheated the Pamunkeys, taking more land than had actually been agreed to in the bill of sale. Anne tried to counteract such trickery by insisting that henceforth they would only lease tribal land to the colonists, but the colonial government in Williamsburg rejected this demand. She had no more luck trying to bar liquor traders from selling their goods in her villages.

By 1711, the tribe was in such impossible financial straits that Anne appealed to the colonial governor to waive the annual tribute. He agreed, on the condition that Anne send her son to be educated at the College of William and Mary in Williamsburg. The college had been founded to educate both the sons of colonists and of the Indian tribes, but the Indians had always been reluctant to send their sons off to be educated by strangers. Besides, when the young men returned, the things they had learned were utterly useless in an Indian village. Nonetheless, Anne sent her son, and another young Pamunkey boy as well.

Today the Pamunkey are one of two Indian tribes still extant in Virginia. They owe their survival in large part to the political skills of Queen Anne.

The Pamunkey River flowed through Anne's traditional homeland.

James Scott

Duke of Monmouth (1649–1685)

James Scott was born in Rotterdam the year King Charles I was executed. His father was the exiled Prince of Wales, Charles, and his mother was the prince's mistress, Lucy Walter. When the monarchy was restored in England, James' father, now King Charles II, publicly recognized the teenage boy as his son and made him duke of Monmouth.

Years went by and it became obvious to everyone in England that King Charles would never have a legitimate child to inherit the kingdom. In response, two factions began to rise in the country: one supported Charles' brother, James, Duke of York. But the duke was a Catholic and many Englishmen were unwilling to see a Catholic become king, even if he was next in line. This discontented party rallied around the duke of Monmouth. True, he was illegitimate, but he was a son of the king and he was Protestant. Several English nobles tried to persuade Charles to legitimize Monmouth, but the king refused. The true right of succession belonged to his brother.

Incredibly, in 1683, Monmouth involved himself in a plot to assassinate his father. The killers would lie in wait for the king at the Rye House at Hoddesdon; as he rode by on his way home from a horse race, they would attack and kill him. The plot went wrong when the king left the race earlier than expected and passed the Rye House before the murderers were in place.

Monmouth escaped to Holland, but three other plotters were executed.

In February, 1685, Charles II died and James II became king. Four months later, Monmouth landed in England, raised his standard, and was proclaimed king at Taunton. Farmers and workingmen joined him, but very few nobles or gentry. At Sedgemoor, Monmouth's army of amateurs was destroyed by professional troops fighting for King James. Monmouth was captured. At his trial, he behaved in an unregal fashion, begging for mercy, but he was condemned and sentenced to be beheaded.

Although Monmouth's uprising against King James II ended in disaster, in 1690, the king's son-in-law, William of Orange, would defeat the king and restore a Protestant monarchy to England.

MASSASOIT

Great Sachem of the Wampanoags (died 1662)

Massasoit means "great sachem." His given name was Wawmegin. Massasoit's tribal land covered present-day Massachusetts and eastern Rhode Island, the areas where the Pilgrims, followed by other English Puritans, first settled.

He was about 40 years old when the Pilgrims arrived at what is now Plymouth, Massachusetts. One of the Pilgrims who met him on his first visit to the settlement described him as, "In his best years, an able body, grave of countenance, and spare of speech."

The Pilgrims arrived late in December—far too late to plant crops. With their supplies aboard the Mayflower dwindling, and having no luck hunting or fishing, the English were on the verge of starvation. Pitying the hapless newcomers, Massasoit sent them generous gifts of food

During that winter of 1620–1621, Massasoit and the Pilgrims worked a simple treaty: they would punish any of their people who hurt or stole from the other. If enemies attacked the Indians, the colonists would come to the aid of their friends, similarly if enemies attacked the colonists, the Indians would come their aid.

In 1623, Massasoit sent a message to his friend Edward Winslow that he was very ill. Winslow packed up medicines and delicacies thought to help the sick and hurried to the sachem's village, accompanied by an Indian interpreter and a fellow colonist. They found Massasoit very sick indeed, his tongue swollen and the inside of his mouth covered with some type of fungus. Winslow scraped away at the nastiness, washed out his mouth, and fed his friend some fruit jam and sassafras tea. Five days later, Massasoit was recovered. "Now I see the English are my friends and love me," he said. "And whilst I live I will never forget this kindness they have showed me." While Massasoit lived, the Indians and the Pilgrims lived in peace and friendship. In the 42 years they lived together, there was only one thing he refused the Pilgrims—he would not let their ministers try to convert his people.

Massasoit signing the earliest recorded treaty with Governor John Carver

Peter the Great

Tsar of All Russia (1672–1725)

Peter the Great was an Enlightenment autocrat. He was envious of European technology, enchanted by the theories of the Enlightenment, but adamant that his Russia would never have a parliament, or a constitution, or a monarchy whose powers were limited by law.

The Russia of the 17th century had not changed since the early Middle Ages. It was overwhelmingly rural, isolated from and suspicious of any ideas from Western Europe, clinging to traditions and modes of behavior that made the Russians appear to visitors as primitive if not barbarous. In his teens, Peter came in contact with communities of foreigners who were living and working in Russia. From them he learned navigation—which became a life-long passion—and heard about the new technologies and advances in science in the West.

As tsar, he made a tour of Holland, England, Germany, and Austria, where he saw the technological superiority of Western Europe. He returned home determined to make dramatic changes. In imitation of the English and the Dutch, he built a navy. He brought in engineers and architects from Western Europe to build him an entirely new city in the latest style out of a bog on the Baltic Sea. He moved his government there, abandoning Russia's medieval capital, Moscow, for the broad boulevards, immense squares, and opulent neoclassical palaces of St. Petersburg.

No detail escaped Peter's notice. He dropped obsolete characters from the Russian alphabet. He started the country's first newspaper. He commanded Russian men to shave their beards and give up their kaftans for European-style dress. To undercut the influence of the Russian Orthodox clergy, he toyed with the idea of introducing Lutheranism into the country. Fearing it would provoke a revolution, he abandoned the idea.

Peter pushed Russia's borders all the way to the Pacific, paving the way for Russia's attempts to colonize Alaska.

While his achievements were epic, in one respect at least, Peter remained as traditional as any of his medieval predecessors: he wanted his people to enjoy the same advantages as any Western European—except the Western notion of freedom.

Peter the Great at the Battle of Poltava

MIR WAIS KHAN HOTAK

King of Kandahar (1673–1715)

In 1700, Afghanistan was under the control of the Persians who imposed higher taxes while pressuring the Afghan tribes to convert from Sunni to Shi'a Islam. In 1704, as rebellion flared up around the country, the Persian shah sent his commander-in-chief, Gurgan Khan, to Kandahar to put down the revolt.

Gurgan defeated the rebels in battle, burnt their villages, executed ringleaders and their supporters, filled the prisons with more suspected rebels, and ruled the province under martial law. His greatest coup was the capture of Mir Wais Khan. He loaded his prisoner down with chains, and sent him to the shah in Isfahan as a prize of war. Everyone, Afghani and Persian, believed this was the last they would see of Mir Wais Khan.

But in Isfahan, Mir Wais Khan's first meeting with the shah went well. Rather than order the rebel chief's immediate execution, the shah kept him as a prisoner. Over a period of weeks and months, Mir Wais Khan won the shah's trust and friendship, and even managed to plant in his mind a few doubts regarding the loyalty and methods of Gurgan Khan. Ultimately the shah released the khan and sent him back to Kandahar.

Now Mir Wais Khan directed his considerable charm against Gurgan Khan. In April 1709, the majority of Persian troops were away from Kandahar, tracking down rebels. Mir Wais Khan sent Gurgan Khan an invitation to a banquet at his country estate, Kokaron, outside the city. Mir Wais Khan served his guests a wide array of rich dishes, accompanied by fine wines of which, in spite of Islam's prohibition against alcohol, Gurgan Khan and his entourage drank heavily. When the Persians were drunk, Mir Wais Khan attacked and killed Gurgan Khan.

News of the murder stunned the Persian shah. He sent ambassadors to Kandahar to make inquiries; Mir Wais Khan had them arrested and thrown in prison. The shah sent a Persian army against the rebels in Kandahar, but Mir Wais Khan defeated it. Uncertain what to do next, the Persian shah decided to do nothing.

Mir Wais Shah spent the last few years of life trying to convince the Afghan tribes to unite so they would no longer be susceptible to invasions. He died peacefully in his bed in 1715, and was buried in a mausoleum in the garden where he killed Gurgan Khan.

View of Kandahar

CHARLES XII

King of Sweden (1682–1718)

Charles spent almost his entire life at war; it was the activity he loved best, but it ruined his country. When Charles became king in 1697, Sweden was one of the great powers of northern Europe. When he died in 1718, Sweden was a bankrupt Scandinavian backwater.

He had just become king at age 14 when Sweden's three greatest threats, Poland, Denmark, and Russia, formed a triple alliance to take advantage of the boy-king, destroy his army, and cripple his kingdom. Thus began the Great Northern War that dragged on for 21 years.

Charles learned military tactics from General Rehnskjold. By age 20, he was ready to lead his army personally, and he demonstrated how well he had been taught by scoring victories in Saxony and Poland (where he installed a new, pro-Swedish king). Then he turned his attention to Russia.

For the rest of his life, Charles would be at war almost continually with his nemesis, Peter the Great. Both men had splendid armies, and both were determined to be the greatest power in northern Europe. Charles had one more ambition—to prevent Russia from ever acquiring a port on the Baltic Sea, thereby preventing her from easy access to the markets of Western Europe.

The war in Russia in 1708–1709 was a disaster. After surviving the brutal Russian winter, Charles' army was destroyed at the Battle of Poltava. Peter the Great took 10,000 Swedish prisoners whom he sent off as forced labor to the mines in the Urals and to the immense construction site that would become St. Petersburg. Charles, with 1,000 officers and men, escaped to Ottoman territory where he tried to persuade the sultan to declare war on Russia.

Sweden's defeat at Poltava emboldened Denmark and Saxony to rise up against Charles, joined by Norway, Prussia and Hanover. In 1718, Charles was campaigning in Norway. Outside Frederiksten, he peered over a parapet to investigate the siege works when a sniper spotted Charles, took aim, and shot the king in the head, killing him.

Charles XII (front, right) and the Swedish royal family escape from their burning castle, 1697.

Mohammed III
ben Abdellah al-Qatib

Sultan of Morocco (1710–1790)

Mohammed III was an innovator. For decades, the reigns of his predecessors had been marred by feuds between rival Berber and Bedouin tribes and wars against the English and the Spanish. Perhaps because he did not become sultan until he was 47 years old, Mohammed had time to study conditions in his own country as well as the international situation, and he was ready to make some changes.

He immobilized the contentious tribes and restored all power to the monarchy. His policy was to bring peace and prosperity to Morocco. He began by signing treaties with the great European powers. Then he sent his own fleet into the Mediterranean against the Barbery pirates who were interfering with international commerce and committing all manner of atrocities against ships' crews and passengers who fell into their hands.

On Morocco's Atlantic coast, at a place convenient for English, French, Dutch, Spanish and Portuguese shipping, he built a new city, Essaouira. It was intended as a commercial center, and he invited Jewish merchants to settle there, and let it be known in Europe that businessmen of any nationality were welcome.

In 1776, the thirteen English colonies along America's Atlantic coast surprised the world by declaring their independence from Great Britain. The next year, 1777, Mohammed surprised the world by being the first ruler to recognize the United States of America as a sovereign nation.

In 1786, Mohammed III and Thomas Jefferson signed a treaty that has endured for more than 220 years. No other treaty between America and a foreign nation has endured so long unbroken.

Mohammed III brought strength and stability to his dynasty, peace and prosperity to his people, and gave legitimacy and friendship to a fledgling nation across the sea.

The ancient city of Essaouira

MARIA THERESA

Holy Roman Empress (1717–1780)

Maria Theresa's impressive list of titles include Holy Roman Empress, Queen of Hungary, Bohemia, Croatia and Slavonia, Archduchess of Austria, Duchess of Parma and Piacenza, Grand Duchess of Tuscany. When she was 23 years old, her father, Emperor Charles, died and Maria Theresa inherited it all. In the interest of keeping their lands and power intact, the Hapburgs had decreed that in the absence of a male heir, the eldest daughter could inherit everything. With her only brother and her father dead, Maria Theresa was next in line.

Very quickly the young empress discovered that both her finances and her army were in deplorable condition. Then, in an attempt to seize Hapsburg territory and perhaps the crown itself, Bavaria, Spain, Saxony, and Prussia, supported by France, declared war. Maria Theresa, supported by George II of England, defended her empire. She drove back the invaders, and, in the peace treaty of the 1748, she held on to her lands and her title, and conceded virtually nothing to her enemies.

Maria Theresa's policy was "enlightened absolutism." As empress, she would not permit her power to be questioned, but she introduced a host of reforms inspired by the Enlightenment. She outlawed torture, the burning of witches, and the death penalty. She made it compulsory for all children to go to school. To encourage inoculation against smallpox in her empire, she, her husband Francis, and all 13 of their surviving children received the smallpox vaccination.

In other respects, Maria Theresa was a woman of her time. She could not imagine a policy of complete freedom of religion in her empire, but she was unwilling to engage in religious persecution. Her solution was to declare that the Protestant faith would be tolerated in Transylvania, and she commanded all Protestants who wished to worship freely to migrate there.

Like Queen Victoria a century later, Maria Theresa married off her children to the great royal houses of Europe. All of them have been forgotten, except the youngest daughter, Marie Antoinette, the tragic queen of France.

Wedding breakfast of Empress Maria Theresa of Austria and Francis of Lorraine

BONNIE PRINCE CHARLIE

Pretender to the Crowns of England and Scotland (1720–1788)

Bonnie Prince Charlie's grandfather was James II, who, because he was a Catholic, was deposed in 1690 and replaced by his Protestant daughter Mary and her Dutch husband, William. The Scots longed for the restoration of the Stuarts (Charlie's family name) since originally they had been the royal family of Scotland, but in England, the overwhelmingly Protestant population feared that the Catholic Stuarts would attempt to impose Catholicism on the nation. And the fact that the Stuarts had settled in Rome, where they were supported financially by the pope, did nothing to allay those fears.

In 1745, when Prince Charlie was twenty-five, the king of France promised him an army to reclaim his throne. So he sailed to the Hebrides, where he told a hopeful yet anxious crowd of well-wishers, "I am come home, and I will not return to France, for I am persuaded that my faithful Highlanders will stand by me." The Highlanders, many of whom were Catholic, did rally to the prince, and the army marched south toward England.

Things got off to a good start at Prestonpans, where Charlie's army defeated an English force. Then the army marched across the border into England. Without firing a shot in its own defense, the city of Derby surrendered to the prince. While the government in London was beginning to feel nervous, Charlie and his followers were beginning to worry, too—the English had not flocked to his banner, and the promised French army was nowhere in sight.

Charlie and his army withdrew into Scotland, where they defeated the English at Falkirk. Then, on April 16, 1746, at Culloden Moor near Inverness, Charlie faced the army of the duke of Cumberland. The duke's army bore muskets and was supported by artillery; most of Charlie's men carried swords and shields. The English guns killed between fifteen hundred and two thousand Scots. Within forty minutes, the battle was over and Prince Charlie's dream of regaining the crown had ended.

He returned to Italy, where he consoled himself with heavy drinking. The Scots kept Bonnie Prince Charlie's memory alive in poetry and ballads, which tended to portray him as a romantic but doomed figure.

Prince Charles Edward Stuart in Edinburgh

CATHERINE II THE GREAT

Empress of Russia (1729–1796)

From the moment she saw her future husband, Grand Duke Peter, Catherine disliked him: he was childish, conceited, and thoroughly unpleasant. But she married him because someday he would be emperor of Russia and she would be empress.

Peter was enthralled by all things Prussian, and the Prussian king, Frederick the Great, was his hero—this in spite of the fact that Prussia was Russia's greatest enemy. As emperor, Peter outraged the military by returning to Prussia all territories conquered during the Seven Years' War; he antagonized his bodyguards by forcing them to wear exact copies of Prussian uniforms; he threatened the Russian Orthodox Church with his plan to introduce Lutheranism into the country; and he was so contemptuous of Catherine, she feared that in time he would kill her.

On July 9, 1762, Catherine, supported by the regiments of the guards led by her lover Grigory Orlov, seized power and had Peter arrested. It was said he died accidentally in a scuffle with his guards; it is probable that he was killed outright.

Catherine was a woman of wide interests and was especially influenced by the writings of Voltaire and Diderot. True to Enlightenment principles, she opened schools, fostered religious tolerance, offered free smallpox inoculation to the people, and contemplated abolishing serfdom but could not see how Russia would function without it. Adjacent to the Winter Palace in Saint Petersburg, she built the Hermitage to house her magnificent, and growing, collection of fine art.

Even before she came to power, Catherine had lovers, often attractive military men. It is likely that her children, Paul and Anna, ostensibly fathered by Peter, were actually fathered by Grigory Orlov. Her greatest love was Grigory Potemkin, a nobleman who became her political partner. The couple may have married secretly.

Potemkin died five years before Catherine, and in her last, lonely years, she came to realize that her son Paul was a reactionary who shared none of her ideas for a more progressive Russia. She died fearing he would undo everything she had accomplished.

Siraj al-Dawlah

Nawab of Bengal (1733–1757)

The British East India Company was founded in the sixteenth century as a joint-stock company to promote commerce with East India (present-day Indonesia), India, and eventually China. In the eighteenth century, this mercantile organization was beginning to take over the countries, not just sell to them. The East India Company had a military and a government bureaucracy that was well established in India, and growing.

Siraj became nawab at a time when the company was gearing up to take over Bengal. He was an unsympathetic character: he amused himself by publicly belittling and humiliating distinguished visitors; his closest friends were stupid, dissolute men; and he was indifferent to the sufferings of others, which has made some historians wonder if there was a touch of the sociopath in Siraj.

Bad character aside, Siraj understood that his kingdom was in jeopardy. He complained to the governors of the East India Company that they were in violation of their agreement: the Company had expanded their fortress at Calcutta, Fort William; they had defrauded the Bengal government of customs duties; and they were sheltering Siraj's enemies. The governors of the Company ignored the nawab's grievances, so he marched his army to Calcutta and took it from the British.

After his victory, Nawab Siraj supposedly rounded up 146 British subjects and crammed them into a dungeon in Fort William. The cell was so small—twenty-four by eighteen feet—that overnight 123 of the prisoners suffocated. Only one survivor of what became known as "the Black Hole of Calcutta" left an account of that night, and it has been suspect for many years, not least because 146 adults could never have fit into such a small cell. The revised figures are that about 70 were imprisoned in the Hole, 46 of whom suffocated during the night.

The East India Company retaliated by sending in its army, led by Robert Clive, who bribed many of the nawab's men to throw down their weapons once the battle began. Betrayed by his army, Siraj fled but was captured by one of Clive's Indian allies, who beheaded him.

With Siraj's defeat and execution, the East India Company was one step closer to conquering all of India.

Robert Clive meets his Indian allies after the defeat of Siraj al-Dawlah

George III

King of Great Britain (1738–1820)

For two hundred years, George III was notorious as the hard-hearted, hardheaded king whose thoughtless policies cost Great Britain its colonies in America. The debut of the 1994 film, *The Madness of King George*, rehabilitated his image, making him seem a more sympathetic figure.

King George was not entirely responsible for the decisions that drove the American colonies to revolution. He relied heavily on his ministers, who instigated many of the taxation policies the Americans found so odious. George, for example, initially called for the repeal of the Stamp Act, which imposed a tax on everything from newspapers to wills. But when colonists in Boston dumped a valuable shipment of tea into the harbor, the king no longer sympathized with a people he now regarded as ruffians and vandals.

After war broke out in 1775 between the colonies and the mother country, George gave unwavering support to his chief minister, Lord North, who demanded complete submission from the American colonies and rejected any call for compromise. The king's intransigence played into the colonists' hands: before all the world he acted like a tyrant, which gave the Americans the moral justification they needed to convince countries such as France and Spain that their cause was just.

In October 1788, the king suffered an attack that appeared to be a sudden descent into madness. In fact it was porphyria, a rare metabolic disorder. He suffered three bouts of the disease, in 1801, 1804, and 1810; the final attack lasted until his death ten years later. Between these attacks, George was an able administrator who defended Great Britain against the threats of the French Revolution and Napoleon. During the last ten years of his life, however, his son George served as prince regent.

George was not a daring or innovative king, even in matters that seemed perfectly obvious. To off-set recurring uprisings in Ireland, the king's prime minister, William Pitt, suggested lifting the penal laws that kept Irish Catholics as second-class citizens in their own country. George rejected the idea. When no amount of discussion or argument would alter his position, Pitt resigned.

Joseph Brant (Thayendanegea)

War Chief of the Iroquois (1743–1807)

Thayendanegea lived his entire life with one foot in the world of the Indian and the other in the world of the whites. As a boy, he was educated at the Rev. Eleazar Wheelock's school in Lebanon, Connecticut, joined the Anglican Church, and took the name Joseph Brant. He was introduced to some of the most influential colonial officials in New York thanks to his sister Mary (called Molly), the wife of Sir William Johnson, Great Britain's decidedly pro-Indian superintendent of Indian affairs.

When the American Revolution broke out in 1775, the Iroquois Confederacy had voted to remain on the sidelines, but Brant convinced the Iroquois to enter the war on the side of the British. With an army of Iroquois and colonists loyal to Great Britain, he attacked forts and settlements in New York's Mohawk Valley, southern New York, and northern Pennsylvania. He ambushed and inflicted heavy casualties on American militia at Oriskany, and his men massacred settlers, including women and children, at the Pennsylvania settlements of Cherry Valley and Wyoming Valley (Brant insisted that he had not participated).

At the end of the war, the British betrayed Brant and the Iroquois in a treaty with the Americans that did not mention the Indians or make any effort to protect their right to their lands. But the British Crown granted the Indians two thousand acres of good land in Ontario, along the Grand River, and Brant and many other Iroquois moved there. Later Brant traveled to London, where he secured from the government financial compensation for Indians who had lost land and property during the war.

By now it was obvious to Brant that for the Indians to survive they must form a large confederacy, negotiating as a single people with the United States government. Such solidarity was elusive, and the Americans exploited divisions among the tribes to purchase almost all of Ohio.

Brant never abandoned the rituals of his tribe, but in almost every other respect he lived as an English gentleman, in a manor house with servants in livery. He urged his people to assimilate into European society, but not completely—a balancing act most found impossible to accomplish.

Brant intercedes to prevent the death by torture of a captured American captain

LOUIS XVI AND MARIE-ANTOINETTE

King (1754–1793) and Queen (1755–1793) of France

No one was prepared for the extraordinary violence of the French Revolution. The royal family and aristocracy, the Catholic Church in France, and countless ordinary French citizens were overwhelmed by radical ideologies for which nothing in their training or life experience could have prepared them.

Louis had been raised by his grandfather, Louis XV, a domineering old man who considered his grandson and heir a fool; consequently, Louis matured into a shy, well-meaning but awkward adult. Marie-Antoinette, the youngest daughter of the thirteen children of Francis I and Maria Theresa of Austria, was affectionate and high-spirited, but also a spendthrift and naive in political matters. Neither one was equipped to handle the crises that tore France apart: the remnants of feudalism that dehumanized the peasantry, the recurring fiscal emergencies made worse by bad harvests and famines, and the age-old privileges that exempted the nobles and the church from paying taxes. Neither was the royal couple any good at public relations. Marie-Antoinette was especially bad at it, pursuing a frivolous life playing shepherdess at her play farm at Versailles while real shepherdesses and their families lived in poverty.

The success of the American Revolution—which Louis XVI had supported with money, arms, and troops—may have been an inspiration for revolutionaries in France. In 1789, a Paris mob stormed the Bastille prison, a symbol of despotism, released the seven prisoners inside, and beheaded the prison governor. From that moment, events accelerated rapidly as the National Assembly became increasingly radical. Louis attempted to place himself at the head of the revolution, but it was an empty gesture received by the mob with derision.

In 1792, Louis, Marie-Antoinette, their fourteen-year-old daughter, and their seven-year-old son were imprisoned in the Temple fortress in Paris. In 1793, the revolutionary government found Louis guilty of crimes against the state and had him guillotined in what is now the Place de la Concorde. Nine months later Marie-Antoinette was dragged into court; as a particular object of the revolutionaries' hatred, she was charged with treason and incest with her son, and likewise sent to the guillotine.

Louis XVI giving instructions to the French explorer, the Count of La Perouse

KAMEHAMEHA I

King of the Hawaiian Islands (1758–1819)

Kamehameha was twenty years old when the explorer Captain James Cook visited Hawaii. One of the lieutenants in Cook's party was struck by the young man, recording that he had "as savage a face as I ever saw, [yet he was] good natured and humorous."

Kamehameha's family had ruled the island of Hawaii for generations. When Kamehameha became king in 1782, he set out to conquer all the Hawaiian islands. He recruited two English sailors, John Young and Isaac Davis, to teach him and his followers how to use muskets and cannons. With these advantages, Kamehameha took the islands of Maui, Molokai, and Lanai.

On Hawaii, a rival chief, Keoua, rebelled against Kamehameha. The uprising was neutralized when a volcano erupted and the poisonous fumes and hot ash killed a third of Keoua's men. Hawaiians interpreted this timely intervention as a sign that the volcano goddess favored Kamehameha.

In 1795, Kamehameha led an army to Oahu. In an epic battle against enemy chiefs, Kamehameha's men drove the warriors of Oahu off Nuuanu cliff. The last two islands in the archipelago, Kauai and Niihau, surrendered without a fight.

Previously, Hawaiian warrior kings had waged total war, sparing no one. But Kamehameha's law broke with the past, and he declared, "Let every elderly person, woman and child lie by the roadside in safety." In other words, his army was to spare noncombatants. The king broke another Hawaiian tradition when he outlawed human sacrifice.

As supreme king, Kamehameha kept all the traditions of his people, but he was eager to trade with Europeans and Americans who sailed their ships into the lovely bays of Hawaii. He imposed port duties that enriched his kingdom.

At his death, Kamehameha had a traditional Hawaiian funeral, although the human sacrifice was omitted. Then his remains were taken to a secret place and buried. The location of his grave has never been revealed.

An enemy warrior breaks a canoe paddle against Kamehameha's skull

GIA LONG

Emperor of Vietnam (1762–1820)

At age fifteen, Gia Long, a member of Vietnam's Nguyen dynasty, saw his entire family massacred in a peasant revolt. He escaped, fleeing deep into southern Vietnam, where a French Catholic missionary bishop, Pierre-Joseph-Georges Pigneau de Béhaine, hid him in a seminary. Bishop Pigneau became Gia's champion with the French government (at this time France was interested in acquiring colonies in Southeast Asia). The bishop provided practical support to enable Gia to reclaim his position in Vietnam—he acquired European weapons for Gia's followers, and taught them how to make grenades. He also arranged for French officers to train Gia's army and teach the Vietnamese how to construct stronger fortresses and build bronze-plated ships that were virtually unsinkable. The bishop's efforts were not entirely selfless—if he succeeded in helping Gia regain the throne of Vietnam, chances were excellent that the emperor would be generous to the Catholic missionaries in his country.

With his well-trained, well-armed army and his invincible navy, Gia first consolidated his power in southern Vietnam, then defeated his enemies in the north. It took twenty-five years of nonstop warfare for Gia to eliminate his enemies and be crowned emperor. Sadly, Bishop Pigneau did not live to see it. At the bishop's death in 1799, Gia Long led a funeral that included the royal family, the twelve thousand men of his bodyguard, and forty thousand mourners. Gia gave the eulogy, praising the bishop as "the most illustrious foreigner ever to appear at the court of Cochinchina" (as Vietnam was known in the eighteenth century).

Gia Long never became a Catholic; instead, he fostered the teachings of Confucius, instructing his subjects to live virtuous lives in pursuit of duty to family and to their emperor.

Inexplicably, he closed Vietnam to foreign trade, refusing to grant concessions to the British, the Dutch, or even his beloved French. In general, he regarded commerce as demeaning.

When Gia Long moved the seat of government to Hue, he built this citadel into a fortress stronghold, which was defended by guns, moats, and 800 elephants

TECUMSEH

War Chief of the Shawnee (1768–1813)

At age fourteen, Tecumseh joined his older brother Cheeseekau on raids against white settlers in the Ohio Valley and the lands south of the Ohio River. He was a lifelong opponent of American encroachment into Ohio, but isolated raids by a single tribe were unlikely to halt the Americans' movement west. Then, in 1805, Tecumseh's brother Tenskwatawa had a profound religious experience in which it was revealed to him that the Americans were children of the Great Serpent, the Shawnee personification of evil, and the tribe must have no dealings with them.

Tenskwatawa's vision sparked a religious revival among the Shawnee and other tribes, and they flocked to his village to hear his message. Tecumseh used these mass meetings to encourage chiefs and warriors to form a pan-tribal confederation that swore to sell no more land to the Americans, to negotiate with the state and federal governments as a single entity rather than as individual tribes or villages, and to be prepared to fight as one if they had no other option.

During the War of 1812, Tecumseh and his confederation sided with the British in Canada, hoping they would come to the Indians' aid in keeping Ohio clear of American settlers. But time and again, the British disappointed Tecumseh with halfhearted assistance and feeble efforts on the battlefield, in spite of the aid the Indians gave to them, including helping them capture Detroit.

In October 1813, Tecumseh and his warriors were with British and Canadian troops at the Thames River near present-day Moraviantown, Ontario, when word came up the line that an American force was approaching. The commander of the British and Canadians, Brigadier General Henry Procter, wanted to fall back. Tecumseh called him a coward and told him to run away but at least leave the guns and ammunition so the Indians could fight. Procter stayed, but after firing three volleys, he led his men in retreat.

Tecumseh and his men remained on the battlefield, where the chief was shot and killed. Kentucky militiamen mutilated his body, then threw it in a mass grave.

NAPOLEON

Emperor of France (1769–1821)

Napoleon was a man of tremendous ability, tremendous charm, and tremendous ego. In the late 1790s, France's revolutionary government made him a commander, and Napoleon rewarded their trust by scoring victories over the Italians, the Austrians, and the Egyptians. This was the beginning of Napoleon's drive to make France the greatest power in Western Europe.

As a man who already imagined himself a new Charlemagne, Napoleon wanted to be emperor of France. In 1804, he brought the pope to Paris to have him crown Napoleon and his empress-to-be, Joséphine, in Notre-Dame Cathedral. At the last moment, Napoleon took the crown from the pope's hands, crowned himself, and then crowned his wife. Five months later, he traveled to Milan to have himself crowned King of Italy.

Napoleon defeated the Austrians and Russians at Austerlitz, and the Prussians at Jena, but he lost control of the seas to the British at the Battle of Trafalgar. He invaded Spain, but between the Spanish guerrillas and the British and Portuguese troops led by the Duke of Wellington, his grip on the country was never firm.

Then in 1812, Napoleon invaded Russia. The Russians, relying on the vastness of their country, kept retreating, drawing Napoleon deeper and deeper into their territory. Rather than surrender Moscow to him, they evacuated the city and set it on fire. Napoleon occupied the ruined city, but Tsar Alexander I refused to negotiate with him. As winter was coming on, Napoleon marched his army back to France. That brutal winter retreat cost Napoleon the lives of 360,000 soldiers.

Back in France, he found himself surrounded by enemies. His marshals refused to fight anymore. Napoleon abdicated and was exiled to the island of Elba in the Mediterranean. In 1815, he escaped and rode to Paris, where for a hundred exciting days it appeared that he would recover everything he had lost. A coalition of British, Prussian, and various German states raised an army to depose Napoleon for good. At Waterloo in modern-day Belgium, the emperor suffered a crushing defeat. This time his enemies sent him to Saint Helena, an island in the Atlantic, twelve hundred miles from any landmass. He remained there until his death. They were difficult years for a man who once said, "Death is nothing but to live defeated and inglorious is to die daily."

Detail of Jacques David's painting of Napoleon crossing the Alps

SEATTLE

War Chief of the Duwamish, Suquamish,
and Lushootseed-speaking tribes (c. 1786—1866)

Seattle grew up at a time when the introduction of firearms and unfamiliar diseases had destabilized the tribes of the Pacific Northwest. One result was much more aggressive behavior between the tribes than had been known previously. Seattle did not stand aloof from these intertribal raids; in fact, he led his last such raid when he was sixty-one years old. But as more American settlers moved into what is now Washington State, Seattle shifted from warfare to diplomacy.

Among his own people, he was renowned as a warrior and as an orator. The chief's most famous oration, known as "Chief Seattle's Speech", especially popular among environmentalists, is probably a fabrication. There is no transcript of the speech from the day Seattle is supposed to have delivered it in 1854. The earliest version dates from 1887, twenty-one years after the chief's death. And there are three other versions from the last half the twentieth century. Whoever wrote it, the speech reads very well, as we see from this excerpt: "There was a time when our people covered the land as the waves of a wind-ruffled sea cover its shell-paved floor, but that time long since passed away with the greatness of tribes that are now but a mournful memory. I will not dwell on, nor mourn over, our untimely decay, nor reproach my paleface brothers with hastening it, as we too may have been somewhat to blame."

As more settlers entered his tribe's territory, Seattle formed friendships and alliances with the most influential men he could find, even converting to Catholicism when he noticed the high esteem in which the priests were held. The first American governor Isaac Stevens acknowledged Seattle's standing by naming him head chief of all the tribes in the region. And in 1853, the leaders of a settlement on the Puget Sound thought to honor the chief by naming the place after him.

SHAKA

King of the Zulus (1787–1828)

Shaka's father was a Zulu chief; he had an affair with Shaka's mother. Soon after Shaka was born, he and his mother were expelled from the chief's village. Unwelcome in other villages, Shaka grew up alone and in difficult circumstances. These early traumas shaped his personality: as an adult his loyalty to his mother was unshakable, he could endure any suffering, and in any contest he would not rest until he dominated his opponent.

Shaka was in his teens when Chief Dingiswayo permitted the boy and his mother to live with the Mthethwa tribe. Once Shaka was old enough to fight, Dingiswayo placed him among his warriors. The chief waged war over weaker tribes to form a confederacy that made the Mthethwas the greatest power in the region. In 1816, with his chief's consent, Shaka plotted to avenge the wrongs done to him and his mother. His father had died, and his half brother was now king of the Zulus; Shaka assassinated his half brother and, backed up by the power of Dingiswayo's army, declared himself king of the Zulus.

Free to act as he wished for the first time in his life, Shaka transformed the Zulus into the most ferocious army in what is now South Africa. He introduced new tactics, including using the traditional tall shields as a weapon, and gave up the long throwing javelin for a shorter jabbing spear, ideal for hand-to-hand combat. He demanded absolute obedience from his warriors, and would not even permit a warrior to marry unless his behavior in battle had earned him the privilege.

He conquered tribe after tribe, then obliterated the chiefdoms and consolidated all power in himself. But he made one major error—he did not expel the European traders and hunters who had founded the Port Natal colony. In time, the Europeans would reach such numbers that they would dominate the Zulus.

In 1827, Shaka's mother died, and he commanded the Zulus to join him in excessive and interminable mourning rituals. The next year Shaka died, assassinated by two of his half brothers and his own personal servant.

Shaka Zulu fighting two men

Yagan

Chief of the Noongars (c. 1795–1833)

In 1829, British settlers arrived at Swan River in western Australia and began establishing farms. The Noongar Aborignal people already inhabited the area, but because the colonists regarded them as nomads, the British made little or no effort to purchase their land. Instead, the colonists fenced off acre upon acre for fields and pasture, trespassing on the Noongars' hunting grounds and sacred sites, and even cutting off their access to water. The Noongars retaliated by stealing the settlers' food, killing their cattle, and setting fire to the bush—their traditional method for flushing out game, which now had the added advantage of damaging the settlers crops and homes.

The first serious conflict between the Noongars and the British occurred in 1831 when a colonist named Thomas Smedley shot and killed a member of Yagan's extended family who was stealing potatoes. Yagan, along with his father, Midgegooroo, and several other warriors of the tribe, attacked a house in the settlement where Smedley lived, but they killed the wrong man, a colonist named Erin Entwhistle.

Yagan and two members of his tribe were captured and sentenced to an undetermined prison term on Carnac Island, a penal colony for Aboriginals. But after a month, Yagan and his friends stole a small boat and escaped to the mainland.

Yagan became a nuisance, breaking into settlers' cabins and demanding food and supplies. After his brother was shot and killed by a colonist, Yagan's assaults became violent. He ambushed a cart full of supplies and speared to death two British colonists. The colonial government set a price on his head—£30, dead or alive.

The money was a powerful temptation for two teenage brothers, William and James Keates, who knew Yagan. On July 11, 1833, when Yagan and several tribesmen visited the Keates farm, the boys saw their chance to claim the reward money. William shot Yagan, his brother James shot another Noongar warrior, then they turned and ran for the river. The other Noongars pursued and stabbed William to death with their spears, but they could not catch James, who dove into the river and swam to safety. By the time he returned with a group of armed settlers, the surviving Noongars were gone. One of the British cut off Yagan's head to keep as a trophy. It was exhibited in London and kept there until 1993, when it was returned to Australia.

Sculpture of Yagan by Robert Hitchcock

Siaosi George Tupou I

King of Tonga (c. 1797–1893)

The kings of Tonga trace their line back to the tenth century. The spiritual leader of the Tongans bore the title Tui Tonga and was considered the supreme chief, or king, of the 171 islands that comprise the kingdom of Tonga. But the Tui Tonga remained aloof from the actual details of running his kingdom—that was the responsibility of two of his brothers. Over the centuries, the descendants of the Tui Tongas and their brothers came to regard themselves as independent royal houses. By the nineteenth century, a civil war had broken out in the kingdom as rival claimants fought for supreme power. One of the contenders was Taufa'ahau, a man who envisioned a new type of leadership in Tonga with a single king who possessed political power and spiritual authority. In 1826, he defeated Laufilitonga, the last of the Tui Tongas. Rather than execute Laufilitonga, Taufa'ahau let him go into exile. From that point, for all intents, Taufa'ahau was king.

In 1830, two British Methodist missionaries arrived in the islands. Taufa'ahau was aware of the growth of the British Empire in Asia and Australia, and feared that the British might take control of his kingdom. To forestall this, he recast himself as a European-style king: he and his wife were baptized, taking the names George and Charlotte, in honor of England's King George III and Queen Charlotte. That same year, Taufa'ahau proclaimed himself king of Tonga under the name Siaosi George Tupou I. He consecrated his kingdom to the Christian God, adopted European dress, and as Methodist Christianity spread among his people, encouraged them to take on a European lifestyle. He issued a new code of laws that banned sexually explicit traditional Tongan ceremonies, outlawed alcohol, and decreed that no work could be performed on Sunday.

George's plan worked; impressed that the island had become a Westernized, Christian nation, the British did not colonize Tonga. But George still worried that Europeans might gain power in his country by acquiring land. To prevent this, he restricted ownership of the land to Tongan men.

George was nearly a hundred years old when he left his house one day to go swimming in the sea. The exertion was too much for him; he died later that day.

Although their King converted to Christianity, some Tonga islanders were hostile to the missionaries

JAMES BROOKE

Raja of Sarawak (1803–1868)

A soldier, an adventurer, and an amateur scientist, James Brooke was the first European to establish a royal dynasty in Asia. He was born in India, educated in England, and fought for the East India Company in Burma. In 1833, he inherited a fortune, which he used to purchase a yacht, then he set out to conduct scientific research in northern Borneo.

Brooke arrived in the country just as the sultan of Brunei was facing a rebellion. Brooke and his crew helped the sultan put down the uprising. As an expression of his thanks, the sultan appointed Brooke governor of Sarawak, a province of forty-eight thousand square miles located in Indonesia along the South China Sea, and gave him the title, Raja of Sarawak. Because he was European, Brooke became known as "the White Raja."

Sarawak's coastal settlements had long suffered raids from pirates known as Sea Dayaks, ferocious fighters and headhunters. Brooke spent the rest of his life trying to clear Sarawak's waters of pirates, but never eliminated them completely.

In addition to the Dayak pirates, some of Brooke's Malay and Iban subjects revolted against his rule. Brooke came to believe that he could not maintain control of Sarawak entirely on his own; consequently he offered his territory to the British government in exchange for British troops, but the British declined the offer. Brooke toyed with the idea of handing over Sarawak to the Dutch, but his nephew, who was his heir, talked him out of it.

Brooke never married, but he fathered at least one illegitimate child with a mistress. Teenage boys were his primary love interests: he had an affair with a Sarawak prince named Badruddin and another with an English boy, Charles Grant. At his death, Brooke passed his title to his nephew, Charles Johnson, who out of respect for his uncle, the raja, renamed himself Charles Brooke. The Brooke family ruled as rajas of Satawak until 1946 when the last raja, Charles Vyner de Windt Brooke, handed over Sarawak to Britain as a crown colony.

Mongkut Rama IV

King of Siam (1804–1868)

Mongkut Rama is best known as the king in the Broadway musical comedy *The King and I.* The play has not found many fans in Thailand (the modern name for Siam), where Rodgers and Hammerstein's humorous portrayal of the king and superficial depiction of Buddhism have given offense.

Before he became king, Mongkut lived for twenty-seven years as monk in a Buddhist monastery in Bangkok. His interest in the West led him to consult American and French missionaries who helped him in his study of the sciences, Western languages, and Western politics. While he was excited by the possibilities Western technology and trade could offer his country, Mongkut feared that either the French or the British, both of whom were working to expand their influence in Southeast Asia, would take over his country and declare it a colony. He made treaties with the United States, Japan, and Great Britain that opened his country to foreign trade, and he succeeded in preserving Siam's integrity by pitting the French and the British against each other.

In 1862, Mongkut invited an English widow, Anna Leonowens, to come live in his court and give his children, wives, and concubines a Western education. Leonowens lived in Mongkut's palace for five years, tutoring his family and advising him on the politics of the Western nations. The king had hoped to extend such an education to his subjects, but was blocked by the majority of his nobles, who rejected Western ideas.

After leaving Siam, Leonowens wrote a memoir, *The English Governess at the Siamese Court,* which became the basis of the stage play, *Anna and the King of Siam,* and then of the musical. Mongkut's biographer, Abbot Low Moffat, has criticized Leonowen's exaggerated description of court life and her characterization of Mongkut as a tyrant.

NAPOLEON III AND EUGÉNIE

Emperor (1808–1873) and Empress (1826–1920) of France

Napoleon III was the nephew of *the* Napoleon. Although France was now a republic, the name Napoleon had lost none of its cache. In 1848, he was elected president of the republic. In 1849, he delighted French Catholics by leading an army to Rome to defend the pope against Italian revolutionaries. When the French legislature rejected a constitutional amendment that would have permitted presidents to be reelected, Napoleon used his popularity to stage a coup that overthrew the republic and reestablished the empire—with himself as emperor. To validate his authority, he called for a referendum: 7.5 million voters approved his actions, as opposed to 650,000 dissenting votes.

As emperor, he sponsored large public works projects such as canals and railroads. He expanded the banking system and made it easier for more people to get credit. And he introduced free trade.

In 1853, the emperor married an enchanting Spanish countess, Eugénia de Montijo. If Victoria of England set the standard for morals, Eugénie set the criterion for style: she single-handedly made hoop skirts unfashionable. But Eugénie's influence was not limited to setting trends. She was a political and social conservative who tried to curb some of her husband's more progressive policies.

In 1870, the Spanish invited a Prussian prince to be their king. Napoleon objected, unwilling to have enemies on both his northern and southern borders. France and Prussia went to war in July, but it was over in September when the Prussian army surrounded Napoleon and his army of eighty thousand men at Sedan. The surrender of the emperor brought down the empire, and France became a republic again. Eugénie and the prince imperial, Louis Napoleon, took refuge in England, where the emperor followed them some months later.

Napoleon died in 1873 from a botched operation to remove a bladder stone. The prince enlisted in the British army and in 1879 was killed fighting the Zulus in South Africa. Eugénie founded a monastery, St. Michael's Abbey, in Farnborough, and had her husband and her son buried in the crypt. She joined them after her death in 1920.

Napoleon III, Eugénie, and Louis Napoleon

COCHISE

War Chief of the Chiricahua Apaches (1810–1874)

The Apaches and the Mexicans had been at war against each other for decades, but Cochise had nothing against the Americans who were settling in Arizona. In 1858, when he met with American government agent Michael Steck, Cochise promised friendship as long as the Americans did not harass the Apaches. In return, Steck gave the Apaches regular and generous gifts of food.

Then, in 1861, a high-handed lieutenant named George Bascom invited Cochise to his tent at Apache Pass. There he accused the chief of kidnapping a white boy. Cochise replied, truthfully, that Bascom had gotten it wrong—it was a different band of Indians who had the child. Bascom would not listen; until the Chiricahuas returned the boy, Cochise would be his prisoner. Before he could be placed under arrest, Cochise drew his knife, slit open the canvas, and ran into the desert. Bascom retaliated by capturing Cochise's wife, son, brother, and two nephews. Cochise took four Americans captive, then sent Bascom a message offering to free his prisoners in exchange for his family. Bascom rejected the offer.

Cochise tortured his captives to death and left their bodies where the American troops would find them. Bascom hanged Cochise's brother and nephews, but spared his wife and son. Eleven years of war followed. After the Americans lured Cochise's closest friend and ally, Chief Mangas Coloradas, to a parley, then tortured and killed him, Cochise swore never to make peace.

But Cochise and his Apaches were outnumbered. By 1871, the chief understood that if he kept fighting, it would end with the annihilation of his people. Through the influence of an army scout, Thomas Jeffords, and the Indian commissioner, General Oliver Howard, both of whom were sympathetic to Cochise, he and his people were given a reservation on their own lands in southeastern Arizona.

OTTO

King of the Hellenes (1815–1862)

It is strange that once Greece, the cradle of democracy, gained its independence from the Turks it installed an absolute monarchy. Stranger still is that the first king of Greece was a German.

Greece had won its revolution thanks to the support of Great Britain, France, and Russia. The three Great Powers agreed (without consulting the Greeks) that Greece should have a monarchy. They offered the crown to sixteen-year-old Prince Otto of Bavaria, ostensibly because among his ancestors were members of the Comnenus dynasty, who had ruled the Byzantine Empire.

Otto arrived in Greece with thirty-five hundred Bavarian troops and three Bavarian advisors. He did not invite any Greeks to join his government. When he married, he chose a German princess and married her in Germany. A devout Roman Catholic, he would not convert to the Greek Orthodox faith, which offended the majority of his subjects.

Greece's finances were in ruins. To pay back loans from the Rothschild bank, Otto was forced to raise taxes higher than they had been under the Turks. Even this was not enough to keep the country afloat. He borrowed 60 million francs from the Great Powers, which gave them the right (they believed) to interfere in Greece's internal affairs.

In 1843, the Greeks were clamoring for a constitution. On September 3 of that year, two respected army officers marched the infantry into the square in front of the palace in Athens. The citizens joined the soldiers and refused to return to their homes until the king granted them a constitution and a national assembly, and included Greeks in his government. Otto gave in to the crowd's demands.

Even after these concessions, Otto had very little support among the Greek people. When Greek rebels led a coup in 1862, Britain, France, and Russia instructed Otto not to resist. A British warship transported the king and queen of Greece back to Germany. The historian Thomas W. Gallant summed up Otto as "neither ruthless enough to be feared, nor compassionate enough to be loved, nor competent enough to be respected."

King Otto enters Athens

THEODORE II

King of Ethiopia (c. 1818–1868)

As a young man, there was a Robin Hood quality to Theodore: he plundered and robbed but gave generously of his loot to the poor. His given name at the time was Kassa, and he came from a line of warlords. His family connections combined with his charisma and his success as a freebooter won him a large following among other violent men. Soon his band of robbers grew to an army that he used to destroy his enemies and conquer central and northern Ethiopia. His power grew so great that he could command the bishops of the Ethiopian Orthodox Church to anoint and crown him king. He took a new name, Theodore, Tewodros in Amharic, the language of Ethiopia; in his people's folklore, it was the name of a legendary king who had ushered in an era of peace and righteousness.

It was Theodore's wish to give his people the technological advances enjoyed in Europe and the United States. He brought into the country engineers to build roads and bridges, and artisans to show the Ethiopians how to manufacture rifles and cannons. But he ran into resistance when he began to tax the aristocracy and the church and expropriated church lands. The privileged classes fought his reforms every step of the way, which forced Theodore to keep a standing army of fifty thousand men to put down petty uprisings among the nobles and bishops. To maintain such a large army, Theodore had to raise taxes even on the peasants, his strongest base of support. As the peasants found it harder and harder to feed their families, they turned against the king, too.

In the 1860s, the nobles in the north defeated Theodore's army just as Ethiopian Muslims in the southern provinces made war on the king. Theodore appealed to the French and the British for aid, but his request was ignored. He wrote a personal letter to Queen Victoria that somehow went astray. Stung by these slights, Theodore lashed out against the Europeans he had invited to help his people. He arrested several dozen, including women and children, and imprisoned them in his mountain fortress, Magdela. Some of the men he tortured, and he threatened all of his prisoners with execution.

When the British government sent an army to rescue the captives, Theodore hunkered down at Magdela. There he discovered that the British artillery was far superior to his own. As British troops poured into the fortress, Theodore killed himself.

Theodore II supervises a work crew building a road through the mountains of Ethiopia.

Alexander II the Tsar-Liberator

Tsar of Russia (1818–1881)

Four years before the American Civil War freed more than 4 million black slaves, Alexander II liberated more than 40 million Russian serfs. Speaking to a group of noblemen who were angry about his policy, Alexander reminded them, "It will be much better if this takes place from above than from below." Under the tsar's radical plan, the serfs were given the land they worked to support themselves (as distinct from the estate land they worked for their master). And they could buy more land if they had the means. But now that the serfs were no longer dependent on their master for all their needs, the government had to step in and provide everything from medical care to road repair.

Alexander's reforms extended to every aspect of Russian society. He introduced the jury system—the first in the history of Russian jurisprudence. He lifted the restrictions on what could be taught or debated in the universities. And he ensured that military conscription—formerly borne largely by the peasants and working classes—drew from every level of Russian society equally. Ironically, Alexander could implement so many dramatic reforms for the simple reason that he was an autocrat.

Yet the radical elements in Russia were not satisfied. Alexander's reforms had not gone far enough to suit them. Groups known as Land and Liberty, the Organization, and the People's Will pushed for more reforms and adopted drastic measures to advance their agendas: in 1866, an assassin fired six shots at Alexander; incredibly, every shot missed. The tsar responded by unleashing the secret police on the extremists, which made them even more fanatical in their opposition to the Russian regime.

On March 1, 1881, Alexander was riding in his carriage along the Catherine Canal in Saint Petersburg when a revolutionary threw a bomb. It missed the carriage, but the explosion killed a Cossack guard, and injured the driver and several bystanders. As the tsar stepped out to comfort the wounded, an assassin threw a second bomb, which landed at his feet. The force of the explosion almost blew off both his legs, yet Alexander was still alive. He was carried back to the Winter Palace, where he died. Alexander's son, Alexander III, built a church at the scene of the assassination; it was dedicated as the Church of the Savior on Spilled Blood.

VICTORIA

Queen of Great Britain, Empress of India (1819–1901)

Victoria was one of those rare monarchs whose influence was so pervasive that she gave her name to an age. Her sixty-four-year-reign—the longest in British history—coincided with the dramatic social and economic upheavals brought on by the Industrial Revolution and the expansion of the British Empire to virtually every corner of the globe.

A small young woman, not even five feet tall, with large blue eyes and a figure that was becoming a bit plump, she was eighteen when she became queen. In 1840, she married her first cousin, Albert, a German duke. During the early years of their marriage, Victoria was reluctant to give her husband any real governmental responsibility. An intelligent, energetic man, Albert hated having nothing of importance to do, but in time, the couple arrived at a compromise as Victoria came to realize how well Albert understood high politics.

The royal couple had nine children, most of whom were married off to the other royal houses of Europe; it was the same story with Victoria and Albert's grandchildren, so that by 1900 virtually every monarch on the Continent was directly related to, or an in-law of, the English queen.

Albert's death in 1861 devastated Victoria. She went into deep mourning, isolating herself from her government to the extent that some politicians began to wonder out loud if the country needed a constitutional monarchy. After several years of seclusion, she did return to public life, but she never gave up wearing black.

Victoria considered her eldest son, Albert Edward, or Bertie, a lazy scapegrace and a rake, and so she gave him no responsibilities. In his boredom, Bertie sank deeper and deeper into frivolous pursuits, which only confirmed his mother's bad opinion of him.

The 1870s were a good decade for the queen: her beloved Benjamin Disraeli became prime minister and secured for her the title of empress of India. He also arranged for England to acquire the Suez Canal, which gave British ships a faster route to India.

In 1897 the nation and the empire celebrated Victoria's diamond jubilee, marking sixty years as queen. She died four years later, calling the name of her son Bertie. He later went on become one of the most popular kings of England.

Queen Victoria at the time of her coronation

Victor Emmanuel II

King of Italy (1820–1878)

In the nineteenth century, there was no unified nation of Italy; instead, the Italian peninsula was carved up into eight petty kingdoms and dukedoms, with the Papal States, the territory ruled by the pope, sprawling across central Italy. To call for a democratic government in any of these states was a sure way to wind up in prison, but the successful revolutions in America, France, Haiti, and Greece led Italian political dissidents to work for the abolition of the autocrats and the establishment of a united Italian republic. By the late 1850s, however, it was becoming clear that a majority of the Italian people were more comfortable with a constitutional monarchy than a republic. The man they rallied around was Victor Emmanuel, the king of Piedmont, Savoy, and Sardinia.

In 1849, at the beginning of his reign, Victor Emmanuel despised revolutionaries, deriding them as a "vile and infected race." But his prime minister, Count Camillo di Cavour, could see that the movement for a united Italy was gaining momentum; it was Cavour who convinced Victor Emmanuel to support the Italian unification movement, with an eye toward becoming king of Italy.

The unification process was a slow and sometimes bloody affair. Lombardy in the north and Naples and Sicily in the south threw their support behind a united Italy. In 1861, Victor Emmanuel was proclaimed king of Italy, but there were still large portions of the peninsula not under his rule, including Venice, Umbria, and Rome and the Papal States. Not until 1871 did Victor Emmanuel take control of the Papal States, but once he did, he declared Rome the capital of the new Italy. The pope lashed back by excommunicating the king (when Victor Emmanuel was dying, the pope lifted the ban so he could receive the last rites and a Christian burial).

Victor Emmanuel was not a brilliant or even charismatic king, yet during the days of the unification movement, Italians imagined he would be an ideal monarch. In fact he was a man of modest talents who happened to be in the right place, with the right pedigree, at the right time.

TAWHIAO

King of the Maori (1822–1894)

Tawhiao became king at the moment when the Maori were losing their independence. Initially, the British colonists had recognized the Maori kingdom as a distinct nation state in New Zealand, but by the 1860s, this Maori kingdom seemed to the British settlers to be an obstruction hindering their settlement of the northern and southern islands of New Zealand.

In 1863, the British colonial government sent fourteen thousand troops into the Maori kingdom. Tawhiao argued that the Maori should wage a guerrilla war against the invaders, but his war chiefs insisted on erecting earthwork fortifications. The British either stormed or simply went around these forts. It is believed that if Tawhiao's strategy had been adopted, the Maori might have had more success; they wouldn't have won the war, but they might have been able to get better terms from the British. The war dragged on until 1881, by which time the British occupied 1 million acres of Maori territory, and Tawhiao had been compelled to move his people farther south to a region that was named for him—King Country.

Hoping to reclaim his lost land, Tawhiao made the long voyage to England to put his case directly to Queen Victoria. Although he was a brother monarch, the queen would not see him; Tawhiao was fobbed off on the secretary of state for the colonies, who told the king that his complaint was a purely internal matter to be settled by New Zealanders.

This failure contributed to the Maori's loss of confidence in Tawhiao. Tribes began to break away, and even those that still respected Tawhiao no longer felt obligated to obey him. His political influence had evaporated.

The king's most enduring influence was religion. Many Maori believe he once prophesied that messengers of God, who spoke the Maori language and traveled in pairs, would cross the Pacific to New Zealand and bring to them a new kind of gospel. When Mormon missionaries from the United States arrived in New Zealand, they were fluent in the Maori language and traveled through the country in pairs. Many of Tawhiao's people took this as the fulfillment of his prophecy and converted. As for Tawhiao, the Church of Jesus Christ of Latter-day Saints has no record that the king ever became a Mormon.

Tawhiao showing ritual facial tattooing

PEDRO II

Emperor of Brazil (1825–1891)

At age nine, Pedro II was emperor of Brazil. Across the Atlantic, his fifteen-year-old sister, Maria II, was queen of Portugal. They came by their titles honestly—they were Braganzas, members of the royal family that had ruled Portugal since the fourteenth century.

The Braganzas arrived in the Portuguese colony of Brazil in 1808 when the Portuguese royal family left the country to escape Napoleon and set up a government in exile. In 1821, when King John VI returned to Europe, he left his son Pedro—Pedro II's father—as emperor of Brazil. Pedro I was too liberal for Brazil's upper class and too conservative for its intellectuals, but the ordinary people liked him, which paved the way for his son to become emperor. Young Pedro was almost universally popular, and he increased his popularity by modernizing Brazil.

Pedro II gave Brazil its first railroad, its first transatlantic telegraph, and its first telephones. He also introduced paved roads to his country. He opened grammar schools, high schools, and universities throughout the country, established libraries, and provided financial support for Brazilian artists and writers. In 1840, he began a gradual process of emancipating Brazil's slaves, starting with the forty slaves he had inherited.

Brazil had a legislature, but under the constitution, the emperor could exercise "moderating power" by vetoing a bill or even dissolving the lower house and calling for new elections.

In spite of his best efforts for his country, Pedro was a political dinosaur, particularly as South America had been swept by recurring waves of revolution since the first years of the nineteenth century. By abolishing slavery, he lost support among the landed elite, and by holding on to his monarchical privileges, he provoked the intellectuals. With his support dwindling, in 1889, a coup drove Pedro from power. He and his family left the country for France, where he died two years later.

In 1920, the bodies of Pedro and his wife, Teresa, were repatriated to Brazil and buried in a chapel of the cathedral of Petrópolis.

Pedro II amid his court

Cetshwayo

King of the Zulus (1826–1884)

The nephew of the great Shaka Zulu, Cetshwayo's reign coincided with the period when the power of the British and the Dutch colonists in South Africa was ready to eclipse the power of the Zulus. When the Dutch put pressure on the Zulus' border along the Transvaal colony, Cetshwayo courted the British in Natal, urging them to mediate. Officials of the British colonial government in Natal agreed that Cetshwayo's complaints were legitimate, but they had instructions from London to do nothing to disrupt good relations with the Dutch colonists in South Africa. So the British stalled, made military preparations in case a war erupted with the Zulus, and then at last gave Cetshwayo a decision that was flagrantly unjust to the Zulus.

War did break out between the British and the Zulus in January 1879. The Zulus won some victories, and plunged England and France into grief when they killed in battle Louis Napoleon, the twenty-three-year-old prince imperial of France. But the Zulus were outgunned, and in August 1879, Cetshwayo surrendered.

The British abolished the Zulu monarchy, stripped Cetshwayo of his authority, exiled him, then set about breaking up the Zulu kingdom into thirteen districts, each ruled by a man picked by the colonial government. While this arrangement succeeded in breaking the unity of the Zulus, it also brought out old hatreds and rivalries. To restore order to Zululand, the British permitted Cetshwayo to travel to London to discuss how to clean up the mess.

He was sent home with a commission to take up residence in the district at the center of Zululand, but his kingship was not restored; the Zulu kingdom was to remain divided. A new war broke out between Zulus who would not accept this settlement and Zulus who acquiesced to the British.

To escape the bloodshed, Cetshwayo took refuge with the British. He died the following year—of heart disease said the coroner, of poison said the king's followers.

FRANZ JOSEPH
Emperor of Austria, King of Hungary (1830–1916)

Franz Joseph spent his sixty-eight-year reign trying to satisfy his subjects' demands for some autonomy while preserving his absolute power and at the same time holding together his empire. The Hungarians, the Bohemians (known today as Czechs), and the Serbs were calling for independence, something the emperor would not grant them. As a compromise, he established constitutional governments in Austria and Hungary that gave each nation control over its internal affairs, but he did nothing to satisfy the nationalism of the Bohemians and the Serbs.

The Serbs, as Slavs and members of the Orthodox Church, appealed to the Russian tsar Alexander II to champion their cause, which he agreed to do. To counterbalance the Russian threat to his empire, Franz Joseph allied himself with the German Kaiser. This was in 1879, and it was the first step toward the polarization of Europe that would lead to World War I.

In his youth, the emperor had intended to marry the Bavarian princess Helene, but he reneged in favor of her younger sister, Elisabeth, a woman of breathtaking beauty. Franz Joseph was deeply in love with her, but Elisabeth hated court life in Vienna—she found the antique formality stifling and spent most of her life traveling to escape it. These absences were painful for the emperor.

More trouble came in 1889 when Franz Joseph's son and heir, Crown Prince Rudolf, killed his mistress, Baroness Maria Vetsera, and then killed himself. In 1898, while visiting Geneva, Empress Elisabeth was stabbed through the heart by an anarchist who explained to the police, "I wanted to kill a royal. It did not matter which one."

The assassination of Franz Ferdinand, next in line to the throne, and his wife, Sophie, by a Serbian nationalist added another sorrow on the overburdened emperor and became the excuse for the First World War.

Franz Joseph died in 1916, in the midst of the war. The Austro-Hungarian Empire survived him, but barely: Franz Joseph was succeeded by his grandnephew, Charles, who reigned only three years before the monarchy and empire were abolished.

SITTING BULL

Chief of the Hunkpapa Sioux (1831–1890)

At age fourteen, Sitting Bull counted his first coup on a Crow warrior—a danger-ous thing since it required him to strike but not injure his enemy. As he matured, he proved to be an especially courageous warrior, but also a deeply religious man. He learned the sacred mysteries of the Sioux (also known as the Lakota), and his back and chest were scarred from his repeated participation in the sacrificial, self-tortur-ing ritual known as the Sun Dance.

Having spent his youth fighting enemy tribes, in his thirties Sitting Bull began years of futile warfare against the Americans who poured into his tribe's territory, mining for gold, starting farms, and building forts. Some bands of Sioux gave up, settled on reservations, and let the federal government in Washington provide them with rations, but Sitting Bull and the Oglala Sioux war chief Crazy Horse would not surrender. They lived as the Sioux always had, following the buffalo in the Yel-lowstone and Powder valleys.

In 1868, the United States government signed a treaty with the Sioux promising to keep settlers out of the tribes' sacred Black Hills. However, when gold was dis-covered there, the treaty and its promises were forgotten. The culminating moment of the Great Sioux War that followed came in 1876 when Sitting Bull and Crazy Horse, riding with thousands of Indians, pinned down Lieutenant Colonel George Armstrong Custer and approximately two hundred men of the Seventh Cavalry at Little Bighorn, and killed them all. By 1881, however, the overwhelming number of American troops and the dwindling number of buffalo forced Sitting Bull to admit defeat. He lived for a time on a reservation until Buffalo Bill Cody hired him as the star attraction of his traveling Wild West show.

In 1890, he retired to the Standing Rock Reservation, where he became one of the spiritual leaders of the religious movement known as the Ghost Dance. The government agent on the reservation called for Sitting Bull's removal. Indian police broke into the chief's cabin and were dragging him away when Sitting Bull's follow-ers intervened. A gunfight erupted, during which one of the Indian police shot and killed Sitting Bull.

Photograph of Sitting Bull in Bismarck, North Dakota

Maximilian I and Carlota

Emperor (1832–1867) and Empress (1840–1927) of Mexico

In 1863, the thirty-two-year-old Austrian archduke Maximilian was idling his time away with his exquisite wife, Charlotte (later known as Carlota), at their palace in Trieste when word reached him that he had been chosen to be emperor of Mexico. In his innocence, Maximilian believed he had been elected emperor by the Mexican people; in fact, he had been hand picked by Napoleon III of France, who wanted to put down a liberal revolution in Mexico and make the country part of France's empire. A French army accompanied the royal couple to Mexico, where they were greeted enthusiastically by conservative Mexicans.

To the horror of his conservative allies, Maximilian embraced policies that were being promoted by the revolutionary Benito Juárez: the emperor called for redistribution of land, freedom of religion, and civilian control of the military, and he extended the right to vote to all classes of Mexicans.

Juárez and his followers were not impressed. Maximilian was still an emperor, and worse yet, a foreigner put in place by a foreign power and backed up by foreign troops. To underscore their contempt for Maximilian, Juárez's followers shot anyone who supported the emperor. Maximilian, contrary to his liberal mind-set, gave orders that Juárez supporters should likewise be shot.

In 1866 the United States began supplying weapons to Juárez's troops. That same year Napoleon III withdrew his army from Mexico. Carlota traveled to Europe and pleaded with kings to send help to her beleaguered husband, but they all found some excuse why they could not get involved. In Queretaro, Juárez's men captured Maximilian, tried him before a court martial, and sentenced him to death. Juárez was flooded with appeals for clemency, even from liberals such as Giuseppe Garibaldi, but he insisted that the execution of Maximilian would send a message to the world to keep out of Mexico's affairs.

On June 19, 1867, Maximilian and two of his generals were executed by firing squad. When Carlota heard the news, she suffered an emotional breakdown from which she never recovered. She spent the rest of her long life in seclusion.

The execution of Emperor Maximilian, seen here wearing a sombrero

CIXI

Empress of China (1835–1908)

Cixi was a concubine of low birth but she did what no other wife or concubine of the emperor of China managed to do—she gave the emperor a son. Soon thereafter the old emperor died, and at the reading of the will, it was learned that Cixi had been named regent. She liked exercising power, but when her son came of age, she retired quietly to Beijing's opulent Summer Palace. A few years later, Cixi's son died, and his cousin, a three-year-old child, was named emperor. Cixi was brought back to be regent once again. When this boy was old enough to reign, Cixi stepped aside, but not for long. In 1898, she staged a palace coup against her nephew and took over the government.

A genius at manipulation, and domineering to the point of despotism, Cixi was overprotective of her power and her privileges. She rejected any suggestion of political or social reform in China. To build her magnificent Summer Palace, she expropriated funds that had been earmarked to build China a navy. When she decided to reorganization the bureaucracy, she began by executing two of its most senior members—the better to ensure that her wishes would be carried out fully.

The Taiping Rebellion revealed to the world what Cixi was willing to do to stay in power. The uprising was led by a madman, Hung Hsiu-chuan, who believed he was the younger brother of Jesus Christ and had been given a mission by the Christian God to destroy the Manchus. The war to destroy the Taipings, as Hung's followers were called, cost the lives of 11 million Chinese.

Hostile to the Western powers that dreamed of adding China to their overseas empires, and suspicious even of Western traders and missionaries, in 1900 Cixi supported the Boxers, a nationalist terrorist organization that called for the restoration of traditional Chinese values by killing all Westerners in the country, as well as any Chinese who were contaminated with Western values, such as Chinese Christians. The British, French, Germans, Russians, Japanese, Americans, Austrians, and Italians raised a multinational army that crushed the Boxers and forced on Cixi a humiliating treaty in which she agreed to pay $333 million in reparations, grant the Western countries valuable trade concessions, and permit them to maintain armed troops in China.

Cixi died in 1908 and was buried in the tomb complex she had constructed—a marvel of temples and pavilions, all covered with gold leaf.

LEOPOLD II
King of Belgium (1835–1909)

Like virtually every other sovereign of the nineteenth century, Leopold II believed that oversea colonies could make a country wealthy and powerful. To the king's disappointment, neither his government nor his people shared his opinion. Then Leopold had a burst of inspiration: he would establish a private colony, fully owned and operated by himself.

In 1876, he hired the explorer Henry Morton Stanley (who five years earlier had tracked down the missing missionary Dr. David Livingstone) to find a suitable location for a colony; Stanley suggested the Congo. At a conference in Berlin in 1884–1885, representatives of the United States and fourteen European nations recognized Leopold as the sole proprietor of the Congo, a territory seventy-six times larger than Belgium. All profits generated in the colony went directly into Leopold's pocket, and to keep order in the Congo, he employed a private army, known, ironically, as the Force Publique.

One of the largest moneymakers in the king's colony was the rubber industry. Leopold's foremen treated Congolese men, women, and children as slaves. Anyone who defied the Belgians was tortured or killed outright. During a tour of inspection, the British consul, Roger Casement, found that bosses punished children who would not work, or did not work fast enough, by lopping off a hand. Congolese who did not deliver their weekly quota of food or woven baskets were flogged so viciously that they carried the scars for the rest of their lives. And then there were the epidemics of smallpox and other diseases that swept through the villages and camps where the slave laborers, too weak and malnourished to fight off the infections, died by the thousands. At least 2 million Africans died working for King Leopold, although some researchers claim the number is as high as 15 million.

Casement's report sparked the world's first international human rights campaign, which concluded when the Belgian parliament forced Leopold to sign over the Congo to the nation of Belgium.

Leopold died in 1909. As the hearse bearing his body rolled through the streets of Brussels, the crowd booed.

LILIUOKALANI

Queen of the Hawaiian Islands (1838–1917)

By the time Liliuokalani was born, the Hawaiian royal family was living in a style that imitated the monarchs of Europe. She received a Western-style education at a school run by American missionaries, where she showed a particular talent for music and poetry. During her lifetime, Liliuokalani wrote 150 songs, including the classic, "Aloha Oe."

In 1887, while her brother Kalakaua was king, Liliuokalani traveled to England to join the other monarchs of the world in celebrating Queen Victoria's golden jubilee. When she returned to Hawaii, she learned that her brother had signed a new constitution that made Hawaiian monarchs little more than figureheads. In 1891, Kalakaua died and Liliuokalani became queen.

American residents in Hawaii, known as annexationists, were eager for the islands to become a United States territory. Liliuokalani, however, wanted to maintain her homeland's independence. Her attempt to pass a new constitution that would restore to the Hawaiian monarchs their rights and powers gave the annexationists the excuse they had been waiting for. The U.S. minister to the island brought in American troops "to protect American life and property," while the annexationists staged a coup that drove Liliuokalani from the throne. She did not fight back, but appealed to President Grover Cleveland to restore her rights and her country's independence. Cleveland was sympathetic, but declined to use any of his political capital to restore the queen.

In 1894, soon after the annexationists established the Republic of Hawaii, native Hawaiians rebelled against the new government; Liliuokalani may have been involved in the insurrection. After the insurgency was suppressed, Liliuokalani accepted the new status quo, took an oath of allegiance to the republic, and retired from public life. The territorial legislature voted her an annual pension of $4,000 and gave her a 6,000-acre sugar plantation to supplement her income. In her will, she left her fortune to the Queen Liliuokalani Trust to assist needy and orphaned children. The Trust is still in existence.

A photograph of Liliuokalani, inscribed by the queen for the U.S. Secretary of the Navy

JOSEPH

Chief of the Nez Percé (1841–1904)

Under the terms of a treaty signed by Nez Percé chiefs and representatives of the United States government, all members of the tribe were confined to a small reservation in present-day Oregon. Originally the Nez Percé reservation had been much larger, but as miners and other settlers poured into Oregon, demanding more land, the federal government decided to open up for settlement lands that had been promised to the Indians.

Chief Joseph's father felt betrayed and led his band east of the Rockies to buffalo country; other Nez Percé chiefs did the same. Joseph grew up there, married, and started a family that included five girls and four boys. Joseph became chief in 1871. Then, in 1877, the federal authorities insisted that all bands of Nez Percé return to the reservation; Joseph and several other chiefs obeyed. But en route to the reservation in Oregon, a band of Nez Percé warriors killed several settlers. Joseph and his fellow chiefs, fearful that federal troops would punish the entire tribe for the killings, turned around and headed east.

In four months, five hundred Nez Percé traveled a thousand miles across Idaho and Montana with the aim of getting across the border into Canada, where the U.S. soldiers could not pursue them. They fought a running war, and inflicted several defeats on the U.S. troops. Joseph would not permit his warriors to harm white women and children, or to mutilate the bodies of fallen soldiers and settlers—a policy that won him admiration and sympathy back east. But the odds were against the Nez Percé. By October 1877, Joseph was the only chief still alive or not in Canada, and although the border was only thirty miles away, the women, children, and elderly were too sick and weak to make the final run toward safety. As he surrendered his rifle to General Nelson Miles, he delivered a moving speech that has become a classic of American oratory. "It is cold and we have no blankets. The little children are freezing to death," he said. "Hear me, my chiefs. I am tired. My heart is sick and sad. From where the sun now stands, I will fight no more forever."

Joseph hoped the U.S. government would send him back to the Wallowa Valley in Oregon; instead he was confined on reservations in Kansas, then Oklahoma, and finally at Nespelem, Washington, where he died in his sleep.

Edward VII

King of Great Britain, Emperor of India (1841–1910)

His parents, Victoria and Albert, considered their son Bertie (as they called him), too irresponsible to be trusted with any political power. When Bertie was eighteen, his father wrote, "It grieves me when one considers that he might be called on at any moment to take over the reins of government." Stung by this lack of confidence, Bertie acted even more irresponsibly, frittering away the years carousing, attending sporting events, setting the standard for male fashion, and chasing women. He genuinely loved his wife, Alexandra, but could not resist the attractions of beautiful women such as the celebrated actress Lillie Langtry.

But if he was a disappointment at the palace, in the country and abroad Bertie was popular and well respected. He knew personally, and was related to, virtually every king and queen on the Continent, and he used these ties to arbitrate between contending kingdoms. He developed a reputation as a peacemaker, and historians believe that it was Bertie who forestalled the First World War.

By the time he came to throne in 1901, he was sixty years old, stout, bald, and in poor health. In the nine years of his reign, he had little time to make the type of impact his mother had made upon the nation and the world, but he achieved several important foreign successes—an alliance with Japan, an *entente* with France, and friendly relations with Russia. Arrayed against these powers was the Triple Alliance of Germany, Austria, and Italy, forged by the king's bellicose, megalomaniacal nephew Kaiser Wilhelm.

In Edward's day, kings and emperors still visited one another, the aristocracy of Europe still stood at the pinnacle of society, and the wealth and power of the upper classes went virtually unchallenged. All that would be swept away by World War I and the Russian Revolution. Yet at Edward's death, it seemed as if the old days would be gone forever—his body was escorted to the grave by no fewer than nine kings.

Photograph of Edward VII taken the year before he became king

Muhammad Ahmad

The Mahdi (1844–1885)

In Islam, the Mahdi is a messianic figure who will restore the faith to its purest form and establish a final age of justice on earth just before the end of the world. In the late nineteenth century in the Sudan, a mystic named Muhammad Ahmad declared that he was the Mahdi, and that part of his mission was to drive out of the Sudan the Ottoman Turks, the Egyptians, and the British. "I am the Mahdi, the Successor of the Prophet of God," he told his followers, "Cease to pay taxes to the infidel Turks and let everyone who finds a Turk kill him, for the Turks are infidels." The authorities in Egypt sent troops into the desert to find Muhammad Ahmad's camp and arrest him, but the Mahdi's followers—called the *ansar*, or the "helpers"—ambushed and massacred almost the entire army.

In 1883, the Mahdi won stunning victories. First his men, armed only with spears and swords, overwhelmed four thousand professional Egyptian troops. The Egyptians responded by sending an army of eight thousand, led by a British officer, William Hicks, into the Sudan to punish the Mahdi, but this army was destroyed by forty thousand *ansar*. Each victory increased Muhammad Ahmad's standing among his people: they were triumphing over old enemies, therefore, he must be the Mahdi.

Finally, the *ansar* defeated four thousand British troops, a victory that convinced the British government to abandon the Sudan and limit their involvement to securing the ports along the Red Sea, including Khartoum. In 1884, the government sent General Charles Gordon, an unconventional but highly successful military man, to evacuate Europeans and Egyptians from Khartoum. Gordon got twenty-five hundred non-Sudanese out before the Mahdi and the *ansar* surrounded and cut off the city.

After a nine-month siege, a resident of Khartoum who supported the Mahdi secretly opened the gates along the Nile, and the *ansar* swarmed into the city. In the slaughter that ensued, the entire garrison was killed, and Gordon was hacked to death, beheaded, and his head was mounted in a tree where passersby could see it.

Six months after his victory at Khartoum, the Mahdi died. Without his leadership, his movement fell into disarray and the *ansar* were defeated and scattered by British and Ethiopian armies.

LUDWIG II THE MAD

King of Bavaria (1845–1886)

In the English-speaking world, Ludwig is known as "the Mad" because he was deposed on the grounds that he was mentally unstable. In German-speaking lands, however, he is known as *der Märchenkönig*, the fairy-tale king, because of his attachment to German folklore and his passion for medieval-style castles.

It is true that Ludwig was a man whose enthusiasms had an all-consuming quality. He was especially passionate about the operas of Richard Wagner, and became not just his most ardent fan but also his patron. Ludwig was nineteen when he met his hero, and Wagner was as impressed by the prince as the prince was by the composer. "Alas, he is so handsome and wise, soulful and lovely," Wagner wrote, "that I fear that his life must melt away in this vulgar world like a fleeting dream of the gods." In 1872, Ludwig began construction of a festival theater designed especially for the performance of Wagner's operas. There he attended private performances of early versions of Wagner's Ring cycle. But he also had an even more intimate setting for performances: at Linderhof Palace he built a grotto where opera singers sang to the king while he was rowed about in a boat shaped like a shell.

Castles were Ludwig's second greatest passion. His finest architectural achievement was the construction of Neuschwanstein Castle atop a mountain crag. Above the battlements soar fairy-tale towers, and the walls are adorned with frescoes of scenes from Wagner's operas. Ludwig used his own resources to pay for these and other construction projects, but by 1885 he was 14 million marks in debt. His extravagances distressed his ministers, and they began to collect a file of eccentric behavior as well as servants' gossip, all of which they used as evidence of the king's insanity. Two days after Ludwig was deposed, he went for a walk along a lakeshore with the doctor who had declared him mentally unfit to rule. Hours later, the bodies of the king and the doctor were discovered floating in shallow water. To this day, no one knows what happened at the lakeshore, if Ludwig and the doctor were murdered by unknown persons, or if the king killed the doctor and then drowned himself.

MEIJI
Emperor of Japan (1852–1912)

Beginning in the seventeenth century, Japan sealed itself off from the outside world, permitting only limited trade and no other contact with Europe, America, or even other Asian nations. For nearly 250 years, Japan remained frozen in time, a medieval world of lords whose every word and action went unquestioned, samurai warriors who clung to a rigid military code, and submissive peasants. In this world, the emperor was venerated as having descended from the gods, but politically he was a figurehead. When an American, Commodore Matthew Perry, sailed his battleships into what is now known as Tokyo Bay and forced the Japanese to end their isolation, the imperial court was among the first to support this daring innovation.

Meiji was born the year Commodore Perry stepped ashore in Japan. He was given an education that drew upon non-Japanese sources, which revealed to him that kings in Europe wielded real power. The boy emperor's education was the beginning of the end of medieval Japan and of docile Japanese emperors.

When Meiji came to power, he took a new oath that he had apparently composed for himself: he swore to establish a legislature, abolish feudalism, and to model Japan's government administration, economy, and military on Western models.

The emperor wore Western-style clothes, ate Western food, worked very hard at bringing his country into the modern world, and set an example for living simply without any imperial ostentation.

It was difficult for many Japanese to adjust to the dramatic and unfamiliar changes Meiji imposed on them, and so the emperor developed another strategy. Although he had power now and exercised it, he positioned himself as a godlike figure, the living embodiment of the kingdom. Poor judgment, ineffectual policies, or bad legislation would be the fault of the ministers and legislators, but never of the emperor, who was above such petty concerns.

By the time of Meiji's death, the modernization process was virtually completed, so much so that in 1905 Japan utterly defeated Russia in war.

Emperor Meiji (seated on the right) with his family.

RUDOLF

Crown Prince of Austria (1858—1889)

Prince Rudolf's brief life was not a happy one. His liberal political and social ideas put him at odds with his father, Emperor Franz Joseph, who almost considered his only son a subversive. The emperor and his prime minister, Count Eduard von Taaffe, struck back by excluding the prince from all affairs of state. As for Rudolf's mother, the Empress Elisabeth, she shared many of his ideas, including granting more autonomy to the ethnic groups within the empire, but she had always been emotionally aloof from her son. It did their relationship no good when the empress dismissed Rudolf's wife, Princess Stéphanie of Belgium, as an oaf. By the time Rudolf and Stéphanie had a child, a daughter they named Elisabeth Marie, their marriage had soured, and the prince began to look for female companionship elsewhere.

Desperate to do something constructive, Rudolf began writing anonymous articles for a politically radical newspaper. He sponsored an epic reference work on the every facet of life in the Austro-Hungarian Empire. And he toyed with the idea of convincing the Poles to elect him their king, or perhaps—and this was a long shot—persuading his father to make him king of Hungary. Nothing came of these royal ambitions, and Rudolf began to suffer bouts of depression.

In 1887, Rudolf acquired Mayerling, a manor house outside Vienna that he used as a hunting lodge. That same year he met seventeen-year-old Baroness Maria Vetsera, the daughter of an Austrian diplomat. They began an affair that lasted about eighteen months.

On January 29, 1889, Rudolf's driver took the couple to Mayerling. The next morning they were found in Rudolf's room, dead. For more than a century, conspiracy theories have swirled around the deaths, but most likely Rudolf shot and killed Maria, then turned his gun on himself.

Neither Franz Joseph nor Elisabeth ever recovered from the murder-suicide. Some historians have argued that with the death of Rudolf, the collapse of the Austro-Hungarian Empire was inevitable, since there was no other heir who shared the crown prince's reforming zeal.

WOVOKA

Prophet of the Ghost Dance (1858–1932)

On January 1, 1887, Wovoka, a Northern Paiute, was ill with a fever when his soul was transported to the afterlife, where he received his Great Revelation. God commanded him to dance the traditional Round Dance (later known as the Ghost Dance) and promised him power over the natural world and political power equal to that the of the president of the United States. Wovoka's followers said that after this vision he was able to make ice appear on the hottest days of summer, and he was impervious to gunpowder. It was the second "miracle" that led to the creation of Ghost Shirts, sacred garments that were believed to keep the wearer safe from bullets. At Wounded Knee in 1890, two hundred Lakota men, women, and children were wearing Ghost Shirts when they were shot and killed by U.S. troops.

Representatives of many tribes visited Wovoka to discuss his visions and his message, and over time his message became confused with that of other Indian mystics. The Lakota, for example, believed Wovoka promised that the Ghost Dance would eradicate all the whites and bring back from the dead all their fallen family members and friends. There was another Paiute prophet named Wodziwob who had promised such a thing, but it is not clear if Wovoka taught this, too.

Wovoka had grown up on a ranch that belonged to the Wilson family and his name in white society was Jack Wilson. Between the devout Presbyterian beliefs of the Wilsons and the outdoor revivals led by traveling preachers, Wovoka's religious message was a mix of Christian and traditional Indian elements. Crowds of Indians came to see him work miracles, and then, like a congregation at a revival, they would take up a collection for him.

After the disaster at Wounded Knee, many Indians dismissed Wovoka as a fraud, while others threatened to kill him. For his own safety, he stopped preaching, but he welcomed visitors and passed on his message to them privately. He also sold them eagle feathers, red ochre, and even the ten-gallon Stetson hats he favored, all of which were said to have healing powers. And his reputation for making miracles survived: at the outset of World War I, some Indians believed Wovoka would help President Woodrow Wilson by making the Atlantic Ocean freeze so American troops could walk to France.

Wovoka with actor Tim McCoy

WILHELM II
Emperor of Germany (1859–1941)

Wilhelm II was one of the strangest and most dangerous royals of the modern era. He craved the attention of his English relatives—his grandmother Queen Victoria, his uncle Edward VII, his cousin George V. But he had nothing but contempt for his own father and mother, who planned to introduce a constitutional monarchy in Germany.

Wilhelm wanted to wield power like his cousin the tsar. Furthermore, he imagined himself a great military commander in the tradition of Frederick the Great; in fact, he had no leadership skills, and his military experience was limited to a fascination with uniforms and military ceremonies. One of the first things Wilhelm did upon becoming emperor was to dismiss Otto von Bismarck. For decades Bismarck had kept Germany out of war, and the kaiser was itching for combat.

His militaristic posturing and his rearmament of the German navy distressed Wilhelm's grandmother, Victoria, who like her son Edward VII, feared that the kaiser's ego would plunge Europe into war. When World War I erupted across Europe, Wilhelm was entirely unqualified to lead. Soon his troops were fighting on two fronts: Great Britain and France to the west, Russia to the east. When the United States entered the war, Germany was in real trouble—the American troops were fresh, there were lots more of them in America, and as opposed to Germany's dwindling supplies, the resources of the United States appeared endless.

On November 9, 1818, two days before the armistice was signed, Wilhelm abdicated and with his family left Germany for an estate in Doorn, Holland. In 1940 Wilhelm sent a telegram to Adolf Hitler congratulating him on the conquest of France. The Führer detested the kaiser; when Nazi troops invaded Holland, a column marched right passed Wilhelm's estate in Doorn—but not a single German officer stopped to pay a courtesy call on the ex-emperor.

Franz Ferdinand

Archduke of Austria (1863–1914)

The suicide of Austria's crown prince Rudolf made Archduke Franz Ferdinand next in line to inherit the Austro-Hungarian Empire. Unlike his uncle, Emperor Franz Joseph, Franz Ferdinand believed the empire was on the brink of a major crisis. Rising nationalism among the various ethnic groups—Serbs, Bohemians, Bosnians, Croats, Hungarians—was straining the unity of the empire. Franz Ferdinand's solution was to create a new "United States of Austria," which would recognize sovereign states drawn up along ethnic lines

Franz Joseph didn't much care for this proposal, just as he didn't much care for Franz Ferdinand's wife, Sophie. Because she was not of royal blood, the emperor had tried to stop the marriage. Franz Ferdinand insisted, however, and so the emperor played the only card he had left: Sophie would not receive any royal title, she could never be crowned empress, and her children would not be in line for the throne.

The assassination of Franz Ferdinand and Sophie was the result of their driver taking a wrong turn. During the couple's visit to Sarajevo, a Serbian assassin threw a grenade at their open car. He missed, and the grenade bounced off the hood to explode behind the automobile. Franz Ferdinand and Sophie insisted upon being taken to the hospital where the injured were being treated. En route, their driver lost his bearings and turned up a side street just as another assassin, Gavrilo Princip, was walking along. He pulled out his pistol, hurried over to the car, and fired twice, striking Sophie in the stomach and Franz Ferdinand in the neck.

As Sophie slumped over, unconscious, her husband cried, "Sophie dear! Sophie dear! Don't die! Stay alive for the sake of the children." As help arrived, the archduke fell forward, saying over and over again, "It is nothing. It is nothing." They were his last words.

Franz Ferdinand and his wife Sophie approaching their car moments before their assassination

ELIZABETH

Grand Duchess of Russia (1864–1918)

Like her younger sister, Alexandra, Elizabeth's fate was tied to that of the Romanovs. Alexandra married Nicholas II, the last tsar; Elizabeth married Nicholas's uncle, the Grand Duke Sergei.

Elizabeth and Sergei had known each other as children; their relationship had always been friendly but not romantic, yet when Sergei proposed, Elizabeth accepted.

The marriage fell apart quickly. Sergei was a homosexual, a heavy drinker, and given to fits of jealousy. The rest of the imperial family felt sorry for Elizabeth (whom they called Ella); she was a lovely young woman who deserved better. To everyone's surprise, Elizabeth seemed to genuinely love Sergei.

In February 1905, Sergei was riding in a coach through the Kremlin when a revolutionary threw a bomb. The force of the explosion was so great that it literally blew the grand duke's body to bits. Ella, who was in a palace inside the Kremlin, ran outside when she heard the explosion; she found nothing but a bloody mess scattered across the snow.

After four years of mourning and wondering what she should do with her life, Ella sold off her jewels and all her other possessions and built a convent in Moscow, with herself as abbess. The women who joined her called themselves the Sisters of Sts. Martha and Mary. They operated a hospital, an orphanage, and a dispensary for the poor. From time to time, Ella visited the imperial family, but her last visit, in 1916, ended badly. She had gone to see her sister Alexandra to explain that Rasputin was undermining the monarchy and to persuade her to give him up. Instead, Alexandra cut off all contact with Ella.

In 1918, a year after the fall of the tsar and his government, Lenin ordered the arrest of Ella and five of her Romanov relatives. Red Guards herded them into carts, then drove them into the woods outside the town of Alapayevsk. There the guards threw their prisoners into an abandoned mine shaft, dropped in hand grenades to kill the wounded, then shoved burning brush and timber into the shaft to finish off anyone who was still alive. A few weeks later, the Whites, Russians loyal to the tsar, recovered the bodies. Wrapped around the head of one of the Romanov princes was Ella's handkerchief—she had bandaged the wound before she died.

ELIZABETH

KIN

Nicholas II and Alexandra

Tsar (1868–1918) and Tsarina (1872–1918) of Russia

As monarchs with a seventeenth-century worldview, Nicholas and Alexandra were entirely unsuited to rule at the beginning of the twentieth century. Even as revolution spread across Europe and took root in Russia, Nicholas rejected all calls for schools, decent working conditions in the factories, access to doctors, freedom of religion, and rights for ethnic minorities. After the revolution of 1905, he made one concession: he granted Russia a Duma, or parliament of the people's elected representatives, but he maintained the power to shut it down whenever he liked.

Nicholas and Alexandra had four daughters and one son, Alexis. The discovery that the boy had hemophilia devastated the family. In desperation, Alexandra turned to Siberian mystic Grigory Rasputin, who on several occasions when Alexis had suffered an accident had stopped the bleeding. So fierce was her attachment to Rasputin that she would not believe any report that exposed him for what he really was—a drunken, lecherous, blaspheming lout. It was whispered throughout Russia that Rasputin violated Alexandra and her daughters, yet still she would not give him up.

World War I was the death knell of the tsars. Russia did not have the railroads, the factories, or the technology to fight the highly mechanized armies of Germany and Austria. What Russia had was millions of men, but the country could not keep them supplied with weapons, ammunition, food, warm clothes, or even boots. At the front, troops surrendered in droves to the enemy, or deserted. In the cities there were riots and strikes as the civilian population suffered from shortages of food and fuel.

In March 1917, members of the Duma had had enough; they established a provisional government and called upon Nicholas to abdicate in favor of his son. Fearing for the boy's health, Nicholas abdicated on behalf of Alexis, too. The new government hoped to get the royal family out of Russia, but before they could do so, Lenin overthrew the provisional government, established a Bolshevik state, and sentenced Nicholas, Alexandra, and the five children to death. In 1918, a Communist death squad shot and killed the entire family, along with a handful of their servants, in the cellar of a run-down house in Ekaterinburg.

A portrait of the Russian Imperial Family

MARIE

Queen of Romania (1875–1938)

Glamour, scandal, and courage all attended the life and reign of Marie of Romania. As a granddaughter of Queen Victoria, she was a desirable match for any prince in Europe; her choice was Crown Prince Ferdinand, future king of Romania, whom she married in 1893.

Marie had six children, three sons and three daughters, although how many were fathered by Ferdinand is up for debate. There was also a "mystery child." In 1897, only four years into her marriage, Marie had an affair with an army officer named Cantacuzene. When she discovered that she was pregnant, she traveled to Coburg, Germany, where she remained with her mother until she had given birth. Whether the baby was a boy or a girl, and what became of it, is a secret Marie took to her grave.

As the years went by, Marie found that she could barely tolerate her husband. In a letter to a friend, Gerte Fuller, she wrote of "distaste, which grew to revulsion." She began an affair with Prince Barbu Stirbey, Romania's prime minister; it was likely that the prince fathered Marie's son Mircea and her daughter Ilena. Her daughter Maria may have been fathered by Grand Duke Boris of Russia—at least that is what Marie told her father-in-law, King Carol. In 1903, when she was about to deliver her son Nicholas, Pauline Astor came from America to Romania to be with Marie during the birth. Given the queen's track record, this led to speculation that the baby's father was Pauline's brother, Waldorf Astor. As for Ferdinand, he accepted all of Marie's children as his own.

During World War I, Marie emerged as an ardent Romanian patriot. The German army had overrun most of the kingdom, and some officers in the Romanian army were calling for an all-out retreat into Russian territory. Instead, Marie and several commanders worked out a strategy in which they concentrated the army on one vital portion of the country, from which there would be no retreat.

After the war, the Romanian government hoped it would be able to claim portions of Austro-Hungarian and Russian territory that had large populations of ethnic Romanians. To ensure that these territories would be annexed to Romania, Marie traveled to Versailles, where she used her glamour and charm—along with some judicious arm-twisting—to get everything she wanted.

FAISAL I
King of Iraq (1885–1933)

As the Ottoman Empire crumbled, Faisal, son of one of the most distinguished Muslim families in Arabia, saw an opportunity for home rule for the Arabs. In 1915, he went to Istanbul to argue his cause, but although their empire was on life support, the Ottomans refused to make any concessions to the Arabs. Faisal's next stop was Damascus, where he and other Arab leaders drew up the Damascus Protocol in which they pledged to assist the British war effort by leading an Arab revolt against the Ottomans. In return, the British would support the creation of independent Arab states in Arabia and Mesopotamia.

In 1916, the Arab Revolt was proclaimed in Mecca, Islam's holiest city. Faisal led his army against the Ottomans while the British invaded Palestine (modern-day Israel). Allied with Faisal was a twenty-eight-year-old Anglo-Irish intelligence officer and amateur archaeologist with strong Arab sympathies, T.E. Lawrence, better known as Lawrence of Arabia. Together they disrupted Turkish railway lines and captured the port of Aqaba. Lawrence was invaluable in getting British military supplies for Faisal's men, and after the war Lawrence advised the British Middle East Department to install Faisal as king of what is now Iraq.

In 1919, Faisal met with Chaim Weizmann, head of the World Zionist Organization. Together they hammered out an agreement in which Faisal agreed to accept Jewish immigration to Palestine if Weizmann guaranteed that the Jewish settlers would respect the religious rights and property of Arab farmers. Faisal believed the Arab state the British had promised him in Mesopotamia would balance Jewish settlement in Palestine.

To give his reign validity, Faisal called for a referendum, and 96 percent of voters confirmed him as king of Iraq. Their trust was well placed: Faisal proved to be a shrewd king who was able to keep happy British colonial officials, Arab nationalists, and tribal sheikhs. Sadly, after his death, Iraq sank into decades of unrest and instability.

Faisal and his advisors at the Versailles peace conference. Standing behind the King on his left is Lawrence of Arabia

HAILE SELASSIE I

Emperor of Ethiopia (1892–1975)

The most dramatic moment of Haile Selassie's life came in 1936. Italy, led by Benito Mussolini, had just conquered Ethiopia in a brutal invasion during which the Italians used poison gas on the Ethiopians. Driven out of his kingdom, the emperor traveled to Geneva, where he asked the League of Nations for help. "At a time when my people are threatened with extermination, when the support of the League may ward off the final blow, may I be allowed to speak with complete frankness, without reticence, in all directness such as is demanded by the rule of equality as between all States Members of the League? . . . I ask what measures do you intend to take?"

The League of Nations did nothing. But in 1941, the British liberated Ethiopia and Haile Selassie returned home.

The royal family of Ethiopia was unique in the world: it claimed to be descended directly from the offspring of King Solomon and the Queen of Sheba. They ruled over a land that was religiously divided between Orthodox Christians and Muslims (with a large population of Ethiopian Jews), was dominated by tradition, and where modern technology was virtually unknown. Haile Selassie wanted to give his country a written constitution, update the financial system, bring the army into the twentieth century, and introduce his people to the luxuries and conveniences that were taken for granted in the West. But rigid traditionalists in Ethiopia believed he was going too fast, introducing innovations that no one needed or wanted, and undermining the unique character of their country. Rather than fight the traditionalists, Haile Selassie slowed down the pace of his reforms.

He still encouraged Ethiopian students to attend universities overseas, but once they returned home, the graduates found few opportunities to put their education to work for the good of their country.

The late 1960s and early 1970s brought a string of disasters to Ethiopia—economic stagnation, rising urban poverty, famine, and then the Arab oil embargo, which sent fuel prices soaring. In 1974, a military junta arrested the eighty-two-year-old emperor and took him to prison. No one knows how he died, or when, or where he was buried.

Haile Selassie in full coronation regalia

EDWARD VIII

King of Great Britain, Emperor of India (1894–1972)

Edward VIII reigned for 326 days, more than enough time for him to get to Westminster Abbey and be crowned king. But there was a hitch—Edward was in love with a twice-divorced American whom he wanted to marry and have crowned queen. The British government, the Church of England, and a good part of the British people felt the lady in question was not a suitable candidate. So, in 1937 Edward renounced the throne, then made a radio address in which he explained, "I have found it impossible to carry the heavy burden of responsibility and to discharge my duties as king as I would wish to do without the help and support of the woman I love." At the time many people around the world viewed Edward's abdication in a romantic light, but over the years, as biographers have uncovered more information about Edward and his wife, Wallis Warfield Simpson, the couple no longer appear nearly so attractive.

After abdicating, Edward traveled to France, where he and Mrs. Simpson married. His brother, King George VI, granted the couple the titles duke and duchess of Windsor, but with the stipulation that the duchess could not be addressed as Your Royal Highness. Edward never forgave his family for this slight, just as they never forgave him for acting selfishly.

The duke and duchess embarked on a life of nonstop pleasure—golfing, cruises, parties, vacations on the Riviera. In 1937, they traveled to Hitler's Germany, which further antagonized the family and the British government—the presence of a former king of England was giving legitimacy to the Nazi regime. When World War II broke out in 1939, the duke offered his services to his country, but there were rumors of a Nazi plot to overthrow the king and queen and replace them with the duke and duchess, who would make peace with Germany. To get his brother out of the way, King George sent Edward to Bermuda as governor-general.

After the war, the duke and duchess returned to Europe and their endless round of amusements. In 1972, as the duke lay dying, Queen Elizabeth, Prince Philip, and Prince Charles visited the couple in Paris. When Edward died, Queen Elizabeth put an end to the rift by insisting on a proper royal funeral at which the duchess was treated with great respect and consideration.

The former king and Wallis Simpson on their wedding day

GEORGE VI AND ELIZABETH

King (1895–1952) and Queen (1900–2002) of Great Britain

The abdication of his brother, Edward VIII, pushed George into the spotlight. He was a shy man with a slight speech impediment that made public speaking an ordeal, but his wife, Elizabeth, was all grace and quiet charisma, at ease anywhere and with everyone. With their two delightful little girls, Elizabeth and Margaret, they seemed a typical English family—except they were now king and queen and princesses. And after the glitz and sophistication of Edward, Mrs. Simpson, and their smart set of friends, the new, utterly ordinary royal family were easily accepted by the people of Great Britain.

It was this family's fate to live in extraordinary times. Three years after George's coronation, Nazi Germany invaded Poland, and the world was plunged into another war. One by one the nations of Europe fell before Hitler's *Blitzkrieg*, and soon England was virtually alone, fighting for survival. Almost every night, waves of Nazi bombers attacked English cities and towns. For safety's sake, some English parents sent their children to live in the country, while others sent them all the way to Canada. During the Blitz, the cabinet urged the queen to take the children and leave London, perhaps even go to Canada themselves. Elizabeth replied publicly: "The children won't go without me. I won't leave the king. And the king will never leave." When Buckingham Palace took several hits from Nazi bombers, the queen, referring to a neighborhood of London that had been especially hard hit, declared, "I'm glad we've been bombed. It makes me feel I can look the East End in the face." Such simple statements of courage and solidarity inspired the beleaguered British public.

After the war, it was George's duty to preside over the dissolution of the British Empire. Palestine became the State of Israel. India, over which he had reigned as emperor, split in two: India and Pakistan.

The worry over World War II and the breakdown of the empire took its toll on George's health. He was diagnosed with several ailments, most seriously lung cancer and arteriosclerosis. King George died in 1952 and was succeeded by his daughter Elizabeth.

Queen Elizabeth lived on for another fifty years, becoming the most popular member of the royal family.

Queen Elizabeth playing the piano as King George looks on

CHARLOTTE
Grand Duchess of Luxembourg (1896–1985)

Charlotte's elder sister, Marie Adélaïde, had ruled as grand duchess during World War I, but her cozy relationship with the German forces of occupation incensed her people and gave confidence to radicals in Luxembourg that the days of the ruling house were numbered.

In 1919, under the pressure of hostile public opinion, Marie Adélaïde abdicated in favor of her sister. It fell to Charlotte to keep the dynasty intact and in power, and Luxembourg independent (many liberals in the country were calling for the unification of Luxembourg with Belgium). Charlotte assured the government that she was willing to serve as a constitutional monarch, but under no circumstances would she approve of Luxembourg's being annexed to Belgium. The government rejected the annexation plan, and in a referendum, 77 percent of the electorate of Luxembourg voted to keep the grand ducal family as head of state. A few weeks after winning this double victory, Charlotte married Prince Félix of Bourbon-Parma. In time they had six children, thereby ensuring the continuance of the dynasty.

In 1940, the Nazis invaded the Netherlands, Belgium, and Luxembourg, all nations that had declared their neutrality. Charlotte and her family escaped to England and then went to Canada, where they remained until the end of the war. From Canada, Charlotte made regular broadcasts to her people via the BBC, urging them to have faith that the Allies would defeat the Nazis, and Luxembourg would be free again. These messages of hope made the grand duchess a very popular figure in her country.

After the war, Charlotte supported the Benelux Economic Union with Belgium and the Netherlands, and she endorsed Luxembourg's entrance into the European Community, the forerunner of the European Union.

In 1963, Charlotte was the longest reigning monarch in Europe. To mark the occasion, President John F. Kennedy and First Lady Jacqueline Kennedy invited the grand duchess to the White House for a splendid state dinner. The following year, Grand Duchess Charlotte abdicated in favor of her eldest son, Jean.

HIROHITO

Emperor of Japan (1901–1989)

Historians and biographers still debate the true character of Emperor Hirohito and his level of involvement in Japan's aggressive militarism in the 1930s and 1940s. Some portray him as timid, more interested in studying marine biology than in government; others insist that Hirohito was privy to and approved of all of his commanders' decisions—including the brutal war in China and the surprise attack on the United States' fleet at Pearl Harbor. The debate rages on.

Hirohito's reign covered some of the most dramatic decades in Japan's history. In 1937, the Japanese military invaded China, the first step in a plan to extend Japan's empire throughout the South Pacific and into mainland Asia. In 1940, Japan signed the Tripartite Pact, which allied the country with Nazi Germany and fascist Italy. In 1945, after atomic bombs destroyed the cities of Hiroshima and Nagasaki, Japan surrendered unconditionally to the Allies, thereby bringing World War II to an end.

The emperor's fate after the war was uncertain. Many in the West felt strongly that Hirohito should stand trial as a war criminal, but U.S. General Douglas MacArthur, the newly appointed supreme allied commander in Japan, believed such an act would provoke the Japanese people and make impossible MacArthur's policy of demilitarizing Japan and installing a democratic government. MacArthur probably saved Hirohito's life, but he also stripped him of any real power. In 1946, the emperor renounced his claim to divinity and his descent from the Sun goddess. In 1947, the new constitution adopted by the Japanese (with MacArthur's encouragement) kept the office of the emperor but reduced him to a purely ceremonial role in Japanese society.

In 1975, during a state visit to the United States, Hirohito offered a formal apology for the pain and suffering his country had inflicted upon the world in World War II. Americans were uncertain how to read the apology—as a formality, or as an acceptance of personal responsibility.

Hirohito with U.S. president Gerald Ford

Puyi

Emperor of China (1906–1967)

On her deathbed, the Empress Cixi named Puyi her heir. He was a few weeks shy of his third birthday when he became emperor of China. The little boy was taken away from his family and installed in the Forbidden City palace complex in Beijing; his wet nurse was allowed to accompany him, but aside from her he was surrounded by strangers—guards, bureaucrats, servants, and a small army of eunuchs who fulfilled his every wish and whim.

In 1912, when Puyi was six years old, a revolution swept across the country and China became a republic. Puyi was permitted to retain the title emperor and was given the northern half of the Forbidden City, along with the Summer Palace, as his residence. In 1924, he lost that, too, when a warlord named Feng Yuxiang expelled him from the palace. The Japanese offered the ex-emperor a villa in Tianjin in northeastern China.

A decade later, the Japanese found a use for their imperial guest: as part of their campaign to conquer China they established a puppet state in Manchuria, and they installed Puyi as their puppet emperor. At the end of World War II, the Soviet Red Army overran Manchuria and captured Puyi. In 1946, the Russians sent him to Tokyo to testify at war crimes trials, then kept him in a Russian prison until 1950 when Stalin, as a gesture of friendship, handed over the emperor to Mao Zedong. Puyi remained in prison in China until 1959 when Mao granted him amnesty.

The last emperor's life became very ordinary. He found a job at the Beijing Botanical Garden, married a nurse, then found a better job working as an editor for a political organization.

During the Cultural Revolution of the 1960s, Puyi was such an obvious target for the militant Red Guards that the local security force had to give him protection. By this time he was suffering from heart disease and the first stages of cancer. After his death, Puyi's ashes were buried in Beijing's Babaoshan Revolutionary Cemetery, which had been laid out on the traditional burial site of concubines and eunuchs of the imperial court.

JULIANA
Queen of the Netherlands (1909–2004)

International crises and family troubles plagued Queen Juliana, yet her courage and candor in the face of hardship endeared her to the Dutch people. Even members of the antimonarchical Labor Party considered her "one of the people."

On May 10, 1940, Nazi Germany invaded the Netherlands, expecting it to fall within twenty-four hours. Instead, the Dutch army fought so valiantly that Hitler ordered the Luftwaffe to bomb Rotterdam. In fifteen minutes, the planes poured 107 tons of high explosives onto the city, killing 900 civilians, injuring thousands, and leaving 80,000 homeless. And the Germans threatened to do the same to Amsterdam, the Hague, and Utrecht. As the Dutch surrendered, Juliana, her husband, Bernhard, their one-year-old daughter Beatrix, and Juliana's mother, Wilhelmina, fled to England. For the remainder of the war, Bernhard remained in England, raising a Dutch army in exile; Juliana and her daughter continued on to Canada, where they remained until 1945.

After the war, Juliana's family life lurched from one difficulty to another. She fell under the spell of a mystic named Greet Hofmans, so much so that both her husband and her government demanded that she break off the unhealthy connection. In 1964, one of her daughters secretly converted to Catholicism, then married a Spanish prince without obtaining the permission required by law from the Dutch parliament. In 1966, Juliana's daughter Beatrix caused a firestorm of protest when she married Claus von Amsberg, who had served in the Nazi army during World War II. And the revelation in 1976 that her husband, Bernhard, had taken bribes from Lockheed, the American aircraft company, almost cost Juliana her throne. Bernhard rectified the situation by resigning from all his offices in the Dutch armed forces and in private business.

Nonetheless, Juliana survived all these upheavals, and never lost the affection of her people. A Dutch comedian, Wim Kan, used to say that he wanted the Netherlands to become a republic, but only if Juliana were elected its first president.

MOHAMMAD REZA SHAH PAHLAVI

Shah of Iran (1919–1980)

Mohammad Reza Shah Pahlavi could be described as a progressive, even liberal, autocrat. He consolidated all power in his own hands, but he used that power to redistribute land to his country's peasants (conservative Iranian landowners derided him as the "Bolshevik Shah"), emancipate women, open schools in rural areas, ban marriage before age fifteen, ban polygamy without the wife's consent, permit women to divorce their husbands, welcome new industries and foreign investment into the country, and encourage his people to adopt Western-style dress. With immense oil deposits and the strongest military in the Middle East, Iran had every appearance of stability.

Conservative Muslims in Iran opposed many of the shah's Western-inspired reforms. In 1963, Ayatollah Ruhollah Khomeini, one of the country's most prominent religious leaders, was imprisoned for his outspoken denunciations of the shah's policies. Protests against Khomeini's arrest turned into riots; the shah's closest advisor, Amir Assadollah Alam, gave the security forces a shoot-to-kill order, and a hundred protesters were gunned down. In the years that followed, there were further crackdowns on Muslim dissidents.

Between 1963 and 1976, the haughty, autocratic side of the shah's personality overshadowed his zeal for reform. He set government policy. He decided how oil revenues would be allocated. And he instituted a one-party political system that, perhaps more than anything else, alienated his supporters among the Westernized intelligentsia and the middle class. If he was making enemies at home, he made many friends abroad: he settled a long-standing border dispute with Iraq, maintained friendly relations with the Soviet Bloc and Israel, and counted the United States as his closest ally.

By 1977, however, the political and religious situation in Iran was becoming critical. Led by the peasants, who counted for half the population, there were widespread calls for a return to Islamic law. In 1978, there was violence in the streets of Iran as demonstrators clashed with security forces. Urged on by Ayatollah Khomeini, an Islamic revolution swept across Iran; the shah, unable to stop it, left the country. Two years later, in exile in Egypt, he died of pancreatic cancer.

Mohammad Reza Shah with his wife Queen Soraya

Farouk I

King of Egypt (1920–1965)

In 1937, the year Farouk was crowned king of Egypt, there were two widespread movements developing in his country. One was the Muslim Brotherhood, which promoted traditional Islamic religious values. The other was Egypt's educated classes' increasing interest in and openness to ideas from the West. Young King Farouk's authoritarianism alienated both groups.

At least since World War I, Britain had considered Egypt within its sphere of influence. At the beginning of World War II, Farouk declared his country's neutrality, but the British felt that in his private communications with the British government, the king should have been more forceful in his expressions of support for the Allied cause. And then there were rumors that the Egyptians were in contact with Benito Mussolini's government, and that the king's cabinet was pro-fascist. In 1942, British tanks surrounded Farouk's palace as the British ambassador called to deliver his country's demands: the king must dismiss his cabinet and install a new one drawn from the populist Wafd party. Farouk complied, and from that day on, respect for him among his own people fell sharply.

With responsibility for his country's affairs essentially out of his hands, Farouk gave up being king and became a full-time playboy. He flaunted his wealth in the streets of Egypt. He gambled, caroused, and chased women. He became dangerously obese. In doing so he offended the Egyptians, especially devoutly religious Muslims. After Israel defeated Egypt in the 1948 war, the king came to symbolize the impotence of his country. In 1952, a cadre of young army officers led by Gamal Abdel Nasser staged a coup that drove Farouk from power.

The king didn't seem to mind. He went into exile in Rome, where he continued living the high life. One evening in 1965, he went to a nightclub where he enjoyed a large meal. Just as he had finished eating, Farouk suffered a heart attack and died.

Farouk (in the foreground) with Arab kings and statesmen

RAINIER III AND GRACE

Prince (1923–2005) and Princess (1929–1982) of Monaco

Theirs was the true fairy-tale wedding. Rainer, the debonair prince of the chic little country of Monaco, married Grace Kelly, a cool blond beauty from Philadelphia who was one of the biggest stars in Hollywood. Alfred Hitchcock, for whom Kelly had made several movies, including *Rear Window*, said he was "very happy that Grace has found herself such a good partner." While the couple had the approval of the Kelly family, Hollywood was more reticent: to get out of her contract so she could become princess of Monaco, Kelly was obliged to let her studio film the wedding and then release it in theaters.

In Monaco the couple lived in a two-hundred-room palace, to which Princess Grace attempted to bring a touch of American domesticity. She cooked meals, did volunteer work, and never flaunted her wealth. She also made many trips home to the United States to visit her family and friends. It was said that she even kept her American dentist.

Prince Rainier had inherited a principality that was known primarily as a luxury playground, but he wanted it to be something more. He attracted new investment by reminding major corporations of the advantage of maintaining their headquarters in Monaco—the country is entirely tax free. Thanks to Rainier's efforts, Monaco experienced a new economic boom, and the country (which is about the size of Central Park in New York City) was getting crowded. So Rainier reclaimed land from the sea and built more high rises and luxury waterfront condos.

Tragedy struck the royal family in 1982. Princess Grace was driving her daughter Stephanie from their home in France back to Monaco when she suffered a stroke and lost control of the car, which rolled down a steep embankment. Stephanie emerged from the crash with minor injuries, but Princess Grace died the next day. The loss of his wife devastated Prince Rainier. He largely withdrew from public life, lived quietly with his grief, and never remarried. Rainier died in 2005 and was buried beside Princess Grace in Monaco's Cathedral of Saint Nicholas.

Abdullah bin Abdul Aziz al Saud

King of Saudi Arabia (1924–)

The House of Saud is the royal family that has ruled Saudi Arabia since the country's creation in 1932, but the family is much more ancient than that—the founder of the line settled in Diriyah outside modern-day Riyadh in the mid-fifteenth century.

As rulers of the land that include Mecca and Medina, the two holiest cities of Islam, the Saudi kings are particularly cautious about enforcing a strict interpretation of their religion. Among other restrictions, alcohol is banned and only Muslim places of worship are permitted within the borders of Saudi Arabia.

Since his installation in 2005, King Abdullah has shown some sensitivity to the way the outside world perceives his country and his religion. He has sponsored conferences at which Muslims, Christians, and Jews discussed concerns as well as principles and beliefs they hold in common. He is especially active in trying to eradicate the idea that Islam justifies acts of terrorism.

Among Muslim extremist groups such as al-Qaeda, the king's overtures to the non-Muslim world and his willingness to permit Westerners to live and work in Saudi Arabia and to let the United States station troops in the country are all seen as a betrayal of Islam. In the wake of a series of terrorist attacks on Westerners and Saudis in Saudi Arabia, Abdullah responded by sentencing convicted terrorists to be beheaded in public.

As one of the wealthiest kings in the world (his fortune is believed to be worth about $21 billion), Abdullah is expected to be a generous philanthropist. After the earthquake in Sichuan, China, in 2008, the king sent a gift of $50 million plus $10 million in relief supplies. That same year he contributed $10 billion to the endowment fund of the new King Abdullah University of Science and Technology.

Saudi Arabia is not a Western secular state, and the king does not rule according to Western secular principles. It is not unknown for his security forces to torture prisoners. The rights of women and homosexuals in Saudi Arabia are extremely limited. As a result, during state visits to Europe or the United States, the king almost always encounters crowds of angry protesters.

ELIZABETH II

Queen of England (1926–)

As of this writing, Elizabeth II has reigned for fifty-seven years, which means she is edging up on the record of sixty-four years set by her ancestor, Queen Victoria. As a constitutional monarch, she exercises no real power, but she has influence; she has always been conscientious about studying state papers, and her knowledge of domestic and international affairs is impressive, even moreso considering that she has more than half a century of government experience to draw upon.

From a distance Elizabeth projects an image of calm and dignity, but since 1970 she has engaged in what have come to be known as "walkabouts," stepping out of her vehicle to meet and make conversation with the crowds. Invariably the people are won over by her down-to-earth manner, which has led the queen to quip, "I have to be seen to be believed."

For generations the royal family of England has attempted to be a role model for the nation—not always very successfully. Of Elizabeth's four children, three have been divorced from their spouses. In the case of Prince Charles, his split from his wife, the wildly popular Princess Diana, was exacerbated by his affair with Camilla Parker Bowles (whom he married in 2005).

Elizabeth respects tradition, but she knows when to keep up with the times. In 1992, when a fire severely damaged the royal residence at Windsor Castle, she announced that she, not the government, would pay for the restoration. Even more surprising was her declaration that she and her family were giving up their tax-exempt status.

When her former daughter-in-law Diana died in a car crash in 1997, the queen followed the protocol that was proper for such an occasion and went into seclusion. The British people, who were deep in mass hysteria, read the queen's detachment as callous and unfeeling. The backlash came as a shock, but Elizabeth recovered, made an address to the nation the day before the funeral, and when Diana's coffin passed, led her family in a stately bow, a gesture of respect reserved for royalty.

She remains popular at home and abroad. It is unlikely that she will step down, but if she did, people wonder, would she hand the crown to her son, now over sixty years old, or to her grandson William?

Queen Elizabeth II at the opening of Parliament

Jaber III al-Ahmad al-Jaber al-Sabah

Emir of Kuwait (1926–2006)

Oil production did not begin in Kuwait until 1946. That same year the royal family surprised the world by announcing that the revenue from the oil fields would be distributed among the citizens of Kuwait. Emir Jaber took it a step further, setting up a Fund for Future Generations against the day when the oil wells dry up. He funneled 10 percent of the oil revenues into the fund; at the time of his death the balance in the fund stood at $63.8 billion.

Jaber was a low-key emir. In the 1980s, he liked to leave the palace incognito to do his own shopping. He had to give that up after an assassin recognized him on the street and tried to kill him.

During the Iran-Iraq War, Jaber supported Iraq, but in 1990, Saddam Hussein began threatening Kuwait, demanding a share of the country's oil money. Jaber funneled billions of dollars to Iraq in an attempt to buy off Saddam. It was money wasted—on August 2, 1990, Saddam's army surged across the Kuwaiti border. As the royal family scrambled to escape into Saudi Arabia, an Iraqi sniper shot and killed the emir's young brother Fahad.

From the safety of Saudi Arabia, Jaber watched helplessly as cable news stations reported the Iraqi troops' acts of savagery against the Kuwaitis.

In 1991, a coalition of armed forces from the United States, Great Britain, and many other nations entered Kuwait and drove out the Iraqis in a matter of days. When Jaber returned home, he found a devastated land; the Iraqis had looted millions of dollars in cash and property, and before they retreated, they set fire to almost all seven hundred of Kuwait's oil wells.

Jubilant crowds welcomed the emir home, but within months, Kuwaitis were grumbling that the restoration of basic services was creeping along too slowly. Furthermore, the liberal reforms the emir had promised had not materialized. It was not until 1999 that Jaber introduced legislation to grant women the right to vote and hold office. Six more years of argument and foot-dragging followed until the new election law was passed in 2005, just months before the emir died.

Jaber III and U.S. president George W. Bush at Al Hamra's guest palace discussing the Gulf War

HUSSEIN

King of Jordan (1935–1999)

Hussein became king at a tumultuous moment in the history of the Middle East: the State of Israel had been established in Palestine; Arab nations who had gone to war to destroy the Jewish state had been soundly defeated; and Arab, or Palestinian, refugees had swarmed across the border into Jordan. Complicating the situation were the West Bank of the Jordan River and East Jerusalem, land that was part of Jordan but was coveted by Israel. Experienced statesmen wondered how an eighteen-year-old king could be expected to defend his borders against Israel, fend off his powerful Arab neighbors, and feed and house the refugees?

The first thing Hussein did was gain the support of the Jordanian army. With the military behind him, he was in a less vulnerable position. Supported by influential political and tribal leaders, the king began consolidating his power. To strengthen his support among ordinary Jordanians, he opened more schools and worked to attract new businesses to the country. Then, in 1967, Hussein made a serious mistake—he joined with Egypt and attacked Israel. In what became known as the Six-Day War, Hussein lost the West Bank, which accounted for half of the population of his country and half of its economic activity. If the defeat was humiliating, the aftermath was worse, as new Palestinian guerrilla movements sprang up in Jordanian refugee camps. Every time these guerrillas attacked Israel, Israel responded by bombing the camps in Jordan.

From 1967 until 1973, Jordan was in turmoil with fighting between Jordanian troops and Palestinian guerrillas, bombing raids from Israel, and the threat of a Syrian invasion. Hussein began what would be a decades-long quest to bring peace to his country. All manner of proposals were presented; all of them failed. Then, in 1994, he negotiated directly with the Israeli government and produced a treaty, putting an end to forty-six years of hostility between Israel and Jordan. It was a bold move that secured King Hussein's reputation as a peacemaker.

King Hussein with his wife Queen Noor

JUAN CARLOS I AND SOFÍA

King (1938–) and Queen (1938–) of Spain

In 1969, General Francisco Franco, the dictator who had run Spain since 1939, announced that at his retirement or death the head of state would be Prince Juan Carlos. There had been no king in Spain since 1931, when Juan Carlos's grandfather Alfonso XIII had been forced out, but Franco believed that the Spanish people would unite around a constitutional monarch.

It was the prince's wife, Sofía (the daughter of the king of Greece—another exiled monarch), who had encouraged Juan Carlos to establish friendly ties with Franco. She also came up with a new title suitable for a prince waiting to become a constitutional monarch—prince of the Spanish State.

After Franco's death in 1975, Juan Carlos and Sofía helped the government make a peaceful transition from dictatorship to democracy: political parties and trade unions were permitted, strikes were legal, and every Spanish man and woman had the right to vote. Under a new constitution, the prime minister was chief executive, and the king was commander-in-chief of the armed forces. In 1981, a group of army officers staged a coup to give Juan Carlos real political power, but it failed because the king refused to participate, and even called out officers and troops loyal to him to defend the government.

Juan Carlos is not popular only in Spain; a 2008 poll found that people in South and Central America rate him the most popular world leader, while a 2006 poll taken in Portugal found that 28 percent of Portuguese were willing to see their country unite with Spain if Juan Carlos could be their king.

In the twenty-first century, we are accustomed to kings and queens uttering polite platitudes in public, but Juan Carlos and Sofía are outspoken. In a 2008 interview, Sofía defended her traditional views regarding marriage and family. And in 2007, while attending a summit in Chile, Juan Carlos took on the unpredictable and inflammatory president of Venezuela, Hugo Chávez. As Chávez ranted that Spain's prime minister José María Aznar was a "fascist," the king cut him off, saying, "Why don't you shut up?"

Hassanal Bolkiah Mu'izzaddin Waddaulah

Sultan of Brunei (1946–)

In 1997, *Forbes* magazine named Sultan Hassanal Bolkiah the world's wealthiest man—and the wealthiest royal. His fortune at the time was estimated to be $55.6 billion. Twelve years later, the sultan's fortune has dropped to about $20 billion, which puts him in fourth place on the list of the world's richest monarchs.

Arriving at an exact figure for Hassanal Bolkiah's personal wealth is difficult because it fluctuates with the markets: he has absolute control over Brunei's finances and he has unlimited access to his country's oil revenue.

Furthermore, the sultan has powers that monarchs have not enjoyed since the Middle Ages. As head of state, he has full executive power over the country; for good measure, he is prime minister and minister of defense and of finance. In 2006, he amended the Brunei constitution to declare that his actions were infallible. Yet in 2004, he reestablished the Brunei legislature that had been dissolved forty-two years earlier. Given the sultan's power over the state, it is difficult to gauge the influence of the legislature on government affairs.

Hassanal Bolkiah is renowned as an avid collector of fine automobiles. According to Guinness World Records, his collection of five hundred Rolls-Royces is the largest in the world—and it includes the very last Phantom VI ever made. The car collection is housed in five aircraft hangars and is serviced by a team of specialists.

The sultan lives in the world's largest palace: covering 2.1 million square feet, it features more than 1,700 rooms, including at least 250 bathrooms.

Hassanal Bolkiah has twelve children—seven daughters and five sons. At present he has two wives: Raja Isteri Pengiran Anak Hajah Saleha, his first wife, is also the sultan's cousin. His third wife, Pengiran Isteri Azrinaz Mazhar, was a newscaster on Malaysian television. The sultan's second wife, Pengiran Isteri Mariam, had been a Royal Brunei Airlines flight attendant; Hassanal Bolkiah divorced her in 2003 and stripped her of her royal titles. His heir is Crown Prince Al-Muhtadee Billah, the first-born son of his first wife.

DIANA

Princess of Wales (1961–1997)

Between 1981, when she became engaged to Prince Charles, until her tragic death in 1997, the world watched as Diana evolved from a camera-shy future princess to one of the most poised and self-confident women of her time. It has often been said that the press hounded Diana, and it is certainly true that she always made excellent tabloid fodder. But Diana was not only a victim of the press, she was also a skillful manipulator of the press. No matter where she went or what she did, she could expect to be followed by a horde of reporters and paparazzi recording her every move. She used this coverage to advance her favorite charities and her efforts to enforce a worldwide ban on land mines, and to show her compassion for children suffering from AIDS.

Her marriage to Charles began under the watchful eye of the cameras, and that is where it ended. In 1994, first the prince, and then the princess gave candid interviews about their troubled marriage. The most memorable moment came when Diana referred to her husband's longtime mistress, Camilla Parker Bowles, "Well, there were three of us in this marriage, so it was a bit crowded." The TV interviews were the final blow—Queen Elizabeth suggested to her son and daughter-in-law that they consider getting a divorce.

In 1997, Diana began a romance with Dodi al-Fayed, an Egyptian billionaire film producer and son of Mohamed al-Fayed, owner of the landmark British department store, Harrods. On the evening of August 31, 1997, the couple were on their way to al-Fayed's apartment in Paris when their driver lost control of the car. Diana and al-Fayed, as well as the driver, died in the crash.

Her death shocked the world, and sent the people of Britain into an emotional tailspin with tens of thousands sobbing in the street outside her palace. The royal family, led by the example of Queen Elizabeth, went into seclusion, but distressed crowds demanded that the queen come outside and mourn with them. The queen defused the volatile situation by going out to the crowd and by making a radio address to the nation in which she said, "No one who knew Diana will ever forget her. Millions of others who never met her, but felt they knew her, will remember her."

Diana cradles a sick child during her visit to Imran Khan's cancer hospital in Pakistan in April 1996

INDEX